MILITARY AND VETERAN ISSUES

U.S. NAVY FORCE STRUCTURE AND FORWARD PRESENCE OVERSEAS

PLANS AND CONSIDERATIONS

MILITARY AND VETERAN ISSUES

Additional books in this series can be found on Nova's website under the Series tab.

Additional e-books in this series can be found on Nova's website under the e-book tab.

MILITARY AND VETERAN ISSUES

U.S. NAVY FORCE STRUCTURE AND FORWARD PRESENCE OVERSEAS

PLANS AND CONSIDERATIONS

AGNES S. JENNINGS
EDITOR

nova publishers
New York

NOTICE TO THE READER

Library of Congress Cataloging-in-Publication Data

ISBN: 978-1-63482-939-7

Published by Nova Science Publishers, Inc. † New York

CONTENTS

PREFACE

This book provides background information and presents potential issues for Congress concerning the Navy's ship force-structure goals and shipbuilding plans. The planned size of the Navy, the rate of Navy ship procurement, and the prospective affordability of the Navy's shipbuilding plans have been matters of concern for the congressional defense committees for the past several years. Decisions that Congress makes on Navy shipbuilding programs can substantially affect Navy capabilities and funding requirements, and the U.S. shipbuilding industrial base. Moreover, in support of its mission to deter conflict or fight in wars if necessary, the Navy considers it a core responsibility to maintain a forward presence—to keep some of its fleet far from U.S. shores at all times in areas that are important to national interests. This book discusses preserving the Navy's forward presence with a smaller fleet, as well as provides an analysis of the Navy's fiscal year 2015 shipbuilding plan. Finally, it examines the long-term effect of crew rotation on forward presence.

In: U.S. Navy Force Structure ...
Editor: Agnes S. Jennings

ISBN: 978-1-63482-939-7

Chapter 1

NAVY FORCE STRUCTURE AND SHIPBUILDING PLANS: BACKGROUND AND ISSUES FOR CONGRESS*

Ronald O'Rourke

SUMMARY

The Navy's proposed FY2016 budget requests funding for the procurement of nine new battle force ships (i.e., ships that count against the Navy's goal for achieving and maintaining a fleet of 306 ships). The nine ships include two Virginia-class attack submarines, two DDG-51 class Aegis destroyers, three Littoral Combat Ships (LCSs), one LPD-17 class amphibious ship, and one TAO(X) class oiler. The Navy's proposed FY2016-FY2020 five-year shipbuilding plan includes a total of 48 ships, compared to a total of 44 ships in the FY2015-FY2019 five-year shipbuilding plan.

The planned size of the Navy, the rate of Navy ship procurement, and the prospective affordability of the Navy's shipbuilding plans have been matters of concern for the congressional defense committees for the past several years. The Navy's FY2015 30-year (FY2015-FY2044) shipbuilding plan, like many previous Navy 30-year shipbuilding plans, does not include enough ships to

* This is an edited, reformatted and augmented version of a Congressional Research Service publication RL32665, prepared for Members and Committees of Congress dated March 3, 2015.

fully support all elements of the Navy's 306-ship goal over the entire 30-year period. In particular, the Navy projects that the fleet would experience a shortfall in amphibious ships from FY2015 through FY2017, a shortfall in small surface combatants from FY2015 through FY2027, and a shortfall in attack submarines from FY2025 through FY2034.

The Navy delivered its narrative report on the FY2015 30-year shipbuilding plan to CRS on July 3, 2014. The Navy estimates in the report that the plan would cost an average of about $16.7 billion per year in constant FY2014 dollars to implement, including an average of about $15.7 billion per year during the first 10 years of the plan, an average of about $19.7 billion per year during the middle 10 years of the plan, and an average of about $14.6 billion per year during the final 10 years of the plan.

A December 2014 Congressional Budget Office (CBO) report on the Navy's FY2015 30-year shipbuilding plan estimates that the plan will require about 13% more funding to implement than the Navy estimates, including about 6% more than the Navy estimates during the first 10 years of the plan, about 14% more than the Navy estimates during the middle 10 years of the plan, and about 20% more than the Navy estimates during the final 10 years of the plan. Over the years, CBO's estimates of the cost to implement the Navy's 30-year shipbuilding plan have generally been higher than the Navy's estimates. Some of the difference between CBO's estimates and the Navy's estimates, particularly in the latter years of the plan, is due to a difference between CBO and the Navy in how to treat inflation in Navy shipbuilding. The program that contributes the most to the difference between the CBO and Navy estimates of the cost of the 30-year plan is a future destroyer that appears in the latter years of the 30-year plan.

Potential issues for Congress in reviewing the Navy's proposed FY2015 shipbuilding budget, its proposed FY2015-FY2019 five-year shipbuilding plan, and its FY2015 30-year (FY2015- FY2044) shipbuilding plan include the following:

- the potential impact on the size and capability of the Navy of limiting DOD spending through FY2021 to the levels set forth in the Budget Control Act of 2011, as amended;
- the appropriate future size and structure of the Navy in light of budgetary and strategic considerations; and
- the affordability of the 30-year shipbuilding plan.

Introduction

This report provides background information and presents potential issues for Congress concerning the Navy's ship force-structure goals and shipbuilding plans. The planned size of the Navy, the rate of Navy ship procurement, and the prospective affordability of the Navy's shipbuilding plans have been matters of concern for the congressional defense committees for the past several years. Decisions that Congress makes on Navy shipbuilding programs can substantially affect Navy capabilities and funding requirements, and the U.S. shipbuilding industrial base.

Background

Navy's Ship Force Structure Goal

January 2013 Goal for Fleet of 306 Ships

On January 31, 2013, in response to Section 1015 of the FY2013 National Defense Authorization Act (H.R. 4310/P.L. 112-239 of January 2, 2013), the Navy submitted to Congress a report presenting a goal for achieving and maintaining a fleet of 306 ships, consisting of certain types and quantities of ships.[1] The goal for a 306-ship fleet is the result of a force structure assessment (FSA) that the Navy completed in 2012.

306-Ship Goal Reflects 2012 Strategic Guidance and Projected DOD Spending Shown in FY2013 and FY2014 Budget Submissions

The 2012 FSA and the resulting 306-ship plan reflect the defense strategic guidance document that the Administration presented in January 2012[2] and the associated projected levels of Department of Defense (DOD) spending shown in the FY2013 and FY2014 budget submissions. DOD officials have stated that if planned levels of DOD spending are reduced below what is shown in these budget submissions, the defense strategy set forth in the January 2012 strategic guidance document might need to be changed. Such a change, Navy officials have indicated, could lead to the replacement of the 306-ship plan of January 2013 with a new plan.

Table 1. Current 306 Ship Force Structure Goal Compared to Earlier Goals

Ship type	306-ship plan of January 2013	~310-316 ship plan of March 2012	Revised 313-ship plan of September 2011	Changes to February 2006 313-ship plan announced through mid-2011	February 2006 Navy plan for 313-ship fleet	Early-2005 Navy plan for fleet of 260-325 ships		2002-2004 Navy plan For 375-Ship Navy[a]	2001 QDR plan for 310-ship Navy
						260 - ships	325-ships		
Ballistic missile submarines (SSBNs)	12[b]	12-14[b]	12[b]	12[b]	14	14	14	14	14
Cruise missile submarines (SSGNs)	0[c]	0-4[c]	4[c]	0[c]	4	4	4	4	2 or 4[d]
Attack submarines (SSNs)	48	~48	48	48	48	37	41	55	55
Aircraft carriers	11[e]	11[e]	11[e]	11[e]	11[f]	10	11	12	12
Cruisers and destroyers	88	~90	94	94[g]	88	67	92	104	116
Frigates	0	0	0	0	0	0	0	0	
Littoral Combat Ships (LCSs)	52	~55	55	55	55	63	82	56	0

Ship type	306-ship plan of January 2013	~310-316 ship plan of March 2012	Revised 313-ship plan of September 2011	Changes to February 2006 313-ship plan announced through mid-2011	February 2006 Navy plan for 313-ship fleet	Early-2005 Navy plan for fleet of 260-325 ships		2002-2004 Navy plan For 375-Ship Navy[a]	2001 QDR plan for 310-ship Navy
Amphibious ships	33	~32	33	33[h]	31	17	24	37	36
MPF(F) ships[i]	0[j]	0[j]	0j	0[j]	12[i]	14[i]	20[i]	0[i]	0[i]
Combat logistics (resupply) ships	29	~29	30	30	30	24	26	42	34
Dedicated mine warfare ships	0	0	0	0	0	0	0	26[k]	16
Joint High Speed Vessels (JHSVs)	10[l]	10[l]	10[l]	21[l]	3	0	0	0	0
Other[m]	23	~23	16	24n	17	10	11	25	25
Total battle force ships	**306**	**~310-316**	**313**	**328**	**313**	**260**	**325**	**375**	**310 or 312**

Sources: Table prepared by CRS based on U.S. Navy data.

Note: QDR is Quadrennial Defense Review. The "~" symbol means approximately and signals that the number in question may be refined as a result of the Naval Force Structure Assessment currently in progress.

Table 1. (Continued)

a. Initial composition. Composition was subsequently modified.

b. The Navy plans to replace the 14 current Ohio-class SSBNs with a new class of 12 next-generation SSBNs. For further discussion, see CRS Report R41129, Navy Ohio Replacement (SSBN[X]) *Ballistic Missile Submarine Program: Background and Issues for Congress*, by Ronald O'Rourke.

c. Although the Navy plans to continue operating its four SSGNs until they reach retirement age in the late 2020s, the Navy does not plan to replace these ships when they retire. This situation can be expressed in a table like this one with either a 4 or a zero.

d. The report on the 2001 QDR did not mention a specific figure for SSGNs. The Administration's proposed FY2001 DOD budget requested funding to support the conversion of two available Trident SSBNs into SSGNs, and the retirement of two other Trident SSBNs. Congress, in marking up this request, supported a plan to convert all four available SSBNs into SSGNs.

e. With congressional approval, the goal has been temporarily be reduced to 10 carriers for the period between the retirement of the carrier *Enterprise* (CVN-65) in December 2012 and entry into service of the carrier *Gerald R. Ford* (CVN-78), currently scheduled for September 2015.

f. For a time, the Navy characterized the goal as 11 carriers in the nearer term, and eventually 12 carriers.

g. The 94-ship goal was announced by the Navy in an April 2011 report to Congress on naval force structure and missile defense.

h. The Navy acknowledged that meeting a requirement for being able to lift the assault echelons of 2.0 Marine Expeditionary Brigades (MEBs) would require a minimum of 33 amphibious ships rather than the 31 ships shown in the February 2006 plan. For further discussion, see CRS Report RL34476, *Navy LPD-17 Amphibious Ship Procurement: Background, Issues, and Options for Congress*, by Ronald O'Rourke.

i. Today's Maritime Prepositioning Force (MPF) ships are intended primarily to support Marine Corps operations ashore, rather than Navy combat operations, and thus are not counted as Navy battle force ships. The planned MPF (Future) ships, however, would have contributed to Navy combat capabilities (for example, by supporting Navy aircraft operations). For this reason, the ships in the planned MPF(F) squadron were counted by the Navy as battle force ships. The planned MPF(F) squadron was subsequently restructured into a different set of initiatives for enhancing the existing MPF squadrons; the Navy no longer plans to acquire an MPF(F) squadron.

j. The Navy no longer plans to acquire an MPF(F) squadron. The Navy, however, has procured or plans to procure some of the ships that were previously planned for the squadron—specifically, TAKE-1 class cargo ships, and Mobile Landing Platform (MLP)/Afloat Forward Staging Base (AFSB) ships. These ships are included in the total shown for "Other" ships.

k. The figure of 26 dedicated mine warfare ships included 10 ships maintained in a reduced mobilization status called Mobilization Category B. Ships in this status are not readily deployable and thus do not count as battle force ships. The 375-ship proposal thus implied transferring these 10 ships to a higher readiness status.

l. Totals shown include 5 ships transferred from the Army to the Navy and operated by the Navy primarily for the performance of Army missions.

m. This category includes, among other things, command ships and support ships.

n. The increase in this category from 17 ships under the February 2006 313-ship plan to 24 ships under the apparent 328-ship goal included the addition of one TAGOS ocean surveillance ship and the transfer into this category of six ships—three modified TAKE-1 class cargo ships, and three Mobile Landing Platform (MLP) ships—that were previously intended for the planned (but now canceled) MPF(F) squadron.

Goal for Fleet of 306 Ships Compared to Earlier Goals

Table 1 compares the 306-ship goal to earlier Navy ship force structure plans.

February 2015 Navy Testimony Referring to Goal for Fleet of 308 Ships

At a February 25, 2015, hearing on Department of the Navy acquisition programs before the Seapower and Projection Forces subcommittee of the House Armed Services Committee, Department of the Navy officials testified that "the FY 2014 update to the 2012 Force Structure Assessment (FSA) to meet the Department of the Navy's required missions in support of the DSG [Defense Strategic Guidance document of January 2012], has increased the objective to 308-ships to account for evolving force structure decisions and real-world changes to assumptions made in 2012."[3] The testimony did not detail the composition of this new 308-ship force-level goal, but one of the officials at the hearing, discussing the anticipated procurement of a 12th LPD-17 class amphibious ship, referred to the amphibious ship force level goal as having been increased from 33 ships to 34 ships.[4]

At a February 26, 2015, hearing on the Department of the Navy's proposed FY2016 budget before the Defense subcommittee of the House Appropriations Committee, Admiral Jonathan Greenert, the Chief of Naval Operations, testified that

> The 2014 update to the "2012 Force Structure Assessment" (FSA) and other Navy analysis describe the baseline of ships needed to support meeting each mission....
>
> According to the FSA, the Navy has a requirement for a force of 11 CVN, 88 large surface combatants (DDG and CG), 48 attack submarines (SSN), 12 SSBN, 11 large amphibious assault ships (LHA/D), 11 amphibious transport docks (LPD), 11 dock landing ships (LSD),52 small surface combatants, 10 JHSV, 29 combat logistics force (CLF) ships, and 24 command and support ships.[5]

The list of ships in the above passage totals 307, and is the same in composition as the 306-ship goal except that it includes one more ship in the "other" category (i.e., 24 ships rather than 23). (The "other" category includes, among other things, command and support ships.)

Together, the Navy's February 25 and 26 testimony suggests that the Navy has a new 308-ship force-level goal that, compared to the 306-ship goal, includes one additional amphibious ship and one additional ship in the "other" category.

Navy's Five-Year and 30-Year Shipbuilding Plans

Five-Year (FY2015-FY2019) Shipbuilding Plan

Table 2 shows the Navy's FY2015 five-year (FY2015-FY2019) shipbuilding plan.

Table 2. Navy FY2016 Five-Year (FY2016-FY2020) Shipbuilding Plan (Battle force ships—i.e., ships that count against 306-ship goal)

Ship type	FY16	FY17	FY18	FY19	FY20	Total
Ford (CVN-78) class aircraft carrier			1			1
Virginia (SSN-774) class attack submarine	2	2	2	2	2	10
Arleigh Burke (DDG-51) class destroyer	2	2	2	2	2	10
Littoral Combat Ship (LCS)	3	3	3	2	3	14
LHA(R) amphibious assault ship		1				1
LPD-17 class amphibious ship	1					1
LX(R) amphibious ship					1	1
Fleet tug/salvage ship (TATS)		1	1	2	1	5
Mobile Landing Platform (MLP)/Afloat Forward Staging Base (AFSB)		1				1
TAO(X) oiler	1		1	1	1	4
TOTAL	**9**	**10**	**10**	**9**	**10**	**48**

Source: FY2016 Navy budget submission.

Notes: The MLP/AFSB is a variant of the MLP with additional features permitting it to serve in the role of an AFSB. The Navy proposes to fund the TATFs and TAO(X)s through the National Defense Sealift Fund (NDSF) and the other ships through the Navy's shipbuilding account, known formally as the Shipbuilding and Conversion, Navy (SCN) appropriation account.

Observations that can be made about the Navy's proposed FY2015 five-year (FY2015-FY2019) shipbuilding plan include the following:

- **Total of 48 ships**. The plan includes a total of 48 ships, compared to a total of 44 ships in the FY2015-FY2019 five-year shipbuilding plan.
- **Average of 8.8 ships per year**. The plan includes an average of 9.6 battle force ships per year. The steady-state replacement rate for a fleet of 306 ships with an average service life of 35 years is about 8.7 ships per year. In light of how the average shipbuilding rate since FY1993 has been substantially below 8.7 ships per year (see **Appendix D**), shipbuilding supporters for some time have wanted to increase the shipbuilding rate to a steady rate of 10 or more battle force ships per year.
- **DDG-51 destroyers and Virginia-class submarines being procured under MYP arrangements**. The 10 DDG-51 destroyers to be procured in FY2013- FY2017 and the 10 Virginia-class attack submarines to be procured in FY2014- FY2018 are being procured under multiyear procurement (MYP) contracts.[6]
- **Flight III DDG-51 to begin with second ship in FY2016**. The second of the two DDG-51s requested for FY2016 is to be the first Flight III variant of the DDG-51. The Flight III variant is to carry a new and more capable radar called the Air and Missile Defense Radar (AMDR).
- **Modified LCS/Frigate to start in FY2019**. The LCS program was restructured in 2014 at the direction of the Secretary of Defense. As a result of the restructuring, LCSs to be procured in FY2019 and beyond are to be built to a more heavily armed design. The Navy has stated that it will refer to these modified LCSs as frigates.
- **12th LPD-17 class ship added to FY2016.** The LPD-17 class ship requested for FY2016 is to be the 12th ship in the class. The Navy had planned on procuring no more than 11 LPD-17s, but Congress has supported the procurement of a 12th LPD-17 by providing unrequested funding for a 12th ship in FY2013 and FY2015. Responding to these two funding actions, the Navy, as a part of its FY2016 budget submission, has inserted a 12th LPD-17 into its shipbuilding plan, and is requesting in FY2016 the remainder of the funding needed to fully fund the ship.
- **TAO(X) procurement to begin FY2016.** The TAO(X) oiler requested for procurement in FY2016 is to be the first in a new class of 17 ships.

30-Year (FY2015-FY2044) Shipbuilding Plan

FY2016 30-Year Plan Not Submitted As of February 24, 2015

The Navy as of February 24, 2015, had not yet submitted its FY2016 (FY2016-FY2045) 30-year shipbuilding plan. Discussion below and elsewhere in this report of the Navy's 30-year shipbuilding consequently is keyed to the Navy's FY2015 (FY2015-FY2044) 30-year shipbuilding plan.

Table 3. Navy FY2015 30-Year (FY2015-FY2044) Shipbuilding Plan

FY	CVN	LSC	SSC	SSN	SSBN	AWS	CLF	Supt	Total
15		2	3	2					**7**
16		2	3	2			1		**8**
17		2	3	2		1		3	**11**
18	1	2	3	2			1	1	**10**
19		2	2	2			1	1	**8**
20		2	3	2		1	1	2	**11**
21		2	3	1	1		1		**8**
22		2	3	2		1	1	2	**11**
23	1	2	3	1			1	3	**11**
24		2	3	2	1	2	1	2	**13**
25		2	3	1			1	1	**8**
26		2		2	1	1	1		**7**
27		2		1	1		1		**5**
28	1	2		2	1	2	1	1	**10**
29		2		1	1	1	1	1	**7**
30		2	1	2	1	1	1	2	**10**
31		2		1	1	1	1	2	**8**
32		2	1	2	1	2	1	3	**12**
33	1	2		1	1	1	1	2	**9**
34		2	1	2	1	1		2	**9**
35		2	1	1	1				**5**
36		2		2		1			**5**
37		2	4	1					**7**
38	1	3	4	2					**10**
39		3	4	1					**8**
40		3	4	2		2			**11**
41		3	4	1					**8**

Table 3. (Continued)

FY	CVN	LSC	SSC	SSN	SSBN	AWS	CLF	Supt	Total
42		3	4	2		1			**10**
43	1	2	4	1			1		**9**
44		2	2	2		2			**8**

Source: FY2015 30-year (FY2015-FY2044) shipbuilding plan.

Key: **FY** = Fiscal Year; **CVN** = aircraft carriers; LSC = surface combatants (i.e., cruisers and destroyers); **SSC**= small surface combatants (i.e., Littoral Combat Ships [LCSs]); **SSN** = attack submarines; **SSGN** = cruise missile submarines; **SSBN** = ballistic missile submarines; **AWS** = amphibious warfare ships; **CLF** = combat logistics force (i.e., resupply) ships; Supt = support ships.

FY2015 30-Year Plan Reflected Proposed Changes in Ship Counting Rules

The Navy's FY2015 30-year shipbuilding plan incorporated a proposed change in the rules for how to count battle force ships. Congress, as part of its markup of the Navy's FY2015 budget, provided direction to the Navy on how the counting rules were to be changed. The discussion below of the Navy's FY2015 30-year shipbuilding plan makes multiple references to the old counting rules and the Navy's proposed counting rules. When the Navy's FY2016 30-year shipbuilding plan is submitted, it will presumably reflect the direction on counting rules that congress provided in marking up the Navy's proposed FY2015 budget. The effect of the congressional direction is to modify the counting rules somewhat, but not as much as the Navy had proposed.

Table 3 shows the Navy's FY2015 30-year (FY2015-FY2044) shipbuilding plan.

In devising a 30-year shipbuilding plan to move the Navy toward its ship force-structure goal, key assumptions and planning factors include but are not limited to the following:

- ship service lives;
- estimated ship procurement costs;
- projected shipbuilding funding levels; and
- industrial-base considerations.

Navy's Projected Force Levels Under 30-Year Shipbuilding Plan

Table 4 shows the Navy's projection of ship force levels for FY2015-FY2044 that would result from implementing the FY2015 30-year (FY2015-FY2044) shipbuilding plan shown in **Table 3.**

Table 4. Projected Force Levels Resulting from FY2015 30-Year (FY2015-FY2044) Shipbuilding Plan

Where two figures are shown, the first is the figure using existing rules for counting battle force ships, and the second is the figure using the Navy's proposed modified rules for counting battle force ships

	CVN	LSC	SSC	SSN	SSGN	SSBN	AWS	CLF	Supt	Total
306 ship plan	**11**	**88**	**52**	**48**	**0**	**12**	**33**	**29**	**33**	**306**
FY15	10	85	19/26	54	4	14	30	29	29/32	**274/284**
FY16	11	88	23/30	53	4	14	31	29	27/30	**280/290**
FY17	11	90	27/34	50	4	14	32	29	29/32	**286/296**
FY18	11	91	31/38	52	4	14	33	29	29/32	**295/304**
FY19	11	93	35/40	51	4	14	33	29	31/34	**301/309**
FY20	11	95	36/37	49	4	14	33	29	33/36	**304/308**
FY21	11	96	36/33	49	4	14	33	29	32/35	**304**
FY22	11	97	38/36	48	4	14	33	29	32/35	**306/307**
FY23	12	98	39	49	4	14	33	29	33/36	**311/314**
FY24	12	98	41/40	48	4	14	34	29	33/36	**313/315**
FY25	11	98	43	47	4	14	34	29	34/37	**314/317**
FY26	11	97	46	45	2	14	36	29	34/37	**314/317**
FY27	11	99	49	44	1	13	35	29	34/37	**315/318**
FY28	11	100	52	41	0	13	36	29	34/37	**316/319**
FY29	11	98	52	41	0	12	35	29	34/37	**312/315**
FY30	11	95	52	41	0	11	35	29	34/37	**308/311**
FY31	11	91	52	43	0	11	34	29	34/36	**305/307**
FY32	11	89	52	43	0	10	34	29	35/37	**303/305**
FY33	11	88	52	45	0	10	35	29	35/37	**305/307**
FY34	11	86	52	46	0	10	34	29	35/37	**303/305**
FY35	11	87	52	48	0	10	32	29	35/37	**304/306**
FY36	11	88	52	49	0	10	32	29	35	**306**
FY37	11	90	52	51	0	10	33	29	34	**310**
FY38	11	91	52	50	0	10	33	29	35	**311**

Table 4. (Continued)

	CVN	LSC	SSC	SSN	SSGN	SSBN	AWS	CLF	Supt	Total
FY39	11	92	52	51	0	10	33	29	34	**312**
FY40	10	90	52	51	0	10	32	29	34	**308**
FY41	10	89	52	51	0	11	33	29	34	**309**
FY42	10	87	52	52	0	12	32	29	34	**308**
FY43	10	84	52	52	0	12	31	29	34	**304**
FY44	10	83	52	52	0	12	31	29	34	**303**

Source: FY2015 30-year (FY2015-FY2044) shipbuilding plan.

Note: Figures for support ships include five JHSVs transferred from the Army to the Navy and operated by the Navy primarily for the performance of Army missions.

Key: **FY** = Fiscal Year; **CVN** = aircraft carriers; **LSC** = surface combatants (i.e., cruisers and destroyers); **SSC** = small surface combatants (i.e., frigates, Littoral Combat Ships [LCSs], and mine warfare ships); **SSN** = attack submarines; **SSGN** = cruise missile submarines; **SSBN** = ballistic missile submarines; **AWS** = amphibious warfare ships; **CLF** = combat logistics force (i.e., resupply) ships; Supt = support ships.

As part of its FY2015 budget submission, the Navy is proposing to modify the rules for what ships to include in the count of the number of battle force ships in the Navy. In its FY2015 budget submission, the Navy has presented figures for projected Navy ship force levels using both the existing rules and the proposed modified rules. **Table 4** and **Table 6** show figures using both the existing rules and the proposed modified rules.

Observations that can be made about the Navy's FY2015 30-year (FY2015-FY2044) shipbuilding plan and resulting projected force levels included the following:

- **Total of 264 ships; average of about 8.8 per year**. The plan includes a total of 264 ships to be procured, two less than the number in the FY2014 30-year (FY2014-FY2043) shipbuilding plan. The total of 264 ships equates to an average of about 8.8 ships per year, which is slightly higher than the approximate average procurement rate (sometimes called the steady-state replacement rate) of about 8.7 ships per year that would be needed over the long run to achieve and maintain a fleet of 306 ships, assuming an average life of 35 years for Navy ships.

- **Proposed modified counting rules affect small surface combatants and support ships**. As can be seen in **Table 4**, the Navy's proposed modified rules for what ships to include in the count of the number of battle force ships (see "Oversight Issues for Congress for FY201") would affect the reported figures for small surface combatants during the period FY2015-FY2024 and the reported figures for support ships during the period FY2015-FY2035.
- **Eleven cruisers proposed for some form of reduced operating status included in count**. As part of its FY2015 budget submission, the Navy is proposing to put 11 of its 22 Aegis cruisers into some form of reduced operating status starting in FY2015, and then return them to service years from now. The 11 cruisers proposed for some form of reduced operating status are included in the count of battle force ships shown in **Table 4** and **Table 6** during the years that they are in reduced operating status.
- **Projected shortfalls in amphibious ships, small surface combatants, and attack submarines**. The FY2015 30-year shipbuilding plan, like many previous Navy 30-year shipbuilding plans, does not include enough ships to fully support all elements of the Navy's 306-ship goal over the entire 30-year period. In particular, the Navy projects that the fleet would experience a shortfall in amphibious ships from FY2015 through FY2017, a shortfall in small surface combatants from FY2015 through FY2027, and a shortfall in attack submarines from FY2025 through FY2034.
- **Ballistic missile submarine force to be reduced temporarily to 10 boats**. As a result of a decision in the FY2013 budget to defer the scheduled procurement of the first Ohio replacement (SSBN[X]) ballistic missile submarine by two years, from FY2019 to FY2021, the ballistic missile submarine force is projected to drop to a total of 10 or 11 boats—one or two boats below the 12-boat SSBN force-level goal—during the period FY2029-FY2041. The Navy says this reduction is acceptable for meeting current strategic nuclear deterrence mission requirements, because none of the 10 or 11 boats during these years will be encumbered by long-term maintenance.[7]

Table 5. Ship Procurement Quantities in First 10 Years of 30-Year Shipbuilding Plans Years shown are fiscal years

FY of 30-year plan (year submitted)	01	02	03	04	05	06	07	08	09	10	11	12	13	14	15	16	17	18	19	20	21	22	23	24
FY01 plan (2000)	8	8	8	8	7	5	6	6	6	7														
FY02 plan (2001)		6	n/a	n/a	n/a	n/a	n/a	n/a	n/a	n/a	n/a													
FY03 plan (2002)			5	5	7	7	11	n/a	n/a	n/a	n/a	n/a												
FY04 plan (2003)				7	8	7	7	9	14	15	13	14	15											
FY05 plan (2004)					9	6	8	9	17	14	15	14	16	15										
FY06 plan (2005)						4	7	7	9	10	12	n/a	n/a	n/a	n/a									
FY07 plan (2006)							7	7	11	12	14	13	12	11	11	10								
FY08 plan (2007)								7	11	12	13	12	12	10	12	11	6							
FY09 plan (2008)									7	8	8	12	12	13	13	12	12	13						
FY10 plan (2009)										8	n/a	n/a	n/a	n/a	n/a	n/a	n/a	n/a	n/a					
FY11 plan (2010)											9	8	12	9	12	9	12	9	13	9				
FY12 plan (2011)												10	13	11	12	9	12	10	12	8	9			
FY13 plan (2012)													10	7	8	9	7	11	8	12	9	12		
FY14 plan (2013)														8	8	7	9	9	10	10	10	11	14	
FY15 plan (2014)															7	8	11	10	8	11	8	11	11	13

Source: Navy 30-year shipbuilding plans supplemented by annual Navy budget submissions (including 5-year shipbuilding plans) for fiscal years shown. n/a means not available—see notes below.

Notes: The FY2001 30-year plan submitted in 2000 was submitted under a one-time-only legislative provision, Section 1013 of the FY2000 National Defense Authorization Act (S. 1059/P.L. 106-65 of October 5, 1999). No provision required DOD to submit a 30-year shipbuilding plan in 2001 or 2002, when Congress considered DOD's proposed FY2002 and FY2003 DOD budgets. (In addition, no FYDP was submitted in 2001, the first year of the George W. Bush Administration.) Section 1022 of the FY2003 Bob Stump National Defense Authorization Act (H.R. 4546/P.L. 107-314 of December 2, 2002) created a requirement to submit a 30-year shipbuilding plan each year, in conjunction with each year's defense budget. This provision was codified at 10 U.S.C. 231. The first 30-year plan submitted under this provision was the one submitted in 2003, in conjunction with the proposed FY2004 DOD budget. For the next several years, 30-year shipbuilding plans were submitted each year, in conjunction with each year's proposed DOD budget. An exception occurred in 2009, the first year of the Obama Administration, when DOD submitted a proposed budget for FY2010 with no accompanying FYDP or 30-year Navy shipbuilding plan. Section 1023 of the FY2011 Ike Skelton National Defense Authorization Act (H.R. 6523/P.L. 111-383 of January 7, 2011) amended 10 U.S.C. 231 to require DOD to submit a 30-year shipbuilding plan once every four years, in the same year that DOD submits a Quadrennial Defense Review (QDR). Consistent with Section 1023, DOD did not submit a new 30-year shipbuilding plan at the time that it submitted the proposed FY2012 DOD budget. At the request of the House Armed Services Committee, the Navy submitted the FY2012 30-year (FY2012-FY2041) shipbuilding plan in late-May 2011. Section 1011 of the FY2012 National Defense Authorization Act (H.R. 1540/P.L. 112-81 of December 31, 2011) amended 10 U.S.C. 231 to reinstate the requirement to submit a 30-year shipbuilding plan each year, in conjunction with each year's defense budget.

Table 6. Projected Navy Force Sizes in First 10 years of 30-Year Shipbuilding Plans

Years shown are fiscal years; where two figures are shown, the first is the figure using existing rules for counting battle force ships, and the second is the figure using the Navy's proposed modified rules for counting battle force ships.

FY of 30-year plan (year submitted)	01	02	03	04	05	06	07	08	09	10	11	12	13	14	15	16	17	18	19	20	21	22	23	24
FY01 plan (2000)	316	315	313	313	313	311	311	304	305	305														
FY02 plan (2001)		316	n/a	n/a	n/a	n/a	n/a	n/a	n/a	n/a	n/a													
FY03 plan (2002)			314	n/a	n/a	n/a	n/a	n/a	n/a	n/a	n/a	n/a												
FY04 plan (2003)				292	292	291	296	301	305	308	313	317	321											
FY05 plan (2004)					290	290	298	303	308	307	314	320	328	326										
FY06 plan (2005)						289	293	297	301	301	306	n/a	n/a	305	n/a									

FY of 30-year plan (year submitted)	01	02	03	04	05	06	07	08	09	10	11	12	13	14	15	16	17	18	19	20	21	22	23	24
FY07 plan (2006)							285	294	299	301	306	315	317	315	314	317								
FY08 plan (2007)								286	289	293	302	310	311	307	311	314	322							
FY09 plan (2008)									286	287	289	290	293	287	288	291	301	309						
FY10 plan (2009)										287	n/a	n/a	n/a	n/a	n/a	n/a	n/a	n/a	n/a					
FY11 plan (2010)											284	287	287	285	285	292	298	305	311	315				
FY12 plan (2011)												290	287	286	286	297	301	311	316	322	324			
FY13 plan (2012)													285	279	276	284	285	292	300	295	296	298		
FY14 plan (2013)														282	270	280	283	291	300	295	296	297	297	

Table 6. (Continued)

FY of 30-year plan (year submitted)	01	02	03	04	05	06	07	08	09	10	11	12	13	14	15	16	17	18	19	20	21	22	23	24
FY15 plan (2014)															274/	280/	286/	295/	301/	304/	304	306/	311/	313/
															284	290	296	304	309	308		307	314	315

Source: Navy 30-year shipbuilding plans supplemented by annual Navy budget submissions (including 5-year shipbuilding plans) for fiscal years shown. n/a means not available—see notes below.

Notes: The FY2001 30-year plan submitted in 2000 was submitted under a one-time-only legislative provision, Section 1013 of the FY2000 National Defense Authorization Act (S. 1059/P.L. 106-65 of October 5, 1999). No provision required DOD to submit a 30-year shipbuilding plan in 2001 or 2002, when Congress considered DOD's proposed FY2002 and FY2003 DOD budgets. Section 1022 of the FY2003 Bob Stump National Defense Authorization Act (H.R. 4546/P.L. 107-314 of December 2, 2002) created a requirement to submit a 30-year shipbuilding plan each year, in conjunction with each year's defense budget. This provision was codified at 10 U.S.C. 231. The first 30-year plan submitted under this provision was the one submitted in 2003, in conjunction with the proposed FY2004 DOD budget. For the next several years, 30-year shipbuilding plans were submitted each year, in conjunction with each year's proposed DOD budget. An exception occurred in 2009, the first year of the Obama Administration, when DOD submitted a proposed budget for FY2010 with no accompanying FYDP or 30-year Navy shipbuilding plan. The FY2006 plan included data for only selected years beyond FY2011. Section 1023 of the FY2011 Ike Skelton National Defense Authorization Act (H.R. 6523/P.L. 111-383 of January 7, 2011) amended 10 U.S.C. 231 to require DOD to submit a 30-year shipbuilding plan once every four years, in the same year that DOD submits a Quadrennial Defense Review (QDR). Consistent with Section 1023, DOD did not submit a new 30-year shipbuilding plan at the time that it submitted the proposed FY2012 DOD budget. At the request of the House Armed Services Committee, the Navy submitted the FY2012 30-year (FY2012-FY2041) shipbuilding plan in late-May 2011. Section 1011 of the FY2012 National Defense Authorization Act (H.R. 1540/P.L. 112-81 of December 31, 2011) amended 10 U.S.C. 231 to reinstate the requirement to submit a 30-year shipbuilding plan each year, in conjunction with each year's defense budget.

Comparison of First 10 Years of 30-Year Plans

Table 5 and **Table 6** below show the first 10 years of planned annual ship procurement quantities and projected Navy force sizes in 30-year shipbuilding plans dating back to the first such plan, which was submitted in 2000 in conjunction with the FY2001 budget. By reading vertically down each column, one can see how the ship procurement quantity or Navy force size projected for a given fiscal year changed as that year drew closer to becoming the current budget year.

OVERSIGHT ISSUES FOR CONGRESS FOR FY2016

Potential Impact on Size and Capability of Navy of Limiting DOD Spending to BCA Caps Through FY2021

One potential issue for Congress concerns the potential impact on the size and capability of the Navy of limiting DOD spending through FY2021 to levels at or near the caps established in the Budget Control Act of 2011 (BCA) as amended. Navy officials state that a decision to reduce DOD's budget to such levels would eventually lead to a smaller and less capable Navy.

Admiral Jonathan Greenert, the Chief of Naval Operations, provided detailed testimony on this question in his prepared statements for hearings before the Senate Armed Services Committee on November 7, 2013, and the House Armed Services Committee on September 18, 2013.8 In further testimony on this issue to the Senate Armed Services Committee on January 28, 2015, Greenert stated:

> A return to sequestration in FY 2016 would necessitate a revisit and revision of the DSG [Defense Strategic Guidance document of January 2012]. Required cuts will force us to further delay critical warfighting capabilities, reduce readiness of forces needed for contingency response, forego or stretch procurement of ships and submarines, and further downsize weapons capability. We will be unable to mitigate the shortfalls like we did in FY2013 [in response to the sequester of March 1, 2013] because [unobligated] prior-year investment balances [which were included in the funds subject to the sequester] were depleted under [the] FY 2013 sequester [of March 1, 2013].
>
> The revised discretionary caps imposed by sequestration would be a reduction of about $10 billion in our FY 2016 budget alone, as compared

to PB-2015. From FY 2016-2020, the reduction would amount to approximately $36 billion. If forced to budget at this level, it would reduce every appropriation, inducing deep cuts to Navy Operation and Maintenance (O&M), investment, and modernization accounts. The Research, Development, Test and Evaluation (RDT&E) accounts would likely experience a significant decline across the FYDP, severely curtailing the Navy's ability to develop new technologies and asymmetric capabilities.

As I testified to this committee in November 2013, any scenario to address the fiscal constraints of the revised discretionary caps must include sufficient readiness, capability and manpower to complement the force structure capacity of ships and aircraft. This balance would need to be maintained to ensure each unit will be effective, even if the overall fleet is not able to execute the DSG. There are many ways to balance between force structure, readiness, capability, and manpower, but none that Navy has calculated that enable us to confidently execute the current defense strategy within dictated budget constraints.

As detailed in the Department of Defense's April 2014 report, "Estimated Impacts of Sequestration-Level Funding," one potential fiscal and programmatic scenario would result in a Navy of 2020 that would be unable to execute two of the ten DSG missions due to the compounding effects of sequestration on top of pre-existing FY 2013, 2014, and 2015 resource constraints. Specifically, the cuts would render us unable to sufficiently Project Power Despite Anti-Access/Area Denial Challenges and unable to Deter and Defeat Aggression. In addition, we would be forced to accept higher risk in five other DSG missions: Counter Terrorism and Irregular Warfare; Defend the Homeland and Provide Support to Civil Authorities; Provide a Stabilizing Presence; Conduct Stability and Counterinsurgency Operations; and Conduct Humanitarian, Disaster Relief, and Other Operations. (Table 2 provides more detail on mission risks.) In short, a return to sequestration in FY 2016 will require a revision of our defense strategy.

Critical assumptions I have used to base my assessments and calculate risk:

- Navy must maintain a credible, modern, and survivable sea-based strategic deterrent
- Navy must man its units
- Units that deploy must be ready
- People must be given adequate training and support services
- Readiness for deployed forces is a higher priority than contingency response forces
- Capability must be protected, even at the expense of some capacity

- Modernized and asymmetric capabilities (advanced weapons, cyber, electronic warfare) are essential to projecting power against evolving, sophisticated adversaries
- The maritime industrial base is fragile—damage can be long-lasting, hard to reverse

The primary benchmarks I use to gauge Navy capability and capacity are DoD Global Force Management Allocation Plan presence requirements, Combatant Commander Operation and Contingency Plans, and Defense Planning Guidance Scenarios. Navy's ability to execute DSG missions is assessed based on capabilities and capacity resident in the force in 2020.

The following section describes specific sequestration impacts to presence and readiness, force structure investments, and personnel under this fiscal and programmatic scenario:

Presence and Readiness

A return to sequestration would reduce our ability to deploy forces on the timeline required by Global Combatant Commands in the event of a contingency. Of the Navy's current battle force, we maintain roughly 100 ships forward deployed, or 1/3 of our entire Navy. Included among the 100 ships are two CSG and two ARG forward at all times. CSGs and ARGs deliver a significant portion of our striking power, and we are committed to keeping, on average, three additional CSGs and three additional ARGs in a contingency response status, ready to deploy within 30 days to meet operation plans (OPLANs). However, if sequestered, we will prioritize the readiness of forces forward deployed at the expense of those in a contingency response status. We cannot do both. We will only be able to provide a response force of one CSG and one ARG. Our current OPLANs require a significantly more ready force than this reduced surge capacity could provide, because they are predicated on our ability to respond rapidly. Less contingency response capacity can mean higher casualties as wars are prolonged by the slow arrival of naval forces into a combat zone. Without the ability to respond rapidly enough, our forces could arrive too late to affect the outcome of a fight.

Our PB-2015 base budget funded ship and aviation depot maintenance to about 80 percent of the requirement in FY 2016-2019. This is insufficient in maintaining the Fleet and has forced us to rely upon Overseas Contingency Operations (OCO) funding to address the shortfall. Sequestration would further aggravate existing Navy backlogs. The impacts of these growing backlogs may not be immediately apparent, but will result in greater funding needs in the future to make up for the shortfalls each year and potentially more material casualty reports (CASREPs), impacting operations. For aviation depot maintenance, the growing backlog will result in more aircraft awaiting maintenance and fewer operational aircraft on the flight line, which would create untenable scenarios in which squadrons would only get their full complement of aircraft just prior to deployment. The situation will lead to less proficient aircrews, decreased combat effectiveness of naval air forces, and increased potential for flight and ground mishaps.

Critical to mission success, our shore infrastructure provides the platforms from which our Sailors train and prepare. However, due the shortfalls over the last three years, we have been compelled to reduce funding in shore readiness since FY 2013 to preserve the operational readiness of our fleet. As a result, many of our shore facilities are degrading. At sequestration levels, this risk will be exacerbated and the condition of our shore infrastructure, including piers, runways, and mission-critical facilities, will further erode. This situation may lead to structural damage to our ships while pierside, aircraft damage from foreign object ingestion on deteriorated runways, and degraded communications within command centers. We run a greater risk of mishaps, serious injury, or health hazards to personnel.

Force Structure Investments

We must ensure that the Navy has the required capabilities to be effective, even if we cannot afford them in sufficient capacity to meet the DSG. The military requirements laid out in the DSG are benchmarked to the year 2020, but I am responsible for building and maintaining capabilities now for the Navy of the future. While sequestration causes significant near-term impacts, it would also create serious problems that would manifest themselves after 2020 and would be difficult to recover from.

In the near term, the magnitude of the sequester cuts would compel us to consider reducing major maritime and air acquisition programs; delaying asymmetric capabilities such as advanced jammers, sensors, and weapons; further reducing weapons procurement of missiles, torpedoes, and bombs; and further deferring shore infrastructure maintenance and upgrades. Because of its irreversibility, force structure cuts represent options of last resort for the Navy. We would look elsewhere to absorb sequestration shortfalls to the greatest extent possible.

Disruptions in naval ship design and construction plans are significant because of the long- lead time, specialized skills, and extent of integration needed to build military ships. Because ship construction can span up to nine years, program procurement cancelled in FY 2016 will not be felt by the Combatant Commanders until several years later when the size of the battle force begins to shrink as those ships are not delivered to the fleet at the planned time. Likewise, cancelled procurement in FY 2016 will likely cause some suppliers and vendors of our shipbuilding industrial base to close their businesses. This skilled, experienced and innovative workforce cannot be easily replaced and it could take years to recover from layoffs and shutdowns; and even longer if critical infrastructure is lost. Stability and predictability are critical to the health and sustainment of this vital sector of our Nation's industrial capacity.

Personnel

In FY 2013 and 2014, the President exempted all military personnel accounts from sequestration out of national interest to safeguard the resources necessary to compensate the men and women serving to defend our Nation and to maintain the force levels required for national security. It was recognized that this action triggered a higher reduction in non-military personnel accounts.

If the President again exempts military personnel accounts from sequestration in FY 2016, then personnel compensation would continue to be protected. Overall, the Navy would protect personnel programs to the extent possible in order to retain the best people. As I testified in March 2014, quality of life is a critical component of the quality of service that we provide to our Sailors. Our Sailors are our most important asset and we must invest appropriately to keep a high caliber all-volunteer force. We will continue to fund Sailor support, family readiness, and education programs. While there may be some reductions to these programs if sequestered in FY 2016, I anticipate the reductions to be relatively small. However, as before, this would necessitate higher reductions to the other Navy accounts.

Conclusion

Navy is still recovering from the FY 2013 sequestration in terms of maintenance, training, and deployment lengths. Only 1/3 of Navy contingency response forces are ready to deploy within the required 30 days. With stable and consistent budgets, recovery is possible in 2018. However, if sequestered, we will not recover within this FYDP.

For the last three years, the Navy has been operating under reduced top-lines and significant shortfalls: $9 billion in FY 2013, $5 billion in FY 2014 and $11 billion in FY 2015, for a total shortfall of about $25 billion less than the President's budget request. Reverting to revised sequester-level BCA caps would constitute an additional $5-10 billion decrement each year to Navy's budget. With each year of sequestration, the loss of force structure, readiness, and future investments would cause our options to become increasingly constrained and drastic. The Navy already shrank 23 ships and 63,000 personnel between 2002 and 2012. It has few options left to find more efficiencies.

While Navy will do its part to help the Nation get its fiscal house in order, it is imperative we do so in a coherent and thoughtful manner to ensure appropriate readiness, warfighting capability, and forward presence—the attributes we depend upon for our Navy. Unless naval forces are properly sized, modernized at the right pace, ready to deploy with adequate training and equipment, and capable to respond in the numbers and at the speed required by Combatant Commanders, they will not be able to carry out the Nation's defense strategy as written. We will be compelled to go to fewer places, and do fewer things. Most importantly, when facing major contingencies, our ability to fight and win will neither be quick nor decisive.

Unless this Nation envisions a significantly diminished global security role for its military, we must address the growing mismatch in ends, ways, and means. The world is becoming more complex, uncertain, and turbulent. Our adversaries' capabilities are diversifying and expanding. Naval forces are more important than ever in building global security, projecting power, deterring foes, and rapidly responding to crises that affect our national security. A return to sequestration would seriously weaken the United States Navy's ability to contribute to U.S. and global security.[9]

Greenert's testimony concluded with the following table:

Mission Impacts to a Sequestered Navy

Quadrennial Defense Review Objectives	Defense Strategic Guidance Missions	Navy Ability to Execute
Project Power and Win Decisively	Project power against a technologically capable adversary	Major challenges to achieve warfighting objectives in denied areas: • Inadequate power projection capacity • Too few strike fighter, command/control, electronic warfare assets • Limited advanced radar and missile capacity • Insufficient munitions
	Execute large-scale ops in one region, deter another adversary's aggression elsewhere	Limited ready capacity to execute two simultaneous large scale ops • 2/3 of required contingency response force (2 of 3 Carrier Strike Groups and 2 of 3 Amphibious Readiness Groups) not ready to deploy within 30 days
	Conduct limited counterinsurgency and other stability operations	Increased risk due to: • Reduced funding to Navy Expeditionary Combat Command • Reduced ISR capacity (especially tactical rotary wing drones)
	Operate effectively in space and cyber space	This mission is fully executable in a sequestered environment • Navy continues to prioritize cyber capabilities
Protect the Homeland	Conduct globally-distributed counter terrorism and irregular warfare operations	Increased risk due to: • Fewer sea base options and less ISR capacity (drones) • Reduced funding to Navy Expeditionary Combat Command
	Conduct humanitarian assistance and disaster relief	Increased risk due to: • Reduction in operations, maintenance, and flying hour accounts
	Defend the Homeland and provide support to civil authorities	Increased risk due to: • Reduction in operations, maintenance, and flying hour accounts
	Maintain a safe, secure, effective nuclear deterrent	This mission is fully executable in a sequestered environment • Navy's top budget priority in any fiscal scenario
	Prevent the proliferation and use of nuclear, biological, and chemical weapons	This mission is fully executable in a sequestered environment
Build Security Globally	Provide a stabilizing presence to influence events, reassure allies, and respond to crises	Increased risk due to: • Less ships forward • Decline of steady state presence & contingency response forces

Table 2: Mission Impacts to a Sequestered Navy

Source: Statement of Admiral Jonathan Greenert, U.S. Navy, Chief of Naval Operations, Before the Senate Armed Services Committee on the Impact of Sequestration on National Defense, January 28, 2015.

Figure 1. Navy Table on Mission Impacts of Limiting Navy's Budget to BC Levels.

APPROPRIATE FUTURE SIZE AND STRUCTURE OF NAVY IN LIGHT OF STRATEGIC AND BUDGETARY CHANGES

A related oversight issue for Congress concerns the appropriate future size and structure of the Navy. Changes in strategic and budgetary circumstances have led to a broad debate over the future size and structure of the military, including the Navy. Changes in strategic circumstances include, among other things, the end of major U.S. ground combat operations in Iraq, the winding down of U.S. combat operations in Afghanistan, China's military (including naval) modernization effort,[10] maritime territorial disputes involving China,[11] Russia's seizure and annexation of Crimea, and the U.S. commitment to counter the Islamic State organization.

The Navy's current goal for a fleet of 306 ships reflects a number of judgments and planning factors (some of which the Navy receives from the Office of the Secretary of Defense), including but not limited to the following:

- U.S. interests and the U.S. role in the world, and the U.S. military strategy for supporting those interests and that role;
- current and projected Navy missions in support of U.S. military strategy, including both wartime operations and day-to-day forward-deployed operations;
- current and projected capabilities of potential adversaries, including their anti- access/area-denial (A2/AD) capabilities;
- regional combatant commander (COCOM) requests for forward-deployed Navy forces;
- the individual and networked capabilities of current and future Navy ships and aircraft;
- basing arrangements for Navy ships, including numbers and locations of ships homeported in foreign countries;
- maintenance and deployment cycles for Navy ships; and
- fiscal constraints.

With regard to the fourth point above, Navy officials testified in March 2014 that a Navy of 450 ships would be required to fully meet COCOM requests for forward-deployed Navy forces.[12] The difference between a fleet of 450 ships and the current goal for a fleet of 306 ships can be viewed as one measure of the operational risk associated with the goal of a fleet of 306 ships.

A goal for a fleet of 450 ships might be viewed as a fiscally unconstrained goal.

Actions by China starting in November 2013 that appear aimed at achieving a greater degree of control over China's near-seas region,[13] followed by Russia's seizure and annexation of Crimea in March 2014, have led to a discussion among observers about whether we are currently shifting from the familiar post-Cold War era of the last 20 to 25 years to a new and different strategic era characterized by, among other things, renewed great power competition and challenges to key aspects of the U.S.-led international order that has operated since World War II. A shift in strategic eras can lead to a reassessment of defense funding levels, strategy, missions, plans, and programs. The shift from the Cold War to the post-Cold War era led to such a reassessment in the early 1990s. A shift from the post-Cold War era to a new strategic era could lead to a new reassessment of defense funding levels, strategy, missions, plans, and programs.[14]

For additional discussion of the relationship between U.S. strategy and the size and structure of U.S. naval forces that can form part of the context for assessing the 30-year shipbuilding plan, see **Appendix C**.

Some study groups have made their own proposals for Navy ship force structure that reflect their own perspectives on the points listed above (particularly the first three and the final one). For purposes of comparison, **Table 7** also shows the Navy's 306-ship goal of January 2013.

A potential key question for Congress concerns whether the U.S. Navy in coming years will be large enough to adequately counter improved Chinese maritime A2/AD forces while also adequately performing other missions of interest to U.S. policymakers around the world. Some observers are concerned that a combination of growing Chinese naval capabilities and budget- driven reductions in the size of the U.S. Navy could encourage Chinese military overconfidence and demoralize U.S. allies and partners in the Pacific, and thereby make it harder for the United States to defend its interests in the region.[15] Potential oversight questions for Congress include the following:

- Under the Administration's plans, will the Navy in coming years be large enough to adequately counter improved Chinese maritime A2/AD forces while also adequately performing other missions of interest to U.S. policymakers around the world?

Table 7. Recent Study Group Proposals for Navy Ship Force Structure

Ship type	Navy's 306- ship goal of January 2013	Project on Defense Alternatives (PDA) (November 2012)	Heritage Foundation (April 2011)	Cato Institute (September 2010)[a]	Independent Panel Assessment of 2010 QDR (July 2010)	Sustainable Defense Task Force (June 2010)	Center for a New American Security (CNAS) (November 2008)	Center for Strategic and Budgetary Assessments (CSBA) (2008)[b]
Submarines								
SSBN	12	7	14[c]	6	14	7	14	12
SSGN	0	6-7	4	0	4	4	0	2
SSN	43	42	55	40	55	37	40	41
Aircraft carriers								
CVN	11	9	11	8	11	9	8	11
CVE	0	0	0	0	0	0	0	4
Surface combatants								
Cruiser	88	72-74	88	22	n/a	85	18	14
Destroyer				65	n/a		56	73
Frigate	0	2-7[j]	28[d]	14	n/a	0	0	9[e]
LCS	52	12[j]		4	n/a	25	48	55
SSC	0	[j]	0	0	n/a	0	40	0[f]
Amphibious and Maritime Prepositioning Force (Future) (MPF[F]) ships								
Amphibious ships	33	≥23	37	23	n/a	27	36	33
MPF(F) ships	0	n/a	0	0	n/a	n/a	0	3g
LSD station ships	0	0	0	0	0	0	0	7h

Table 7. (Continued)

Ship type	Navy's 306- ship goal of January 2013	Project on Defense Alternatives (PDA) (November 2012)	Heritage Foundation (April 2011)	Cato Institute (September 2010)[a]	Independent Panel Assessment of 2010 QDR (July 2010)	Sustainable Defense Task Force (June 2010)	Center for a New American Security (CNAS) (November 2008)	Center for Strategic and Budgetary Assessments (CSBA) (2008)[b]
Other: Mine warfare (MIW) ships; Combat Logistics Force (CLF) ships (i.e., at-sea resupply ships), and support ships								
MIW	0	14[j]	14	11	0	0	0	0
CLF ships	29	n/a	33	21	n/a	36	40	31
Support ships	33	n/a	25	27	n/a			31
TOTAL battle force ships	**306**	**230**	**309**	**241**	**346**	**230**	**300**	**326**[i]

Source: Table prepared by CRS based on the following sources: **For Heritage Foundation**: *A Strong National Defense[:] The Armed Forces America Needs and What They Will Cost*, Heritage Foundation, April 5, 2011, pp. 25-26. **For Cato Institute**: Benjamin H. Friedman and Christopher Preble, *Budgetary Savings from Military Restraint, Washington*, Cato Institute, September 23, 2010 (Policy Analysis No. 667), pp. 6, 8-10, and additional information provided by Cato Institute to CRS by email on September 22, 2010. **For Independent Panel Assessment:** Stephen J. Hadley and William J. Perry, co-chairmen, et al., *The QDR in Perspective: Meeting America's National Security Needs In the 21st Century, The Final Report of the Quadrennial Defense Review Independent Panel*, Washington, 2010, Figure 3-2 on pages 58-59. **For Sustainable Defense Task Force:** Debt, Deficits, and Defense, *A Way Forward[:] Report of the Sustainable Defense Task Force*, June 11, 2010, pp. 19-20. **For CNAS:** Frank Hoffman, *From Preponderance to Partnership: American Maritime Power in the 21st Century*. Washington, Center for a New American Security, November 2008. p. 19 (Table 2). **For CSBA:** Robert O. Work, *The US Navy[:] Charting a Course for Tomorrow's Fleet. Washington, Center for Strategic and Budgetary Assessments*, 2008. p. 81 (Figure 5). **For PDA:** Carl Conetta, Reasonable Defense, Project on Defense Alternatives, November 14, 2012, 31 pp.

Notes: n/a is not addressed in the report. **SSBN** is nuclear-powered ballistic missile submarine; **SSGN** is nuclear-powered cruise missile and special operations forces submarine; **SSN** is nuclear-powered attack submarine; **CVN** is large nuclear-powered aircraft carrier; **CVE** is medium-sized aircraft carrier; **LCS** is Littoral Combat Ship; SSC (an acronym created by CRS for this table) is small surface combatant of 1,000+ tons displacement—a ship similar to late-1990s Streetfighter concept; **MPF**(F) is Maritime Prepositioning Force (Future) ship; LSD is LSD-41/49 class amphibious ship operating as a station ship for a formation like a Global Fleet Station (GFS); **MIW** is mine warfare ship; **CLF** is combat logistics force (i.e., resupply) ship.

a. Figures shown are for the year 2020; for subsequent years, reductions from these figures would be considered.

b. Figures shown are for the year 2028.

c. The report calls for a force of 280 SLBMs, which appears to equate to a force of 14 SSBNs, each with 20 SLBM tubes.

d. The report calls for a force of 28 small surface combatants, and appears to use the term small surface combatants the same way that the Navy does in the 30-year shipbuilding plan—as a way of collectively referring to frigates and LCSs. The small surface combatants (SSCs) called for in the November 2008 CNAS report are separate from and smaller than the LCS.

e. Maritime Security Frigates.

f. Plan includes 28 patrol craft (PCs) of a few hundred tons displacement each, as well as 29 boat detachments and seven riverine squadrons.

g. Plan shows three Mobile Landing Platform (MLP) ships that the Navy currently plans for the MPF(F) squadron, plus 16 existing current-generation maritime prepositioning force (MPF) ships and 17 existing prepositioning ships for Army and other service/agency equipment. Plan also shows 67 other DOD sealift ships.

h. T-LSDs, meaning LSDs operated by the Military Sealift Command (MSC) with a partly civilian crew.

i. The CSBA report shows a total of 488 units by including 162 additional force units that do not count toward the 306-ship goal under the battle force ships counting method that has been used since the early 1980s for public policy discussions of the size of the Navy. These 162 additional force units include 16 existing current-generation maritime prepositioning force (MPF) ships and 17 existing prepositioning ships for Army and other service/agency equipment, 67 other DOD sealift ships, 28 PCs, 29 boat detachments, and certain other small-scale units. The CSBA report proposes a new counting method for naval/maritime forces that includes units such as these in the total count.

Table 7. (Continued)

j. The report "prescribes ending procurement of the LCS with the 12 already purchased. The Reasonable Defense model foresees a future cohort of 28 to 33 small surface combatants, including a mix of the 12 LCS that have already been procured, 14 Mine Counter Measure (MCM) ships already in the fleet, and small frigates or ocean-going corvettes. As the MCM ships age and leave the fleet, the LCS should assume their role. The would leave a post-MCM requirement for 16 to 21 additional small surface combatants. For this, the Navy needs a simpler, less expensive alternative to the LCS."

- What might be the political and security implications in the Asia-Pacific region of a combination of growing Chinese naval capabilities and budget-driven reductions in the size of the U.S. Navy?
- If the Navy is reduced in size and priority is given to maintaining Navy forces in the Pacific, what will be the impact on Navy force levels in other parts of the world, such as the Persian Gulf/Indian Ocean region or the Mediterranean Sea, and consequently on the Navy's ability to adequately perform its missions in those parts of the world?
- To what extent could the operational impacts of a reduction in Navy ship numbers be mitigated through increased use of forward homeporting, multiple crewing, and long-duration deployments with crew rotation (i.e., "Sea Swap")? How feasible are these options, and what would be their potential costs and benefits?[16]
- Particularly in a situation of constrained DOD resources, if enough funding is allocated to the Navy to permit the Navy in coming years to maintain a fleet of 306 ships including 11 aircraft carriers, how much would other DOD programs need to be reduced, and what would be the operational implications of those program reductions in terms of DOD's overall ability to counter improved Chinese military forces and perform other missions?[17]

One observer—the person who until recently was the Navy's lead force-structure planner—stated the following regarding the Navy's approach to fleet design:

> It is time to rethink how we will design the future Fleet in a way that rebalances affordability, platform capability, and deployment processes. We must build it as a whole instead of continuing to "let it happen" one platform requirements decision at a time....
>
> Today the Navy operates about 50 different types of ships and aircraft with individual design-service lives of 20 to 50 years. On average, about two classes of ship or aircraft annually come up for a decision on replacement at the end of their service lives. Each of these decisions, a multi-year joint bureaucratic process with dozens of participating organizations, is made individually. Typically, as a starting point, the new platform must do everything the old one did, except in the more challenging threat environment of the future. All of the decision-making organizations generally advocate for the next-generation platform to have the desired capabilities unmet by the old one—particularly since

any additional unit cost is not their bill. It is no surprise that this process leads to steadily increasing platform and overall Fleet cost....

The future Fleet is being designed ad hoc, one platform at a time, and we cannot afford this. How can we change the trend toward an ever-smaller Fleet of ever-better platforms while maintaining the capability superiority needed to execute our missions? It will take a top- down design to provide a structure in which individual platform requirements can be shaped and disciplined despite all of the pressures. We will have to consider distributing capabilities to a greater extent across a force that is securely networked, at least within line of sight, rather than putting as many as possible on each individual platform and continuing to drive up its size and cost.

We will have to consider separating weapon magazines from the sensors that direct the weapons rather than putting both on the same platform. Another option is increasing reliance on deep-magazine directed energy systems, and on force-wide coordinated soft-kill and counter-targeting techniques, rather than on engaging each threat with ever-larger and more expensive kinetic weapons. We can also think about increasing reliance on penetrating high- threat areas with longer-range weapons or with preprogrammed unmanned systems rather than with manned platforms. Few of these options would rise to the top in the requirements decision-making process for any individual platform. They only start to make sense when considered and competed at a Fleet-wide level.

Developing an overall fleet design to structure and discipline individual platform requirements is no small task. Simply constraining platform cost without dealing with how capabilities might be delivered differently is not sufficient. This is not a once-and-done process, as changes in threat and in our own technology options will never stop. But neither can it be a process that changes the design in some fundamental way every year or two—it will have to influence platform requirements for a long period of time to affect a significant number of new platform designs.

We cannot afford to retire legacy platforms prematurely simply because they are not optimized within our new Fleet design, which will take time to implement and have to be done incrementally. Real and fundamental change in the roles, missions, and interdependencies among platform types, and in the balance between manned and unmanned and between platform and payload, is an inevitable outcome of a Fleet design process. That is the point. Change is hard, and it will have to be authorized and directed by the Navy's leadership or risk not happening.

A number of ideas for a new Fleet design have been offered recently from outside the Navy's decision-making mainstream. However, all have had significant flaws, so they have not received serious consideration. They have assumed things such as beyond line-of-sight networking that has no survivable future in the face of adversary counter-space capability; autonomy of unmanned vehicles in executing lethal missions that is beyond the projected capability of software and U.S. rules of engagement to support; and the use of platforms too small to be capable of global deployment and sustained sea-based operations, which is how the U.S. Navy must deliver global naval power. The future Fleet design must be grounded in technical and operational reality, and it has to come from inside the Navy system....

Developing a rich list of operationally-realistic options supported by rigorous analysis of cost and feasibility is foundational. It could include:

- The use of a common large aviation-ship hull for Navy sea-control/power-projection air wings and for Marine Corps vertical-raid/assault-air wings, reconfigurable between the two missions between the deployments;
- Surface combatants with smaller vertical-launch magazines that can reload at sea from logistic ships or remotely fire weapons carried in supplementary magazines on logistic ships;
- Separate classes of surface combatants optimized for air defense or antisubmarine warfare within a common hull type that can self-defend in peacetime but aggregate to fight offensively in wartime;
- Tactical-combat aircraft that are optimized for endurance and carriage of long-range weapons rather than for penetrating sophisticated defenses carrying short-range weapons;
- Large shore-launched unmanned undersea vehicles that take the place of submarines for preprogrammed missions such as covert surveillance or mine-laying;
- Use of a common hull type for all of the large non-combatant ship missions such as command ships, tenders, hospital ships, ground vehicle delivery, and logistics; and
- Elimination of support models that are based on wartime reliance on reach-back access to unclassified cyber networks connected by vulnerable communications satellites or to an indefensible global internet....

The Navy's long-term force structure requirement is a 306-ship Fleet of the currently- planned designs, of which about 120 (or 40 percent of the force) would be deployed day-to- day. It would also be able to surge an additional 75 ships (another 25 percent) within two months to meet warfighting capacity requirements. In other words, about 65 percent is employed or rapidly employable.

This sounds good, but the reality is that 30 of these 120 deployed ships would be permanently homeported overseas; 26 would be LCSs that use the rotation of their small military crews to keep 50 percent of that class forward deployed; and 40 would be Military Sealift Command support ships that use rotational civilian mariner crewing to keep the ships deployed 75 percent of the time. The remaining 25 of the forward-deployed force will be large and complex multibillion dollar warships with all-military crews, supported out of a rotation base of 140 such ships.

In other words, we plan to buy and operate five of our most expensive ships to keep one deployed. This is not an efficient way to operate. In times of reduced funding our design must address ways to meet our deployment goals with a smaller rotation base while preserving wartime surge capacity.

Many studies and trials have been done over the years on options for reducing the total number of ships needed to sustain the Navy's robust peacetime forward-deployed posture. Increasing forward homeporting in other nations always comes up as the first choice. While it is a good one, few countries beyond those that currently support this (Japan, Spain, Italy, and Bahrain) are willing to tolerate a permanent new U.S. shore footprint. Building new shore-support infrastructure in foreign countries to back this results in a large bill for construction jobs outside the United States, which Congress normally finds unappetizing.

Using rotational crews to keep ships forward for extended periods without long deployments for their sailors is an efficient option that works for ships with small crews like LCSs, legacy mine-warfare ships, or Military Sealift Command support ships. Experiments in which this has been done with military crews on large complex warships have not turned out well. This was due both to the logistics of moving large crews overseas for turnovers and the difficulty of maintaining exact configuration commonality within ships of a class so that a crew arriving on a ship overseas has trained before deployment on an identical ship (or simulator) at home. Conversions of ships from military manning to Military Sealift Command civilian mariner crews that routinely rotate individual crewmembers to sustain ships forward are limited by the law of war concerning what military actions civilians can perform, and there are few legal options left for further expansion of this approach.

What is left in the force-generation model of our current Fleet is a force of our most complex warships—aircraft carriers, submarines, destroyers, and amphibious ships—operating with permanently-assigned military crews in the "Fleet Readiness Program" cycle of maintain- train-deploy with a deployed output of one in five. Future designs must address this model and find ways to get more deployed time out of these expensive ships and crews—without exceeding the current objective of having military crewmembers spend no more than 50 percent of their time away from homeport over a complete multi-year operating cycle. The current limiting factor is the period required to train the crew as a team before deployment following the inactivity and crew turnover of the shipyard maintenance period.

Naval aviation is steadily moving toward the increased use of high-fidelity single and multi- aircraft simulation as a means of developing and sustaining operational proficiency with reduced use of expensive live flying. These simulators are funded as part of the overall fielding plan for the aircraft and were also built for the ballistic-missile submarine force to support its Blue-Gold crew manning concept. There is no equivalent model or set of off-ship simulators for major sections of the crews of conventional surface warships (other than the LCS) for nuclear-aircraft carriers or for attack submarines. A Fleet design that bought such simulation capability as part of its ship production programs—the way that aircraft programs do—would have significant potential for improving operational output by reducing the time to train for deployment after maintenance periods.

Today's Fleet design is the product of many separate and disconnected decisions about the required capabilities of 50 different types of ships and aircraft. While not ineffective, it is definitely too expensive. The budget constraints facing the Navy for the next 20 years are not matched by a projected reduction in the quantity or capability of forces that must be delivered forward every day or surged forward in wartime.

The only way to meet these demands within available resources is to develop a design that provides a structure within which the capabilities of future platforms can be shaped to meet the Fleet's missions efficiently as an overall force. Doing this will require a systems-level approach to defining what it must be able to do, and will mean abandoning some cherished traditions of what each type of platform should do. The alternative is a Navy no longer large or capable enough to do the nation's business.[18]

Affordability of 30-Year Shipbuilding Plan

Another potential oversight issue for Congress concerns the prospective affordability of the Navy's 30-year shipbuilding plan. In assessing the prospective affordability of the 30-year plan, key factors that Congress may consider include estimated ship procurement costs and future shipbuilding funding levels. Each of these is discussed below.

Estimated Ship Procurement Costs

If one or more Navy ship designs turn out to be more expensive to build than the Navy estimates, then the projected funding levels shown in the 30-

year shipbuilding plan will not be sufficient to procure all the ships shown in the plan. Ship designs that can be viewed as posing a risk of being more expensive to build than the Navy estimates include Gerald R. Ford (CVN-78) class aircraft carriers, Ohio-replacement (SSBNX) class ballistic missile submarines, the Flight III version of the DDG-51 destroyer, the TAO(X) oiler, and the LX(R) amphibious ship.

The Navy delivered its narrative report on the FY2015 30-year shipbuilding plan to CRS on July 3, 2014. As shown in the bottom half of **Table 8**, the Navy estimates in the report that the FY2015 30-year plan would cost an average of about $16.7 billion per year in constant FY2014 dollars to implement, including an average of about $15.7 billion per year during the first 10 years of the plan, an average of about $19.7 billion per year during the middle 10 years of the plan, and an average of about $14.6 billion per year during the final 10 years of the plan.

As also shown in the bottom half of **Table 8**, a December 2014 Congressional Budget Office (CBO) report on the Navy's FY2015 30-year shipbuilding plan estimates that the plan will require about 13% more funding to implement than the Navy estimates, including about 6% more than the Navy estimates during the first 10 years of the plan, about 14% more than the Navy estimates during the middle 10 years of the plan, and about 20% more than the Navy estimates during the final 10 years of the plan.[19] Over the years, CBO's estimates of the cost to implement the Navy's 30-year shipbuilding plan have generally been higher than the Navy's estimates.

Some of the difference between CBO's estimates and the Navy's estimates is due to a difference between CBO and the Navy in how to treat inflation in Navy shipbuilding. This difference compounds over time, making it increasingly important as a factor in the difference between CBO's estimates and the Navy's estimates the further one goes into the 30-year period. In other words, other things held equal, this factor tends to push the CBO and Navy estimates further and further apart as one proceeds from the earlier years of the plan to the later years of the plan.

The shipbuilding program that contributes the most to the difference between the CBO and Navy estimates of the cost of the 30-year plan is a future destroyer, called the DDG-51 Flight IV, that appears in the final 15 years of the 30-year plan. As shown in the CBO report, this one program accounts for 38% of the total difference between CBO and the Navy on the estimated cost implement the 30-year shipbuilding plan, making it almost twice as significant as the next-largest contributor to the overall difference (the Ohio replacement program, which accounts for 20%).[20]

Table 8. Navy and CBO Estimates of Cost of FY2014 and FY2015 30-Year Shipbuilding Plans

	First 10 years of the plan	Middle 10 years of the plan	Final 10 years of the plan	Entire 30 years of the plan
FY2014 30-year (FY2014-FY2043) plan (in constant FY2013 dollars)				
Navy estimate	15.4	19.8	15.2	16.8
CBO estimate	16.3	22.6	19.1	19.3
% difference between Navy and CBO estimates	6%	14%	26%	15%
FY2015 30-year (FY2015-FY2044) plan (in constant FY2014 dollars)				
Navy estimate	~15.7	~19.7	~14.6	~16.7
CBO estimate	16.7	22.5	17.5	18.9
% difference between Navy and CBO estimates	6%	14%	20%	13%

Source: **For FY2014 30-year** plan: Congressional Budget Office, *An Analysis of the Navy's Fiscal Year 2014 Shipbuilding Plan*, October 2013, Table 3 (page 13). **For FY2015 30-year plan:** *Report to Congress on the Annual Long-Range Plan for Construction of Naval Vessels for FY2015*, p. 8.

The relatively large contribution of the Flight IV destroyer to the overall difference between CBO and the Navy on the cost of the 30-year shipbuilding plan appears to be due primarily to three factors:

- There are many of these Flight IV destroyers in the 30-year plan—a total of 35, or 13% of the 264 total ships in the plan.
- There appears to be a basic difference between CBO and the Navy over the likely size (and thus cost) of this ship. The Navy appears to

assume that the ship will use the current DDG-51 hull design, whereas CBO believes the growth potential of the current DDG-51 hull design will be exhausted by then, and that the ship will require a larger hull design (either a lengthened version of the DDG-51 hull design, or an entirely new hull design).

- These destroyers occur in the final 15 years of the 30-year plan, where the effects of the difference between CBO and the Navy on how to treat inflation in Navy shipbuilding are the most pronounced.

Future Shipbuilding Funding Levels

It has been known for some time that implementing the 30-year shipbuilding plan would require shipbuilding budgets in coming years that are considerably greater than those of recent years, and that funding requirements for the Ohio-replacement (SSBN[X]) ballistic missile submarine program will put particular pressure on the shipbuilding budget during the middle years of the 30- year plan. The Navy's report on the FY2015 30-year plan states:

> Beginning in FY2020 and running through the end of the 30-year plan horizon, the plan requires an average annual investment of about \$17.2B [billion] (FY14\$) [i.e., in constant FY2014 dollars] to finance, which is ~\$4B/year more than our historical average annual investment of ~\$13B/yr. In particular, for the period while we are procuring the OHIO Replacement (OR) SSBN (essentially FY[20]25-FY[20]34), the Navy will have to provide an average of \$19.7B annually with the peak year in FY[20]32 at slightly more than \$24B. Even if the OHIO Replacement Program (ORP) is removed from the [required] resource total [by funding the program through a different part of the defense budget], the average funding required beginning in FY2020 is ~\$14-15B/yr to build the FSA [Force Structure Assessment] force [i.e., the planned 306-ship fleet]....
>
> While the force structure presented [in this report] describes a battle force that meets the requirements of the National Security Strategy and the 2014 QDR [Quadrennial Defense Review]; it requires funding at an unsustainable level, particularly between FY[20]25 and FY[20]34... The average cost of this plan during the period in which the DON [Department of the Navy] is procuring OR SSBN[s] (~\$19.7B/year [during] FY2025-[FY]2034) cannot be accommodated by the Navy from existing resources—particularly if DOD is required to be funded at the BCA [Budget Control Act] levels....
>
> The DON can only afford the SSBN procurement costs with significant increases in our [budget] top-line or by having the SSBN funded from sources that do not result in any reductions to the DON's current resourcing level....

> If the DON is unable to sustain the average annual shipbuilding budgets of $19.7 billion over the course of the mid-term planning period, which is unlikely to be the case,[21] the battle force will fall far short of meeting the QDR requirements.[22]

In assessing the Navy's ability to reach the higher annual shipbuilding funding levels described above, one perspective is to note that doing so would require the shipbuilding budget to be increased by 30% to 50% from levels in recent years. In a context of constraints on defense spending and competing demands for defense dollars, this perspective can make the goal of increasing the shipbuilding budget to these levels appear daunting.

Another perspective is to note that the additional annual funding needed (roughly $4 billion to $6.7 billion) equates to roughly 0.8% to 1.3% of a defense budget of $521 billion per year (the Budget Control Act figure for defense spending FY2015). Some observers, noting the U.S. strategic rebalancing toward the Asia-Pacific region, have advocated shifting a greater share of the DOD budget to the Navy and Air Force, on the grounds that the Asia-Pacific region is primarily a maritime and aerospace theater for DOD. In discussing the idea of shifting a greater share of the DOD budget to the Navy and Air Force, some of these observers refer to breaking the so-called "one-third, one-third, one-third" division of resources among the three military departments—a shorthand term sometimes used to refer to the more-or-less stable division of resources between the three military departments that existed for the three decades between the end of U.S. participation in the Vietnam War in 1973 and the start of the Iraq War in 2003.[23] In a context of breaking the "one-third, one-third, one-third" allocation with an aim of better aligning defense spending with the strategic rebalancing, shifting 0.8% to 1.3% of the defense budget into the Navy's shipbuilding account would appear to be quite feasible.

More broadly, if defense spending were to remain constrained to the revised cap levels in the Budget Control Act, then fully funding the Department of the Navy's total budget at the levels shown in the current Future Years Defense Plan (FYDP) would require increasing the Department of the Navy's share of the non-Defense-Wide part of the DOD budget to about 41%, compared to about 36% in the FY2014 budget and an average of about 37% for the three-decade period between the Vietnam and Iraq wars.[24] While shifting 4% or 5% of DOD's budget to the Department of the Navy would be a more ambitious reallocation than shifting 0.8% to 1.3% of the DOD budget to the Navy's shipbuilding account, similarly large reallocations have occurred in the past.[25]

Legislative Activity for FY2016

FY2016 Funding Request

The Navy's proposed FY2016 budget requests funding for the procurement of nine new battle force ships (i.e., ships that count against the Navy's goal for achieving and maintaining a fleet of 306 ships). The nine ships include two Virginia-class attack submarines, two DDG-51 class Aegis destroyers, three Littoral Combat Ships (LCSs), one LPD-17 class amphibious ship, and one TAO(X) class oiler. The Navy's proposed FY2016 shipbuilding budget also requests funding for ships that have been procured in prior fiscal years, and ships that are to be procured in future fiscal years.

Appendix A. Comparing Past Ship Force Levels to Current or Potential Future Ship Force Levels

In assessing the appropriateness of the current or potential future number of ships in the Navy, observers sometimes compare that number to historical figures for total Navy fleet size. Historical figures for total fleet size, however, can be a problematic yardstick for assessing the appropriateness of the current or potential future number of ships in the Navy, particularly if the historical figures are more than a few years old, because

- the missions to be performed by the Navy, the mix of ships that make up the Navy, and the technologies that are available to Navy ships for performing missions all change over time; and
- the number of ships in the fleet in an earlier year might itself have been inappropriate (i.e., not enough or more than enough) for meeting the Navy's mission requirements in that year.

Regarding the first bullet point above, the Navy, for example, reached a late-Cold War peak of 568 battle force ships at the end of FY1987,[26] and as of February 24, 2015, included a total of 284 battle force ships (using the new counting rules proposed by the Navy as part of its FY2015 budget submission). The FY1987 fleet, however, was intended to meet a set of mission requirements that focused on countering Soviet naval forces at sea during a potential multi-theater NATO-Warsaw Pact conflict, while the February 2015 fleet is intended to meet a considerably different set of mission requirements centered on influencing events ashore by countering both land- and sea-based military forces of potential regional threats other than Russia, including improved Chinese military forces and non-state terrorist organizations. In addition, the Navy of FY1987 differed substantially from the February 2015 fleet in areas such as profusion of precision-guided air-delivered weapons, numbers of Tomahawk-capable ships, and the sophistication of C4ISR systems and networking capabilities.[27]

In coming years, Navy missions may shift again, and the capabilities of Navy ships will likely have changed further by that time due to developments such as more comprehensive implementation of networking technology, increased use of ship-based unmanned vehicles, and the potential fielding of new types of weapons such as lasers or electromagnetic rail guns.

The 568-ship fleet of FY1987 may or may not have been capable of performing its stated missions; the 284-ship fleet of February 2015 may or may not be capable of performing its stated missions; and a fleet years from now with a certain number of ships may or may not be capable of performing its stated missions. Given changes over time in mission requirements, ship mixes, and technologies, however, these three issues are to a substantial degree independent of one another.

For similar reasons, trends over time in the total number of ships in the Navy are not necessarily a reliable indicator of the direction of change in the fleet's ability to perform its stated missions. An increasing number of ships in the fleet might not necessarily mean that the fleet's ability to perform its stated missions is increasing, because the fleet's mission requirements might be increasing more rapidly than ship numbers and average ship capability. Similarly, a decreasing number of ships in the fleet might not necessarily mean that the fleet's ability to perform stated missions is decreasing, because the fleet's mission requirements might be declining more rapidly than numbers of ships, or because average ship capability and the percentage of time that ships are in deployed locations might be increasing quickly enough to more than offset reductions in total ship numbers.

Regarding the second of the two bullet points above, it can be noted that comparisons of the size of the fleet today with the size of the fleet in earlier years rarely appear to consider whether the fleet was appropriately sized in those earlier years (and therefore potentially suitable as a yardstick of comparison), even though it is quite possible that the fleet in those earlier years might not have been appropriately sized, and even though there might have been differences of opinion among observers at that time regarding that question. Just as it might not be prudent for observers years from now to tacitly assume that the 289-ship Navy of September 2014 was appropriately sized for meeting the mission requirements of 2014, even though there currently are differences of opinion among observers on that question (as reflected, for example, in **Table 7**) simply because a figure of 289 ships appears in the historical records for 2014, so, too, might it not be prudent for observers today to tacitly assume that the number of ships of the Navy in an earlier year was appropriate for meeting the Navy's mission requirements that year, even though there might have been differences of opinion among observers at that time regarding that question, simply because the size of the Navy in that year appears in a table like **Table D-**1.

Previous Navy force structure plans, such as those shown in **Table 1**, might provide some insight into the potential adequacy of a proposed new force-structure plan, but changes over time in mission requirements, technologies available to ships for performing missions, and other force- planning factors, as well as the possibility that earlier force-structure plans might not have been appropriate for meeting the mission demands of their times, suggest that some caution should be applied in using past force structure plans for this purpose, particularly if those past force structure plans are more than a few years old. The Reagan-era plan for a 600-ship Navy, for example, was designed for a Cold War set of missions focusing on countering Soviet naval forces at sea, which is not an appropriate basis for planning the Navy today, and there was considerable debate during those years as to the appropriateness of the 600-ship goal.[28]

APPENDIX B. INDEPENDENT PANEL ASSESSMENT OF 2010 QDR

The law that requires DOD to perform QDRs once every four years (10 U.S.C. 118) states that the results of each QDR shall be assessed by an independent panel. The report of the independent panel that assessed the 2010 QDR was released on July 29, 2010. The independent panel's report recommended a Navy of 346 ships, including 11 aircraft carriers and 55 attack submarines.[29] The report stated the following, among other things:

- "The QDR should reflect current commitments, but it must also plan effectively for potential threats that could arise over the next 20 years.... we believe the 2010 QDR did not accord sufficient priority to the need to counter anti-access challenges, strengthen homeland defense (including our defense against cyber threats), and conduct post-conflict stabilization missions." (Page 54)
- "In this remarkable period of change, global security will still depend upon an American presence capable of unimpeded access to all international areas of the Pacific region. In an environment of 'anti-access strategies,' and assertions to create unique 'economic and security zones of influence,' America's rightful and historic presence will be critical. To preserve our interests, the United States will need to retain the ability to transit freely the areas of the Western Pacific for security and economic reasons. Our allies also depend on us to be fully present in the Asia-Pacific as a promoter of stability and to ensure the free flow of commerce. A robust U.S. force structure, largely rooted in maritime strategy but including other necessary capabilities, will be essential." (Page 51)
- "The United States will need agile forces capable of operating against the full range of potential contingencies. However, the need to deal with irregular and hybrid threats will tend to drive the size and shape of ground forces for years to come, whereas the need to continue to be fully present in Asia and the Pacific and other areas of interest will do the same for naval and air forces." (Page 55)
- "The force structure in the Asia-Pacific needs to be increased. In order to preserve U.S. interests, the United States will need to retain the ability to transit freely the areas of the Western Pacific for security and economic reasons. The United States must be fully present in the Asia-Pacific region to protect American lives and territory, ensure the free flow of commerce, maintain stability, and defend our allies in the region. A robust U.S. force structure, one that is largely rooted in maritime strategy and includes other necessary capabilities, will be essential." (Page 66)
- "Force structure must be strengthened in a number of areas to address the need to counter anti-access challenges, strengthen homeland defense (including defense against cyber threats), and conduct post-

conflict stabilization missions: First, as a Pacific power, the U.S. presence in Asia has underwritten the regional stability that has enabled India and China to emerge as rising economic powers. The United States should plan on continuing that role for the indefinite future. The Panel remains concerned that the QDR force structure may not be sufficient to assure others that the United States can meet its treaty commitments in the face of China's increased military capabilities. Therefore, we recommend an increased priority on defeating anti-access and area-denial threats. This will involve acquiring new capabilities, and, as Secretary Gates has urged, developing innovative concepts for their use. Specifically, we believe the United States must fully fund the modernization of its surface fleet. We also believe the United States must be able to deny an adversary sanctuary by providing persistent surveillance, tracking, and rapid engagement with high-volume precision strike. That is why the Panel supports an increase in investment in long-range strike systems and their associated sensors. In addition, U.S. forces must develop and demonstrate the ability to operate in an information-denied environment." (Pages 59-60)

- "To compete effectively, the U.S. military must continue to develop new conceptual approaches to dealing with operational challenges, like the Capstone Concept for Joint Operations (CCJO). The Navy and Air Force's effort to develop an Air-Sea Battle concept is one example of an approach to deal with the growing anti-access challenge. It will be necessary to invest in modernized capabilities to make this happen. The Chief of Naval Operations and Chief of Staff of the Air Force deserve support in this effort, and the Panel recommends the other military services be brought into the concept when appropriate." (Page 51; a similar passage appears on page 67)

In recommending a Navy of 346 ships, the independent panel's report cited the 1993 Bottom-Up Review (BUR) of U.S. defense plans and policies. **Table B-1** compares the Navy's 306-ship goal of March 2012 to the 346-ship Navy recommended in the 1993 BUR (as detailed partly in subsequent Navy testimony and publications) and the ship force levels recommended in the independent panel report.

Table B-1. Comparison of Navy's 306-ship goal, Navy Plan from 1993 BUR, and Navy Plan from 2010 QDR Review Panel

Ship Type	Navy's 306-ship goal of March 2012	Bottom-Up Review (BUR) (1993)	2010 QDR Independent Review Panel (July 2010)
SSBNs	12-14	18 (SSBN force was later reduced to 14 as a result of the 1994 Nuclear Posture Review)	14
SSGNs	0-4	0 (SSGN program did not yet exist)	4
SSNs	~48	45 to 55 (55 in FY99, with a long-term goal of about 45)	55
Aircraft carriers	11 active	11 active + 1 operational/reserve	11 active
Surface combatants	~145	124 (114 active + 10 frigates in Naval Reserve Force; a total of 110-116 active ships was also cited)	n/a
Cruisers and destroyers	*~90*	*n/a*	*n/a*
Frigates	0 (to be replaced by LCSs)	*n/a*	*n/a*
LCSs	*~55*	*0* *(LCS program did not exist)*	*n/a*
Amphibious ships	~32 (30 operational ships needed to lift 2.0 MEBs)	41 (Enough to lift 2.5 MEBs)	n/a
Dedicated mine warfare ships	0 (to be replaced by LCSs)	26 (LCS program did not exist)	n/a
CLF ships	~29	43	n/a
Support ships	~33	22	n/a
TOTAL ships	**~306**	**346** **(numbers above add to 331-341)**[a]	**346**

Source: Table prepared by CRS. ***Sources for 1993 Bottom-Up Review:*** Department of Defense, *Report on the Bottom-Up Review*, October 1993, Figure 7 on page 28; Department of the Navy, *Highlights of the FY 1995 Department of the Navy Budget*, February 1994, p. 1; Department of the Navy, Force 2001, *A Program Guide to the U.S. Navy*, 1994 edition, p. 15; Statement of VADM T. Joseph

Lopez, U.S. Navy, Deputy Chief of Naval Operations (Resources, Warfare Requirements & Assessments), Testimony to the Military Forces and Personnel Subcommittee of the House Armed Services Committee, March 22, 1994, pp. 2-5. ***Source for independent panel report:*** Stephen J. Hadley and William J. Perry, co-chairmen, et al., *The QDR in Perspective: Meeting America's National Security Needs In the 21st Century, The Final Report of the Quadrennial Defense Review Independent Panel*, Washington, 2010, Figure 3-2 on pages 58-59.

Notes: n/a is not addressed in the report. **SSBN** is nuclear-powered ballistic missile submarine; **SSGN** is nuclear-powered cruise missile and special operations forces submarine; **SSN** is nuclear-powered attack submarine; **LCS** is Littoral Combat Ship; MPF(F) is Maritime Prepositioning Force (Future) ship; **CLF** is combat logistics force (i.e., resupply) ship; **MEB** is Marine Expeditionary Brigade.

a. The Navy testified in 1994 that the planned number was adjusted from 346 to 330 to reflect reductions in numbers of tenders and early retirements of some older amphibious ships.

In a letter dated August 11, 2010, Secretary of Defense Robert Gates provided his comments on the independent panel's report. The letter stated in part:

> I completely agree with the Panel that a strong navy is essential; however, I disagree with the Panel's recommendation that DoD should establish the 1993 Bottom Up Review's (BUR's) fleet of 346 ships as the objective target. That number was a simple projection of the then-planned size of [the] Navy in FY 1999, not a reflection of 21st century, steady-state requirements. The fleet described in the 2010 QDR report, with its overall target of 313 to 321 ships, has roughly the same number of aircraft carriers, nuclear-powered attack submarines, surface combatants, mine warfare vessels, and amphibious ships as the larger BUR fleet. The main difference between the two fleets is in the numbers of combat logistics, mobile logistics, and support ships. Although it is true that the 2010 fleet includes fewer of these ships, they are all now more efficiently manned and operated by the Military Sealift Command and meet all of DoD's requirements....
>
> I agree with the Panel's general conclusion that DoD ought to enhance its overall posture and capabilities in the Asia-Pacific region. As I outlined in my speech at the Naval War College in April 2009, "to carry out the missions we may face in the future... we will need numbers, speed, and the ability to operate in shallow waters." So as the Air-Sea battle concept development reaches maturation, and as DoD's review of global defense posture continues, I will be looking for ways to meet plausible security threats while emphasizing sustained forward presence – particularly in the Pacific.[30]

APPENDIX C. U.S. STRATEGY AND THE SIZE AND STRUCTURE OF U.S. NAVAL FORCES

This appendix presents some observations on the relationship between U.S. strategy and the size and structure of U.S. naval forces that can form part of the context for assessing Navy force structure goals and shipbuilding plans.[31]

Strategic considerations that can be considered in assessing Navy force structure goals and shipbuilding plans include, among other things, the U.S. strategic rebalancing toward the Asia- Pacific region,[32] China's modernization of its maritime military capabilities,[33] and requests from U.S. regional combatant commanders (COCOMs) for forward-deployed U.S. naval forces that the Navy has testified would require a Navy of about 450 ships to fully meet.[34]

More broadly, from a strategic perspective it can be noted that that U.S. naval forces, while not inexpensive, give the United States the ability to convert the world's oceans—a global commons that covers more than two-thirds of the planet's surface—into a medium of maneuver and operations for projecting U.S. power ashore and otherwise defending U.S. interests around the world. The ability to use the world's oceans in this manner—and to deny other countries the use of the world's oceans for taking actions against U.S. interests—constitutes an immense asymmetric advantage for the United States. This point would be less important if less of the world were covered by water, or if the oceans were carved into territorial blocks, like the land. Most of the world, however, is covered by water, and most of those waters are international waters, where naval forces can operate freely. The point, consequently, is not that U.S. naval forces are intrinsically special or privileged—it is that they have a certain value simply as a consequence of the physical and legal organization of the planet.

An additional point that can be noted in relating U.S. naval forces to U.S. national strategy is that most of the world's people, resources, and economic activity are located not in the Western Hemisphere, but in the other hemisphere, particularly Eurasia. In response to this basic feature of world geography, U.S. policymakers for the last several decades have chosen to pursue, as a key element of U.S. national strategy, a goal of preventing the emergence of a regional hegemon in one part of Eurasia or another, on the grounds that such a hegemon could represent a concentration of power strong enough to threaten core U.S. interests by, for example, denying the United

States access to some of the other hemisphere's resources and economic activity. Although U.S. policymakers do not often state this key national strategic goal explicitly in public, U.S. military operations in recent decades—both wartime operations and day-to-day operations—have been carried out in no small part in support of this key goal.

The U.S. goal of preventing the emergence of a regional hegemon in one part of Eurasia or another is a major reason why the U.S. military is structured with force elements that enable it to cross broad expanses of ocean and air space and then conduct sustained, large-scale military operations upon arrival. Force elements associated with this goal include, among other things, an Air Force with significant numbers of long-range bombers, long-range surveillance aircraft, long- range airlift aircraft, and aerial refueling tankers, and a Navy with significant numbers aircraft carriers, nuclear-powered attack submarines, large surface combatants, large amphibious ships, and underway replenishment ships.

The United States is the only country in the world that designs its military to cross broad expanses of ocean and air space and then conduct sustained, large-scale military operations upon arrival. The other countries in the Western Hemisphere do not design their forces to do this because they cannot afford to, and because the United States is, in effect, doing it for them. Countries in the other hemisphere do not design their forces to do this for the very basic reason that they are already in the other hemisphere, and consequently instead spend their defense money on forces that are tailored largely for influencing events in their own local region.

The fact that the United States designs its military to do something that other countries do not design their forces to do—cross broad expanses of ocean and air space and then conduct sustained, large-scale military operations upon arrival—can be important to keep in mind when comparing the U.S. military to the militaries of other nations. For example, in observing that the U.S. Navy has 11 aircraft carriers while other countries have no more than one or two, it can be noted other countries do not need a significant number of aircraft carriers because, unlike the United States, they are not designing their forces to cross broad expanses of ocean and air space and then conduct sustained, large-scale military operations upon arrival.

As another example, it is sometimes noted, in assessing the adequacy of U.S. naval forces, that U.S. naval forces are equal in tonnage to the next dozen or more navies combined, and that most of those next dozen or more navies are the navies of U.S. allies. Those other fleets, however, are mostly of Eurasian countries, which do not design their forces to cross to the other side of the world and then conduct sustained, large-scale military operations upon arrival. The fact that the U.S. Navy is much bigger than allied navies does not necessarily prove that U.S. naval forces are either sufficient or excessive; it simply reflects the differing and generally more limited needs that U.S. allies have for naval forces. (It might also reflect an underinvestment by some of those allies to meet even their more limited naval needs.)

Countries have differing needs for naval and other military forces. The United States, as a country located in the Western Hemisphere with a goal of preventing the emergence of a regional hegemon in one part of Eurasia or another, has defined a need for naval and other military forces that is quite different from the needs of allies that are located in Eurasia. The sufficiency of U.S. naval and other military forces consequently is best assessed not through comparison to the militaries of other countries, but against U.S. strategic goals.

APPENDIX D. SIZE OF THE NAVY AND NAVY SHIPBUILDING RATE

Size of the Navy

Table D-1 shows the size of the Navy in terms of total number of ships since FY1948; the numbers shown in the table reflect changes over time in the rules specifying which ships count toward the total. Differing counting rules result in differing totals, and for certain years, figures reflecting more than one set of counting rules are available. Figures in the table for FY1978 and subsequent years reflect the battle force ships counting method, which is the set of counting rules established in the early 1980s for public policy discussions of the size of the Navy.

As shown in the table, the total number of battle force ships in the Navy reached a late-Cold War peak of 568 at the end of FY1987 and began declining thereafter.[35] The Navy fell below 300 battle force ships in August 2003 and as of February 24, 2015, included 284 battle force ships.

As discussed in **Appendix A**, historical figures for total fleet size might not be a reliable yardstick for assessing the appropriateness of proposals for the future size and structure of the Navy, particularly if the historical figures are more than a few years old, because the missions to be performed by the Navy, the mix of ships that make up the Navy, and the technologies that are available to Navy ships for performing missions all change over time, and because the number of ships in the fleet in an earlier year might itself have been inappropriate (i.e., not enough or more than enough) for meeting the Navy's mission requirements in that year.

For similar reasons, trends over time in the total number of ships in the Navy are not necessarily a reliable indicator of the direction of change in the fleet's ability to perform its stated missions. An increasing number of ships in the fleet might not necessarily mean that the fleet's ability to perform its stated missions is increasing, because the fleet's mission requirements might be increasing more rapidly than ship numbers and average ship capability. Similarly, a decreasing number of ships in the fleet might not necessarily mean that the fleet's ability to perform stated missions is decreasing, because the fleet's mission requirements might be declining more rapidly than numbers of ships, or because average ship capability and the percentage of time that ships are in deployed locations might be increasing quickly enough to more than offset reductions in total ship numbers.

Table D-1. Total Number of Ships in the Navy Since FY1948

FY[a]	Number	FY[a]	Number	FY[a]	Number	FY[a]	Number
1948	737	1970	769	1992	466	FY2014	289
1949	690	1971	702	1993	435		
1950	634	1972	654	1994	391		
1951	980	1973	584	1995	373		
1952	1,097	1974	512	1996	356		
1953	1,122	1975	496	1997	354		
1954	1,113	1976	476	1998	333		
1955	1,030	1977	464	1999	317		
1956	973	1978	468	2000	318		
1957	967	1979	471	2001	316		
1958	890	1980	477	2002	313		
1959	860	1981	490	2003	297		
1960	812	1982	513	2004	291		
1961	897	1983	514	2005	282		
1962	959	1984	524	2006	281		
1963	916	1985	541	2007	279		
1964	917	1986	556	2008	282		
1965	936	1987	568	2009	285		
1966	947	1988	565	2010	288		
1967	973	1989	566	2011	284		

FY[a]	Number	FY[a]	Number	FY[a]	Number	FY[a]	Number
1968	976	1990	547	2012	287		
1969	926	1991	526	2013	285		

Source: Compiled by CRS using U.S. Navy data. Numbers shown reflect changes over time in the rules specifying which ships count toward the total. Figures for FY1978 and subsequent years reflect the battle force ships counting method, which is the set of counting rules established in the early 1980s for public policy discussions of the size of the Navy.

a. Data for earlier years in the table may be for the end of the calendar year (or for some other point during the year), rather than for the end of the fiscal year.

Table D-2. Battle Force Ships Procured or Requested/Programmed, FY1982-FY2020 (Procured FY1982-FY2015; requested or programmed FY2016-FY2020)

82	**83**	**84**	**85**	**86**	**87**	**88**	**89**	**90**	**91**	**92**	**93**	**94**	**95**	**96**	**97**	**98**	**99**	**00**	**01**
17	14	16	19	20	17	15	19	15	11	11	7	4	4	5	4	5	5	6	6
02	**03**	**04**	**05**	**06**	**07**	**08**	**09**	**10**	**11**	**12**	**13**	**14**	***15***	***16***	***17***	***18***	***19***	***20***	
6	5	7	8	4a	5a	3a	8	7	10	11[b]	11[c]	8	8	*9*	*10*	*10*	*9*	*10*	

Source: CRS compilation based on Navy budget data and examination of defense authorization and appropriation committee and conference reports for each fiscal year. The table excludes non-battle force ships that do not count toward the 306-ship goal, such as certain sealift and prepositioning ships operated by the Military Sealift Command and oceanographic ships operated by agencies such as the National Oceanic and Atmospheric Administration (NOAA).

a. The totals shown for FY2006, FY2007, and FY2008, reflect the cancellation two LCSs funded in FY2006, another two LCSs funded in FY2007, and an LCS funded in FY2008.

b. The total shown for FY2012 includes two JHSVs—one that was included in the Navy's FY2012 budget submission, and one that was included in the Army's FY2012 budget submission. Until FY2012, JHSVs were being procured by both the Navy and the Army. The Army was to procure its fifth and final JHSV in FY2012, and this ship was included in the Army's FY2012 budget submission. In May 2011, the Navy and Army signed a Memorandum of Agreement (MOA) transferring the Army's JHSVs to the Navy. In the FY2012 DOD Appropriations Act (Division A of H.R. 2055/P.L. 112-74 of December 23, 2011), the JHSV that was in the Army's FY2012 budget submission was funded through the Shipbuilding and Conversion, Navy (SCN) appropriation account, along with the JHSV that the Navy had included in its FY0212 budget submission. The four JHSVs that were procured through the Army's budget prior to FY2012, however, are not included in the annual totals shown in this table.

c. Figure shown does not reflect potential quantity reduction resulting from March 1, 2013, sequester on FY2013 funding.

Shipbuilding Rate

Table D-2 shows past (FY1982-FY2014) and requested or programmed (FY2015-FY2019) rates of Navy ship procurement.

End Notes

[1] Department of the Navy, *Report to Congress [on] Navy Combatant Vessel Force Structure Requirement*, January 2013, 3 pp. The cover letters for the report were dated January 31, 2013.

[2] For more on this document, see CRS Report R42146, *Assessing the January 2012 Defense Strategic Guidance (DSG): In Brief*, by Catherine Dale and Pat Towell.

[3] Statement of the Honorable Sean J. Stackley, Assistant Secretary of the Navy (Research, Development and Acquisition) and Vice Admiral Joseph P. Mulloy, Deputy Chief of Naval Operations for Integration of Capabilities and Resources and Lieutenant General Kenneth J. Glueck, Jr., Deputy Commandant, Combat Development and Integration & Commanding General, Marine Corps Combat Development Command, Before the Subcommittee on Seapower and Projection Forces of the House Armed Services Committee on Department of the Navy Seapower and Projection Forces Capabilities, February 25, 2015, p. 3.

[4] Source: Spoken testimony of Vice Admiral Mulloy, as reflected in hearing transcript.

[5] Statement of Admiral Jonathan Greenert, U.S. Navy, Chief of Naval Operations, Before the House Subcommittee on Defense, Committee on Appropriations, on FY 2016 Department of the Navy Posture, February 26, 2015, pp. 9 and 11.

[6] For more on MYP contracting, see CRS Report R41909, *Multiyear Procurement (MYP) and Block Buy Contracting in Defense Acquisition: Background and Issues for Congress*, by Ronald O'Rourke and Moshe Schwartz.

[7] For further discussion of this issue, see CRS Report R41129, *Navy Ohio Replacement (SSBN[X]) Ballistic Missile Submarine Program: Background and Issues for Congress*, by Ronald O'Rourke.

[8] See Statement of Admiral Jonathan Greenert, U.S. Navy, Chief of Naval Operations, Before the Senate Armed Services Committee on the Impact of Sequestration on the National Defense, November 7, 2013, pp. 7-11, and Statement of Admiral Jonathan Greenert, U.S. Navy, Chief of Naval Operations, Before the House Armed Services Committee on Planning for Sequestration in FY 2014 and Perspectives of the Military Services on the Strategic Choices and Management Review, September 18, 2013, pp. 6-10.

[9] Statement of Admiral Jonathan Greenert, U.S. Navy, Chief of Naval Operations, Before the Senate Armed Services Committee on the Impact of Sequestration on National Defense, January 28, 2015, pp. 4-9.

[10] For more on the modernization of China's military (particularly naval) capabilities and its potential implications for required U.S. Navy capabilities, see CRS Report RL33153, *China Naval Modernization: Implications for U.S. Navy Capabilities—Background and Issues for Congress*, by Ronald O'Rourke.

[11] For a discussion of these disputes, see CRS Report R42784, *Maritime Territorial and Exclusive Economic Zone (EEZ) Disputes Involving China: Issues for Congress*, by Ronald

O'Rourke. See also CRS Report R42930, *Maritime Territorial Disputes in East Asia: Issues for Congress*, by Ben Dolven, Mark E. Manyin, and Shirley A. Kan.

[12] Spoken testimony of Admiral Jonathan Greenert at a March 12, 2014, hearing before the House Armed Services Committee on the Department of the Navy's proposed FY2015 budget, as shown in transcript of hearing.

[13] For a summary of these actions, see CRS Report R42784, *Maritime Territorial and Exclusive Economic Zone (EEZ) Disputes Involving China: Issues for Congress*, by Ronald O'Rourke.

[14] For a discussion, see CRS Report R43838, *A Shift in the International Security Environment: Potential Implications for Defense—Issues for Congress*, by Ronald O'Rourke.

[15] See, for example, Dan Blumenthal and Michael Mazza, "Asia Needs a Larger U.S. Defense Budget," *Wall Street Journal, July 5, 2011*; J. Randy Forbes, "Defence Cuts Imperil US Asia Role," The Diplomat (http://the-diplomat.com), October 26, 2011. See also Andrew Krepinevich, "Panetta's Challenge," *Washington Post*, July 15, 2011: 15; Dean Cheng, *Sea Power and the Chinese State: China's Maritime Ambitions*, Heritage Foundation Backgrounder No. 2576, July 11, 2011, p. 10.

[16] For further discussion of these options, see CRS Report RS21338, *Navy Ship Deployments: New Approaches— Background and Issues for Congress*, by Ronald O'Rourke.

[17] For further discussion, see CRS Report RL33153, *China Naval Modernization: Implications for U.S. Navy Capabilities—Background and Issues for Congress*, by Ronald O'Rourke.

[18] Arthur H. Barber, "Rethinking The Future Fleet," *U.S. Naval Institute Proceedings*, May 2014: 48-52.

[19] Congressional Budget Office, *An Analysis of the Navy's Fiscal Year 2015 Shipbuilding Plan*, December 2014, Table 3 on page 14.

[20] Congressional Budget Office, An Analysis of the Navy's Fiscal Year 2015 Shipbuilding Plan, December 2014, Table A-1 on page 31.

[21] This can be read as a double negative—that it is *unlikely* the Navy will be *unable* to sustain average annual shipbuilding budgets at this level. The Navy's intent appears to be to state that it is *unlikely* the Navy will be *able* to do this.

[22] *Report to Congress on the Annual Long-Range Plan for Construction of Naval Vessels for FY2015*, June 2014, pp. 5, 6, 7, 9.

[23] The "one-third, one-third, one-third" terminology, though convenient, is not entirely accurate—the military departments' shares of the DOD budget, while more or less stable during this period, were not exactly one-third each: the average share for the Department of the Army was about 26%, the average share for the Department of the Navy (which includes both the Navy and Marine Corps) was about 32%, the average share for the Department of the Air Force was about 30%, and the average share for Defense-Wide (the fourth major category of DOD spending) was about 12%. Excluding the Defense-Wide category, which has grown over time, the shares for the three military departments of the remainder of DOD's budget during this period become about 29% for the Department of the Army, about 37% for the Department of the Navy, and about 34% for the Department of the Air Force.

[24] Since the Defense-Wide portion of the budget has grown from just a few percent in the 1950s and 1960s to about 15% in more recent years, including the Defense-Wide category of spending in the calculation can lead to military department shares of the budget in the 1950s and 1960s that are somewhat more elevated compared to those in more recent years, making it more complex to compare the military departments' shares across the entire period of time since the end of the World War II. For this reason, military department shares of the DOD budget cited in this statement are calculated after excluding the Defense-Wide category. The points made in this statement, however, can still made on the basis of a calculation that includes the Defense-Wide category.

[25] For example, from the mid-1950s to the mid-1960s, reflecting a U.S. defense strategy at the time that placed a strong reliance on the deterrent value of nuclear weapons, the Department of the Air Force's share of the non-Defense-Wide DOD budget increased by several percentage points. The Department of the Air Force's share averaged about 45% for the 10-

year period FY1956-FY1965, and peaked at more than 47% in FY1957-FY1959. As another example, for the 11-year period FY2003-FY2013, as a consequence of combat operations in Iraq and Afghanistan, the Department of the Army's share of the non-Defense-Wide DOD budget increased by roughly 10 percentage points. The Department of the Army's share during this period averaged about 39%, and peaked at more than 43% in FY2008. U.S. combat operations in Iraq and Afghanistan during this period reflected the implementation of U.S. national strategy as interpreted by policymakers during those years.

26 Some publications have stated that the Navy reached a peak of 594 ships at the end of FY1987. This figure, however, is the total number of active ships in the fleet, which is not the same as the total number of battle force ships. The battle force ships figure is the number used in government discussions of the size of the Navy. In recent years, the total number of active ships has been larger than the total number of battle force ships. For example, the Naval History and Heritage Command (formerly the Naval Historical Center) states that as of November 16, 2001, the Navy included a total of 337 active ships, while the Navy states that as of November 19, 2001, the Navy included a total of 317 battle force ships. Comparing the total number of active ships in one year to the total number of battle force ships in another year is thus an apples-to-oranges comparison that in this case overstates the decline since FY1987 in the number of ships in the Navy. As a general rule to avoid potential statistical distortions, comparisons of the number of ships in the Navy over time should use, whenever possible, a single counting method.

27 C4ISR stands for command and control, communications, computers, intelligence, surveillance, and reconnaissance.

28 Navy force structure plans that predate those shown in Table 1 include the Reagan-era 600-ship plan of the 1980s, the Base Force fleet of more than 400 ships planned during the final two years of the George H. W. Bush Administration, the 346-ship fleet from the Clinton Administration's 1993 Bottom-Up Review (or BUR, sometimes also called Base Force II), and the 310-ship fleet of the Clinton Administration's 1997 QDR. The table below summarizes some key features of these plans.

Features of Recent Navy Force Structure Plans

Plan	600-ship	Base Force	1993 BUR	1997 QDR
Total ships	~600	~450/416[a]	346	~305/310[b]
Attack submarines	100	80/~55[c]	45-55	50/55[d]
Aircraft carriers	15[e]	12	11+1[f]	11+1[f]
Surface combatants	242/228[g]	~150	~124	116
Amphibious ships	~75[h]	51[i]	41[i]	36[i]

Source: Prepared by CRS based on DOD and U.S. Navy data.

a. Commonly referred to as 450-ship plan, but called for decreasing to 416 ships by end of FY1999.

b. Original total of about 305 ships was increased to about 310 due to increase in number of attack submarines to 55 from 50.

c. Plan originally included 80 attack submarines, but this was later reduced to about 55.

d. Plan originally included 50 attack submarines but this was later increased to 55. e. Plus one additional aircraft carrier in the service life extension program (SLEP).

f. Eleven active carriers plus one operational reserve carrier.

g. Plan originally included 242 surface combatants but this was later reduced to 228.

h. Number needed to lift assault echelons of one Marine Expeditionary Force (MEF) plus one Marine Expeditionary Brigade (MEB).

i. Number needed to lift assault echelons of 2.5 MEBs. Changing numbers needed to meet this goal reflect in part changes in the design and capabilities of amphibious ships.

[29] Stephen J. Hadley and William J. Perry, co-chairmen, et al., *The QDR in Perspective: Meeting America's National Security Needs In the 21st Century, The Final Report of the Quadrennial Defense Review Independent Panel*, Washington, 2010, Figure 3-2 on page 58.

[30] Letter dated August 11, 2010, from Secretary of Defense Robert Gates to the chairmen of the House and Senate Armed Services and Appropriations Committees, pp. 3 and 4. The ellipsis in the second paragraph appears in the letter.

[31] This appendix adapts material originally presented in Statement of Ronald O'Rourke, Specialist in Naval Affairs, Congressional Research Service, Before the House Armed Services Committee Subcommittee on Seapower and Projection Forces on the Navy's FY2014 30-Year Shipbuilding Plan, October 23, 2013, pp. 1, 17-18.

[32] For more on the strategic rebalancing, see CRS Report R42146, *Assessing the January 2012 Defense Strategic Guidance (DSG)*: In Brief, by Catherine Dale and Pat Towell; and CRS Report R42448, *Pivot to the Pacific? The Obama Administration's "Rebalancing" Toward Asia*, coordinated by Mark E. Manyin.

[33] For more on China's modernization of its maritime military capabilities, see CRS Report RL33153, *China Naval Modernization: Implications for U.S. Navy Capabilities—Background and Issues for Congress*, by Ronald O'Rourke.

[34] Navy officials testified in March 2014 that a Navy of 450 ships would be required to fully meet COCOM requests for forward-deployed Navy forces. (Spoken testimony of Admiral Jonathan Greenert at a March 12, 2014, hearing before the House Armed Services Committee on the Department of the Navy's proposed FY2015 budget, as shown in transcript of hearing.)

[35] Some publications have stated that the Navy reached a peak of 594 ships at the end of FY1987. This figure, however, is the total number of active ships in the fleet, which is not the same as the total number of battle force ships. The battle force ships figure is the number used in government discussions of the size of the Navy. In recent years, the total number of active ships has been larger than the total number of battle force ships. For example, the Naval History and Heritage Command (formerly the Naval Historical Center) states that as of November 16, 2001, the Navy included a total of 337 active ships, while the Navy states that as of November 19, 2001, the Navy included a total of 317 battle force ships. Comparing the total number of active ships in one year to the total number of battle force ships in another year is thus an apples-to-oranges comparison that in this case overstates the decline since FY1987 in the number of ships in the Navy. As a general rule to avoid potential statistical distortions, comparisons of the number of ships in the Navy over time should use, whenever possible, a single counting method.

In: U.S. Navy Force Structure …
Editor: Agnes S. Jennings

ISBN: 978-1-63482-939-7

Chapter 2

PRESERVING THE NAVY'S FORWARD PRESENCE WITH A SMALLER FLEET*

Eric Labs

NOTES

Unless otherwise indicated, all dollar amounts in this report reflect budget authority in 2014 dollars, and all years are federal fiscal years (which run from October 1 to September 30 and are designated by the calendar year in which they end).

Numbers in the text and tables may not add up to totals because of rounding.

SUMMARY

In support of its mission to deter conflict or fight in wars if necessary, the Navy considers it a core responsibility to maintain a forward presence—to keep some of its fleet far from U.S. shores at all times in areas that are important to national interests. Toward that end, at any given time, about one-third of the fleet is deployed overseas. The rest of the Navy's ships are in or near their home ports in the United States for maintenance, training, or

* This is an edited, reformatted and augmented version of a report issued by the Congressional Budget Office, March 2015.

sustainment (a period in which a ship is in port but ready to deploy quickly). Most of the ships that contribute to the Navy's current forward presence of about 100 ships sail from ports in the United States; 31 others are now stationed permanently in foreign countries or at overseas U.S. military bases. In the future, the Navy expects to boost the proportion of ships that it bases abroad.

The Congressional Budget Office estimates that, for the next 30 years, the Navy's 2015 shipbuilding plan (which aims to increase the fleet from 281 ships in 2014 to 306 ships by 2022) would cost about $21 billion annually, on average, in constant 2014 dollars.[1] The Navy's estimates set the figure somewhat lower—at about $19 billion per year.[2] Both estimates are greater than the annual average of almost $16 billion that the Navy has spent for the past three decades, which suggests that the Navy may have difficulty affording its plans. The Chief of Naval Operations' emphasis on forward operations indicates that the Navy has committed to maintaining the largest possible forward presence under any given budget plan.[3]

What Size Fleet Could the Navy Maintain With Smaller Shipbuilding Budgets?

CBO assessed the effects of three smaller annual shipbuilding budgets—$16 billion, $14 billion, and $12 billion—for the next 30 years. In all three cases, by 2044, the fleet would be smaller than would be the case under the Navy's current plan:

- Under the $16 billion budget, by 2044, the fleet would consist of 251 ships, 17 percent fewer than under the Navy's current plan;
- Under the $14 billion budget, it would be 230 ships, 24 percent fewer than under the current plan; and
- Under the $12 billion budget, it would be 208 ships, 31 percent fewer than under the current plan (see Table 1).

Those estimates reflect an assumption that the Navy would reduce the number of its major warships—aircraft carriers, surface combatants, submarines, and amphibious warfare ships—in rough proportion to their current share of the fleet.

Table 1. Fleet Characteristics and Costs of Maintaining the Navy's Forward Presence Under Various Shipbuilding Budgets, 2044

	Average Annual Shipbuilding Budget		
	$16 Billion	**$14 Billion**	**$12 Billion**
Fleet Inventory, 2044	251	230	208
Reduction in Ships From Navy Plan (Percent)	17	24	31
Annual Cost Savings, Operation and Support			
(Billions of 2014 dollars)a	6	10	13
Approach 1: Increase the Length of Deployments for U.S.-Based Ships			
Ships Providing Forward Presence At Any Given Time	113	111	108
	Deployment Length/Operating Cycle (Months)		
Type of Ship			
Aircraft carrier	10/36	6 and 6/36b	7 and 7/36b
Large surface combatant	10/36	6 and 6/36b	7 and 7/36b
Attack submarine	7/24c	7/24c	7/24c
Amphibious warfare ship	8/27	9/27	9/27
Cost (Billions of 2014 dollars) Annual recurring	Less than 0.5	Less than 1	Less than 5
Onetime	0	0	0
	Key Challenges to Implementation - Retention of Sailors Because of Long Deployments - Endurance of Crews in Future Crises - Ship Maintenance		
Approach 2: Base More Ships Overseas and Use More Rotating Crews			
Ships Providing Forward Presence At Any Given Time	113	112	110
	Additional Ships Based Overseas, Additional Ships With Rotating Crews		
Type of Ship			
Aircraft carrier	1, 0	1, 0	2, 0
Large surface combatant	4, 0	4, 6	5, 10
Attack submarine	7, 6	7, 8	9, 10
Amphibious warfare ship	2, 0	2, 2	2, 2
Cost (Billions of 2014 dollars)			
Annual recurring	Less than 1	Less than 5	Less than 10
Onetime	3 to 10	3 to 10	16 to 25
	Key Challenges to Implementation - Building Overseas Capacity - Adapting to New Rotation Procedures - Keeping the Fleet Secure		

Source: Congressional Budget Office.

Note: All costs are in billions of 2014 dollars.

[a] Figures are for operation and support savings before adjustment using either Approach 1 or Approach 2.

[b] The U.S.-based aircraft carriers and large surface combatants would conduct two 6- or 7-month deployments over the 36-month operating cycle.

[c] Some attack submarines would conduct 7-month deployments and some would conduct 6-month deployments.

How Could the Navy Maintain Its Forward Presence under Smaller Shipbuilding Budgets?

The Navy could maximize its forward presence with smaller budgets by expanding the use of three methods that it currently applies to boost overseas operations:

- Deploying ships for longer periods,
- Basing more ships and their crews overseas, and
- Assigning more than one crew to some ships to permit longer deployments.

Even under smaller budgets, CBO found, the Navy could expand its use of each method to maintain the current forward presence, although all three involve costs and pose disadvantages. And even though the Navy might be able to maintain its forward presence by making more use of those methods, smaller fleets would nonetheless reduce the service's ability to implement its war plans in the event of conflict and would limit its flexibility in a crisis short of war.

The Navy also could use different mixes of those methods to maintain its forward presence. To illustrate a range of possibilities, CBO analyzed two basic approaches: The first would simply lengthen many ships' deployments; the second would combine the other two methods into a single approach to increase the efficiency of the ships' use.

Approach 1: Deploy Ships for Longer Periods. Under this approach, the Navy's ships would undertake more frequent and longer deployments. For example, with an annual shipbuilding budget of $16 billion, most large surface combatants (cruisers and destroyers) and aircraft carriers would be deployed for 10 months out of a 36-month operating cycle (or 28 percent of the time—the other 26 months would be devoted to maintenance, training, and sustainment); under a $14 billion budget, those ships would be deployed twice in a 36-month cycle, for 6 months each time (or 33 percent of the time); and under a $12 billion annual budget, the ships would be deployed twice in a 36-month cycle, but for 7 months each time (or 39 percent of the time). By comparison, in 2013, the Navy's destroyers were deployed, on average, for a little longer than 7 months out of a 27-month operating cycle, or about 26 percent of the time.

Longer deployments are more expensive than shorter deployments but, under the scenarios considered in this report, longer deployments are less expensive than buying larger fleets. Costs increase for longer deployments because sailors are paid more while they are at sea, ships consume more fuel, and equipment must be replaced sooner because it wears out faster. But the additional operating costs of longer deployments would be considerably less than the savings that would result from the lower procurement costs and smaller operating budgets required to maintain smaller fleets. As a result, by CBO's estimate, this approach would save between $11 billion and $17 billion per year, depending on the size of the fleet.

Several disadvantages, sometimes with accumulating effects, can arise from longer periods at sea. For example, if the ships must be deployed quickly because of a crisis or a war, crew members who have already been at sea for an extended time could be tired. Longer deployments subject sailors and families alike to added stress, which might hamper the Navy's retention of crew members. Higher sea pay or larger retention bonuses might or might not mitigate that problem. If ships are away from home ports more often or for longer periods, maintenance schedules could be disrupted or altered; if that resulted in less effective or less timely maintenance, ships might not be able to remain in the fleet until the end of their expected service lives. Planning for longer deployments and increasing maintenance may mitigate that problem.

Approach 2: Base More Ships Overseas and Rotate Crews on More Ships. The second approach CBO examined would require the Navy to base another 14 to 18 ships—including aircraft carriers—overseas and to increase by between 12 and 22 (depending on the shipbuilding budget) the number of ships that used rotating crews. Basing more ships overseas can avert some challenges of longer deployments—crews are not as tired and are able to spend more time at home—and ships are more likely to be close to crisis spots. But this approach would save less than the first, mainly because of higher expenses for maintenance and personnel as a result of operating the ships more and using more crews. The increased spending could offset a substantial portion of the savings from smaller procurement and operating budgets, particularly at the lowest of the three budget amounts, but this approach could still save between $10 billion and $12 billion each year, depending on the size of the fleet.

Rotating crews pose several disadvantages, however. Their use on attack submarines, destroyers, and amphibious warfare ships could raise logistical and cultural challenges. In particular, the Navy would need to keep the crews that are not deployed trained and ready to go to sea when their turn arose to operate the ships. Crews might identify less with a particular ship—possibly resulting in lower-quality work or diminished attention to maintaining equipment in the best possible condition. The Navy has overcome such challenges in the past, notably in its staffing of ballistic missile submarines with a pair of crews alternating on fixed-period deployments. The Navy also uses rotating crews on its new littoral combat ships, but widespread application of dual and multiple crewing to other parts of the fleet would present a greater challenge. Expanding the Navy's forward presence by basing more ships abroad might reassure allies or deter potential adversaries, but it also could increase the fleet's vulnerability to attack. For example, a larger concentration of naval forces based overseas would make the fleet more vulnerable to a surprise attack by another nation, by terrorists, or by other nonstate actors. And overseas bases can be closed off relatively quickly if a host government decides it no longer wants U.S. Navy ships based in its harbors. Finally, some challenges could be economic: With more ships based overseas, some areas in the United States near naval bases would see reduced economic activity (while the host countries might see more).

THE NAVY'S 2015 SHIPBUILDING PLAN

In its most recent shipbuilding plan, the Navy proposes to purchase 264 ships over the period from 2015 to 2044: 6 aircraft carriers, 12 ballistic missile submarines, 48 attack submarines, 65 destroyers, 66 littoral combat ships, 21 amphibious warfare ships, and 46 combat logistics and support ships (see Table 2). Taking into account the projected retirements of ships now in the fleet, those purchases would allow the Navy to maintain a fleet of 306 ships or more beginning in 2022 and for most years thereafter through the end of the period.[4] CBO estimates that the Navy's current plan would cost $21 billion per year, on average, for the next 30 years.[5] Such a large shipbuilding budget over a span of three decades has no historical precedent. In constant 2014 dollars, average annual spending over the past decade has been about $14 billion; the annual average for the past 30 years has been roughly $16 billion. Those figures suggest, and the Navy's report explicitly states, that the Navy will find it difficult at best to fully implement its current shipbuilding plan, particularly if the budget for the Department of Defense continues to be subject to significant constraints.

SHIPBUILDING UNDER SMALLER BUDGETS

CBO analyzed possible changes in the composition of the Navy's fleet that would be required under various shipbuilding budgets. For this analysis, CBO chose three basic annual amounts, all in 2014 dollars and each resulting in a smaller fleet than the Navy currently envisions:

- $16 billion (the average ship construction budget over the past 30 years),
- $14 billion (the average ship construction budget for the past 10 years), and
- $12 billion (the average ship construction budget during the 1990s).

CBO's analysis incorporates the assumption that reductions in shipbuilding relative to the Navy's 2015 plan would be distributed in rough proportion to current numbers of major battle force ships: aircraft carriers, large and small surface combatants, submarines, and amphibious warfare ships. The number of combat logistics and support ships also would be reduced, although by smaller percentages. Many of those ships (except oilers) are small and comparatively inexpensive, and their number is not tied directly to the size of the overall fleet. Thus, CBO did not reduce the number of support ships by the same proportion that it reduced the number of combat ships for each budget amount.

Table 2. CBO's Projections of Purchases and Costs of New Battle Force Ships Under Alternative Shipbuilding Budgets, 2015–2044

	Navy's 2015 Plan ($21 Billion)[a]		Average Annual Shipbuilding Budget	
		$16 Billion	$14 Billion	$12 Billion
Combat Ships		Number of Ships Purchased		
Aircraft carriers	6	5	4	3

Table 2. (Continued)

	Navy's 2015 Plan ($21 Billion)[a]	Average Annual Shipbuilding Budget		
		$16 Billion	$14 Billion	$12 Billion
Ballistic missile submarines	12	10	8	6
Attack submarines	48	31	29	27
Destroyers	65	48	41	31
Littoral combat ships	66	47	44	39
Amphibious warfare ships	21	15	12	10
Subtotal	218	156	138	116
Combat Logistics and Support Ships	46	41	37	33
Total	**264**	**197**	**175**	**149**
		Cost (Billions of 2014 dollars)		
Combat Ships				
Aircraft carriers	76	63	57	43
Ballistic missile submarines	92	83	69	54
Attack submarines	144	95	89	84
Destroyers	144	109	91	75
Littoral combat ships	35	25	24	21
Amphibious warfare ships	53	37	31	25
Subtotal	544	412	361	302
Combat Logistics and Support Ships	23	22	20	18
Other Itemsb	55	49	41	39
Total	**621**	**483**	**422**	**359**

Source: Congressional Budget Office.

Note: CBO's analysis includes the assumption that, under all three budget plans, the Navy would buy ships of each type in roughly the same proportion as it would under its 2015 plan.

[a] CBO estimates that the Navy's fiscal year 2015 shipbuilding plan would require an average budget of $21 billion per year over the 2015–2044 period. See Congressional Budget Office, *An Analysis of the Navy's 2015 Shipbuilding Plan* (www.cbo.gov/publication/ 49818). The Navy estimates that its 2015 shipbuilding plan would cost an average of $19 billion per year. That amount covers everything that the Navy pays for from its shipbuilding accounts, including construction of new ships, refueling of nuclear-powered aircraft carriers, ship conversions, construction of training ships, outfitting and postdelivery costs (which include the purchase of many smaller tools and pieces of equipment needed to operate a ship but not necessarily provided by the manufacturing shipyard), and other smaller items.

[b] Other items include funding for refueling nuclear-powered aircraft carriers and the costs of various items that the Navy purchases from its shipbuilding account.

Table 3. Inventory of Battle Force Ships and Fleet Composition in Selected Years Under Alternative Shipbuilding Budgets

	Navy's 2015 Plan				$16 Billion Budget				$14 Billion Budget				$12 Billion Budget			
	2014	2024	2034	2044	2014	2024	2034	2044	2014	2024	2034	2044	2014	2024	2034	2044
	Inventory of Battle Force Ships															
Combat Ships																
Aircraft carriers	10	12	11	10	10	11	11	9	10	11	11	8	10	11	10	7
Ballistic missile submarines	14	14	10	12	14	14	8 †	10	14	14	8	8	14	14	7	6
Attack submarines	54	48	46	52	54	48	39	39	54	48	37	37	54	47	36	35
Guided missile submarines	4	4	0	0	4	4	0	0	4	4	0	0	4	4	0	0
Large surface combatants	85	98	86	83	85	90	72	70	85	89	69	64	85	87	59	55
Small surface combatants and mine countermeasures ships[a]	26	41	52	52	26	35	43	37	26	35	42	32	26	35	39	27
Amphibious warfare ships	31	34	34	31	31	33	31	27	31	33	29	26	31	33	29	25
Subtotal	224	251	239	240	224	235	204 †	192	224	234	196	175	224	231	180	155
Combat Logistics and Support Ships	57	62	64	63	57	64	62	59	57	64	62	55	57	64	59	53
Total	**281**	**313**	**303**	**303**	**281**	**299**	**266 †**	**251**	**281**	**298**	**258**	**230**	**281**	**295**	**239**	**208**

Table 3. (Continued)

	Navy's 2015 Plan				$16 Billion Budget				$14 Billion Budget				$12 Billion Budget			
	2014	2024	2034	2044	2014	2024	2034	2044	2014	2024	2034	2044	2014	2024	2034	2044
	Composition of Battle Force Fleet (Percent)															
Combat Ships																
Aircraft carriers	4	4	4	3	4	4	4	4	4	4	4	3	4	4	4	3
Ballistic missile submarines	5	5	3	4	5	5	3	4	5	5	3	3	5	5	3	3
Attack submarines	19	16	16	17	19	16	15	16	19	16	14	16	19	16	15	17
Guided missile submarines	1	1	0	0	1	1	0	0	1	1	0	0	1	1	0	0
Large surface combatants	30	29	26	27	30	30	27	28	30	30	27	28	30	29	25	26
Small surface combatants and mine countermeasures ships[a]	9	13	18	17	9	12	16	15	9	12	16	14	9	12	16	13
Amphibious warfare ships	11	11	11	10	11	11	12	11	11	11	11	11	11	11	12	12
Subtotal	80	79	78	79	80	79	77	76	80	79	76	76	80	78	75	75
Combat Logistics and Support Ships	20	21	22	21	20	21	23	24	20	21	24	24	20	22	25	25
Total	**100**	**100**	**100**	**100**	**100**	**100**	**100**	**100**	**100**	**100**	**100**	**100**	**100**	**100**	**100**	**100**

Source: Congressional Budget Office. [† On March 17, 2015, CBO corrected this number to increase it by 1.]

[a] Small surface combatants and mine countermeasures ships include littoral combat ships, Oliver Hazard Perry class FFG-7 frigates, and Avenger class mine countermeasures ships.

What Would Smaller Shipbuilding Budgets Buy?

With an average annual budget of $16 billion, the largest of the three amounts considered for this report, CBO estimates that the Navy would purchase 197 battle force ships over the next 30 years—67 fewer than the Navy's 2015 plan calls for. Nearly all of the difference in inventories would come in the second and third decades. Under a $16 billion plan, the fleet would decline gradually from its current 281 battle force ships to 251 ships by 2044—17 percent fewer than the 303 ships envisioned for that year in the Navy's 2015 plan (see the top panel of Table 3 and Figure 1).

In CBO's analysis, the composition of the fleet (that is, the percentage share for each type of vessel) in 2044 under the $16 billion budget would closely resemble the composition proposed in the Navy's 2015 plan (see the bottom panel of Table 3). (CBO assumes that the various ship programs would be cut roughly, but not precisely, by equal proportions.) The largest difference for combat ships would be in the numbers of small surface combatants and mine countermeasures ships, which would account for a share of the fleet that is 2 percentage points smaller than under the Navy's plan. A $16 billion budget would result in a 3 percentage-point increase in the share of combat logistics and support ships. (In CBO's analysis, the percentage of support ships generally increases slightly under all three alternative budgets.)

If the Navy was allocated a $14 billion annual budget for shipbuilding, CBO projects, it could purchase 175 battle force ships, 34 percent fewer than would be purchased under the Navy's 2015 plan. As would be the case for the $16 billion annual budget, in the first decade for this plan, the fleet's composition would be largely similar to that under the Navy's 2015 plan. By 2044, however, the fleet would number 230 ships—24 percent fewer than the number envisioned for that year in the Navy's 2015 plan. Under CBO's assumptions, its composition would be virtually the same as that under the $16 billion budget.

With an average annual budget of $12 billion, CBO projects, the Navy could purchase 149 battle force ships, 44 percent fewer than under the Navy's 2015 plan. That fleet would be slightly smaller in the first decade than under the other two scenarios, and by 2044, the inventory would number 208 ships, 31 percent fewer than under the Navy's 2015 plan.

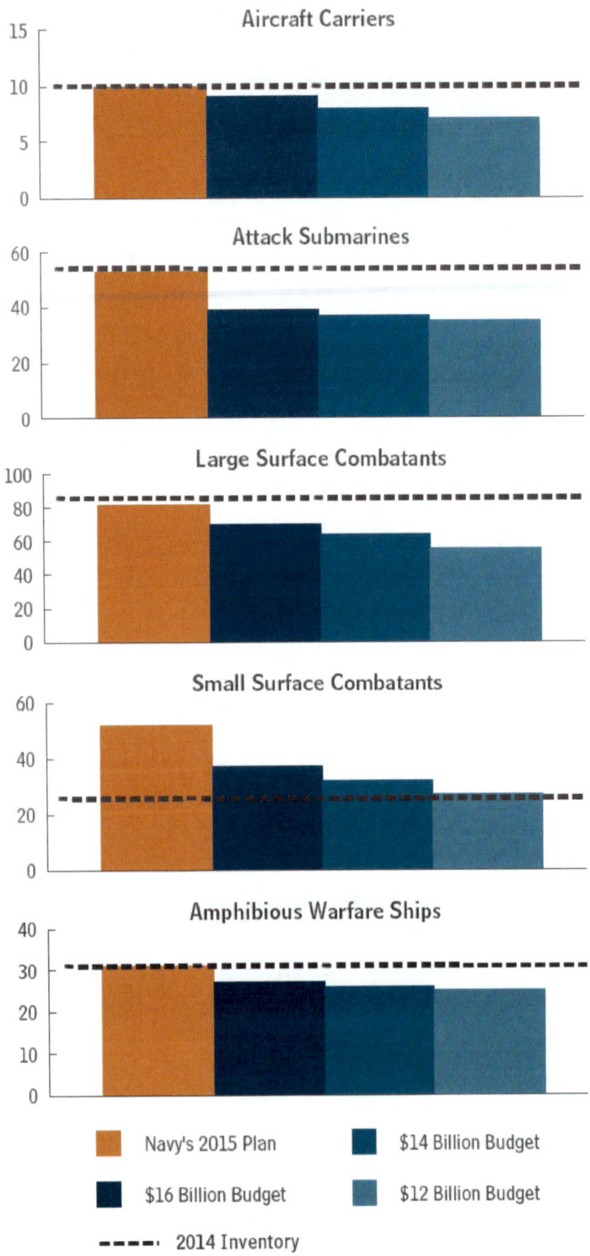

Source: Congressional Budget Office.

Figure 1. Inventories of Selected Ship Types Under Various Annual Shipbuilding Budgets, 2044.

What Would Be the Policy Implications of Smaller Budgets?

Although they would bring the Navy's shipbuilding plan into closer alignment with historical funding, smaller fleets would pose risks that cannot be addressed by maintaining the Navy's forward presence. The Navy would probably have insufficient forces to implement its current wartime plans (which are described only in classified documents). In particular, under each budget amount, the Navy would have fewer ships of all types available to reinforce its fleet in combat for the duration of a conflict. Similarly, smaller fleets would be placed under greater stress in a long crisis that was not a war: If the international environment required the presence of a larger naval force beyond the normal forward presence force for a long time, smaller fleets would struggle more to provide that presence without overtaxing the ships' crews.

CBO's analysis did not include an assumption that the fleets that would be affordable under smaller budgets would forgo certain missions or perform them differently—although those are probable outcomes of smaller shipbuilding budgets. Under such budgetary constraints, the Navy could make choices that are entirely different from the proportionate reductions CBO assumed, doing less overall or emphasizing some types of ships over others to better match its forces to changing demands or wartime priorities. If the Navy was substantially smaller, policymakers in the United States might decide to place more or less emphasis on certain regions, perhaps changing the fleet's composition as a result. A smaller fleet also might cause military leaders to adopt strategies or tactics for achieving objectives different from those that they might pursue with a larger fleet; such differences also could affect the fleet's composition. Thus, for example, it might be argued that if the United States can afford only a small Navy, the fleet should have more submarines relative to aircraft carriers or surface ships because submarines are difficult to detect and can effectively impede another navy's control of the seas.

Some observers have recommended that the Navy increase its reliance on a larger number of smaller ships that are closely networked electronically. In that case, the Navy might purchase ships and have fleets that are markedly different from those considered in this analysis.

What Would Be the Implications for the Shipbuilding Industry?

Although CBO did not specifically analyze the potential effects on naval shipyards, shipbuilding clearly would be curtailed under smaller budgets. Hundreds of companies contribute to the shipbuilding effort at the five large shipyards that produce the Navy's aircraft carriers, large surface combatants, submarines, amphibious warfare ships, and support ships and at the two smaller yards that produce littoral combat ships and small support ships. Those seven shipyards build few ships for the private sector. If funding was increased from its recent levels as envisioned under the Navy's plan, the shipyards' infrastructure could accommodate the resulting increase in orders, and the number of workers would need to increase. In contrast, if spending was less than that in recent years, fewer jobs would be available in the shipyards and related businesses.

There is a tension in determining the most efficient industrial base for shipbuilding. On the one hand, when a given shipyard produces more ships, per-ship overhead costs should decline and workers' skills should increase with each additional unit. On the other hand, if, under smaller shipbuilding budgets, orders were consolidated at fewer yards to preserve efficiency and, as a result, some shipyards closed, there would be less opportunity for competition to reduce the costs.

Over the past decade, the Navy has spent about $14 billion annually to build, on average, 7.7 ships per year. During that time, one major shipyard closed so that its parent company could consolidate its shipbuilding business at another yard to improve efficiency. Under each of the three budget scenarios, rising average costs per ship would reduce average annual ship purchases to 6.5 ships under the $16 billion budget, 5.8 ships under the $14 billion budget, and 5.0 ships under the $12 billion budget—or fewer than one ship per yard per year if all seven yards continued to receive orders from the Navy.

CBO's analysis incorporates the assumption that yards would be closed as needed to produce ships efficiently. Under the $16 billion budget, by the mid-2020s one or two large shipyards and one small shipyard would stop receiving Navy orders. Under the $12 billion budget, two or three large shipyards and one small shipyard probably would stop receiving orders from the Navy. One yard would produce all of the Navy's destroyers if just one was purchased each year for a long period, as would be the case under the $12 billion budget.

CBO's cost analyses incorporate those changes to the extent that the closing of one or more shipyards would affect production rates (and purchase prices) at another shipyard. If the Navy continued to enlist all existing yards in the naval shipbuilding business, costs for each ship would be higher than CBO estimates and the Navy would be able to purchase fewer ships under each budget amount unless savings from competition equaled or exceeded the savings from having some yards produce a larger number of ships.

MAINTAINING A FORWARD PRESENCE WITH A SMALLER FLEET

The Navy routinely deploys slightly more than one-third of its total fleet overseas. In Congressional testimony, Navy officials stated that the service has about 100 ships deployed and operating overseas.[6] Until recently, ships generally deployed with a single crew for 6 or 7 months in a 24- to 32-month operating cycle. (Ships' assignments at sea are limited to the period that the Navy allows a crew to be deployed and away from home—called personnel tempo, or PERSTEMPO.) Cycles consist of phases for maintenance, training in two phases, and deployment, along with a sustainment period during which a ship may be at its home port but available to deploy quickly. The length of the cycle, which has varied over time, depends on the type of ship. Until recently, aircraft carriers followed a 32 month operating cycle, up from 27 months about a decade ago. Surface combatants and amphibious warfare ships followed a 27-month cycle. Attack submarines continue to follow a 24-month cycle. Late last year, the Navy began to phase in its Optimized Fleet Response Plan, which eventually will have all major surface ships deploy for up to 8 months in a 36-month cycle. (Various operating cycles for aircraft carriers are illustrated in Figure 2.)

Single-crewed ships based in the continental United States provide the bulk of the Navy's deployments, but the Navy has used three techniques during the past several decades to sustain or increase its forward presence:

- Deploying ships for longer periods,
- Basing more ships and their crews overseas, and
- Assigning more than one crew to some ships that operate from an overseas port or from a port in the continental United States.

Crew members' families typically live where a ship is based—at the ship's official home port. If a ship operates from and receives maintenance at an overseas port but has a U.S. home port, families reside in the United States.

Fleet Response Plan (2013)

Maintenance	Training	Deployment	Sustainment
32 Weeks	47 Weeks	30–43 Weeks	17–30 Weeks

Total Cycle: 139 Weeks (32 months)

Optmized Fleet Response Plan (2015 and Beyond)

Maintenance	Training	Deployment	Sustainment
26 Weeks	30 Weeks	35 Weeks	65 Weeks

Total Cycle: 156 Weeks (36 months)

Enhanced Carrier Presence Plan (CBO Alternative Based on Earlier Navy Proposal)

Maintenance	Training	Deployment	Dwell	Deployment
35 Weeks	30 Weeks	26–30 Weeks	31–39 Weeks	26–30 Weeks

Total Cycle: 156 Weeks (36 months)

Forward Deployed Naval Force (Japan-Based Carrier)[a]

Maint.	Deployment
17 Weeks	35 Weeks

Total Cycle: 52 Weeks (12 months)

Source: Congressional Budget Office based on data from the Navy.

Note: A ship is considered to be in *sustainment* if it is able to put to sea and go on deployment within a short period. Under the Enhanced Carrier Presence Plan, when a ship is in its *dwell* phase between deployments, it mostly remains in its home port to allow its crew members to rest and spend time with their families.

a. The aircraft carrier in this example is currently based in Japan. It is the Navy's only overseas-based aircraft carrier, and it is considered to be deployed and available to perform missions when it is not in maintenance, even if it is in its home port.

Figure 2. Current and Notional Operating Cycles for a Nuclear-Powered Aircraft Carrier.

Table 4. Major Deployments of U.S.-Based Combat Ships, 2007–2013

	Aircraft Carriers	Attack Submarines	Large Surface Combatants	Small Surface Combatants [a]	Amphibious Warfare Ships
Total Number of Deployments	30	125	236	112	87
Number of Deployments by Length					
6 months or longer	23	113	198	81	62
7 months or longer	16	15	111	14	46
8 months or longer	4	2	26	2	10
Average Length of Deployment (Days)	191	179	190	172	181
Deployments of the Same Ship in					
Consecutive Years	15	21	76	57	41
Average Number of Ships in the					
Navy's Inventory	10	51	71	30	28

Source: Congressional Budget Office based on data from the Department of the Navy.

Note: Excludes ships that operate from overseas bases, such as Japan or Guam, as well as ballistic missile submarines, guided missile submarines, and mine countermeasures ships.

[a] Small surface combatants are Oliver Hazard Perry class FFG-7 frigates.

Increasing the Length and Frequency of Deployments

The Navy can increase its forward presence most quickly by boosting the frequency or the duration of ships' deployments, as it has in the recent past. Under normal peacetime operations in the 1990s, ships were deployed for 6 months about every two years. However, between 2007 and 2013 (the period for which CBO has data), nearly half of all deployments of the Navy's aircraft carriers, large surface combatants, and amphibious warfare ships lasted at least 7 months (see Table 4). Furthermore, a substantial number of surface ships are now deployed every year, rather than once in a cycle of 24 to 32 months, although some of those deployments are for periods of only 2 or 3 months each.

The principal advantage of instituting more frequent or longer deployments is that such a change is relatively quickly and easily accomplished. Ships need not carry additional supplies, for example, because they generally are resupplied at sea or in overseas ports. If it is known in advance that a deployment will be longer than normal, the Navy could plan for additional maintenance; ordinarily, little other additional preparation is necessary.

The disadvantages include the stress borne by crew members and their families and the potential for accelerated deterioration of the ships, especially if longer deployments become routine. If deployments commonly last longer than six months, recruitment and reenlistment— particularly among sailors with specialized or difficult-toreplace skills—could suffer. For that reason, the Navy has tried to keep most deployments of attack submarines to six months. Submariners constitute a relatively small proportion of the total sailing force, but they are among the most highly skilled—they are trained to operate and maintain nuclear-powered ships—and the Navy makes extra efforts to retain them.

Despite those concerns, the extent to which more frequent and longer deployments affect reenlistment has not been studied extensively. A recent analysis of data from 2008 to 2013 for 11 Navy ships—6 deployed for six months each and 5 deployed for longer periods—showed no substantial difference in retention among sailors in either group.[7]

Overall retention data do not provide a clearer picture. Retention for the attack submarine force, for example, is higher than the Navy average, but submarines generally are not deployed for more than six months at a time. Conversely, although half of all large surface combatant deployments from 2007 to 2013 were at least seven months long, retention among sailors on those ships was above the Navy's average and nearly the same as that among the submarine crews. Deployments of the aircraft carrier force were as long as those for the surface combatant force, yet retention among those sailors was below average in every year for the period. And the amphibious force, which consistently has the longest deployments, had below-average retention for three of the six years but above-average retention for the other three years.

Surveys of sailors indicate anecdotally that their primary concern for reenlistment is not the length of deployment as such, but the lack of predictability. In the past, most deployments of longer than 7 months were unscheduled, and sailors learned of them only after they were at sea.[8] To address that difficulty, early in 2014 the Navy unveiled its Optimized Fleet Response Plan, which would change the operating cycle for all surface warships. By having one deployment of up to 8 months out of a 36-month cycle, the new cycle—which the Navy has recently implemented for aircraft carriers and surface combatants—will provide more predictability and stability in crew deployments. Previous cycles had carriers and surface ships deployed for 6 to 7 months out of 32, but over the past two years, ships increasingly have been deployed for longer periods.[9] If the Navy adheres to the new cycle and the schedule it implies, sailors will be deployed for less time, on average, than they have been in recent years, when many have been at sea for longer than 7 months at a time. The disadvantage is that, at 8 months, deployments typically will be scheduled for a month longer than they have been in the past. The Navy's Fleet Forces Command considers that the new operating cycle defines the limit on the demands that can be placed on ships' crews without undermining the service's ability to retain experienced sailors. Deployments of 8 months out of 36 provide almost the same forward presence as that provided by deployments of 7 months out of 32.

Although it is commonly assumed that ships that are deployed routinely for longer periods will require more maintenance, there is not much evidence either to support or to refute that belief. According to a study published by the CNA Corporation, failure to perform adequate maintenance would shorten the service life of surface ships.[10] However, that conclusion does not mean that lengthier deployments will require maintenance in excess of what otherwise would be scheduled. One assumption that is incorporated into CBO's analysis is that there is a direct relationship between the amount of time spent on deployment and the costs of maintenance. For example, amphibious warfare ships currently spend about one day in maintenance for every three days' deployment. Under the alternative approaches discussed in the final section of this report, CBO estimates the costs for maintaining amphibious warfare ships at that rate regardless of whether the additional time is the result of a longer deployment with single or multiple crews. The same types of assumptions were applied to all cases in which deployments were anticipated to exceed those of the Navy's current plan or the Navy's Optimized Fleet Response Plan.

Basing More Ships Overseas

Much more forward presence is possible when ships are based overseas or operated from overseas bases than is possible if those ships are based in the United States.[11] When a ship is already overseas, no time is required for transit. (In many cases, it can take from one to five weeks to sail from a U.S.

base to an overseas operating area and the same amount of time to return home.) Because of this, unless they are in maintenance, ships based overseas are considered to be on deployment even when they are in their home ports. With their different operating cycles, such ships can spend more time at sea conducting missions and still meet the guidelines for the period a crew is permitted to be away from its home port. A ship that is based in Japan, for example, can triple its forward presence compared with the amount it would supply if based in the continental United States.[12]

Since the end of World War II, the Navy has based a portion of its fleet outside the continental United States and Hawaii. At the end of 2013, the Navy had 29 ships, or about 10 percent of its fleet, stationed overseas (see Table 5). The largest concentration is in Japan, which is home to a carrier strike group consisting of one nuclear-powered aircraft carrier and nine cruisers and destroyers, and another group of amphibious warfare ships, consisting of one large amphibious assault ship and three smaller amphibious transport docks or dock landing ships. One command ship and four mine countermeasures ships also are based in Japan. In 2013, the Navy also had ships stationed in the U.S. territory of Guam, at the leased island of Diego Garcia (in the Indian Ocean), in Bahrain, and in Italy.

Over the next decade, the Navy plans to increase to 44 the number of ships based overseas. Four destroyers are scheduled to operate from Spain by the end of 2015 (2 were transferred in 2014; 2 will be transferred this year), and 16 littoral combat ships will ultimately operate from overseas bases (8 to replace retiring mine countermeasures ships, and 8 to be added to the Navy's overseas fleet). The Navy also announced in April 2013 that it would transfer one additional attack submarine to Guam in 2015.[13] More recently, the Navy announced it would base two additional destroyers in Japan—one in 2015 and one in 2017.

The major impediment to overseas basing is in obtaining permission from host governments; basing agreements for existing ships are renegotiated periodically, sometimes resulting in fewer ships' being based overseas or leading to higher costs. For example, in response to a report released in August 2012 by the Center for Strategic and International Studies, the government of Australia explicitly rejected the center's suggestion that the United States base aircraft carriers in that country.[14] And even if agreements are reached, changes in a foreign government's priorities can end a long-standing overseas-basing arrangement, as was the case for U.S. naval and air bases in the Philippines in the early 1990s. Political constraints are less likely to affect overseas bases in a U.S. territory, such as Guam, or at a leased location, such as Diego Garcia.

Table 5. Number of Battle Force Ships Operating From Overseas Bases, by Location and Type

	2013	2024 (Projected)
Japan		
Aircraft carriers	1	1
Cruisers and destroyers	9	11
Amphibious ships	4	4
Command ships	1	1
Mine countermeasures ships[a]	4	n.a.
Littoral combat ships[b]	n.a.	4
Subtotal	19	21
Guam		
Attack submarines	3	4
Fleet tender	_ 1	_ 1
Subtotal	4	5
Bahrain Mine countermeasures ships[a]	4	n.a.
Littoral combat ships[b]	n.a.	8
Subtotal	4	8
Italy Command ships	1	1
Diego Garcia Fleet tender	1	1
Spain Destroyers	0	4
Singapore		
Littoral combat ships[b]	n.a.	4
Total	**29**	**44**

Source: Congressional Budget Office based on data from the Department of the Navy.

Notes: For its 2015 shipbuilding plan, the Navy changed the rules for counting battle force ships. Under that plan, small patrol craft based in Bahrain are counted in the battle force, but the same patrol craft based in the United States are not. In 2013, the Navy had four patrol craft based in Bahrain. Patrol craft are excluded from this table because in 2013 they were not counted as part of the Navy's battle force and by 2025 all patrol craft will have been retired from the fleet.

n.a. = not applicable.

[a] All mine countermeasures ships will be retired by 2024.

[b] In 2013, the Navy had no littoral combat ships based overseas.

The expense of operating overseas presents another area of difficulty. For example, some initial investment is necessary to set up support facilities, and costs can vary widely depending on the number and type of ships at a base and whether infrastructure is already available. In addition, ships cost more to operate from an overseas base: Sea pay, fuel, and maintenance costs are higher, for example, because ships based overseas usually spend more time at sea than ships based in the United States. The Navy estimates that the annual cost of operating a ship based in Japan is about 20 percent greater than the cost of operating a U.S.-based ship. That expense could be justified by the threefold increase in forward presence, however, and in some cases the costs are offset by support from the host country; the government of Japan contributes substantially to the support of U.S. military bases located there.[15]

Basing ships overseas also changes economic activity in the United States, thus creating an indirect cost.

Typically, crew members' families live where a ship is based, and much of the economic activity that comes from maintaining ships overseas (purchases of food, fuel, and some repair activities) and some of the families' household spending would occur in and benefit host countries. When ships are based in the United States, such economic activity stays in the area around the ships' home ports.

Rotating Crews

The third and most technically challenging method that the Navy uses to increase its forward presence is to rotate crews on and off its ships, whether they are based in the United States or operating from overseas ports.[16] The Navy currently employs various crewing arrangements and has experimented with others. The standard model has a single crew that stays with a ship during the maintenance, training, and deployment phases of the operating cycle. In other cases, two or more crews can be assigned to a single ship. For example, since the early 1960s, the Navy's ballistic missile submarines have been staffed by dual crews.[17] Thus, on today's Ohio class submarines, a pair of crews—designated blue and gold—alternates in deployments of two and a half months, with an intervening maintenance period of about a month per rotation. The Navy has adapted that construct for other ships in the fleet (see Table 6). The length of deployment varies by ship class, but the result is the same: When crews alternate and maintenance time is shared, a ship can provide more forward presence than is possible with a single crew.

Another approach is a multiple-crewing arrangement in which crews rotate among ships of the same class; thus, one crew could staff a different ship each time it goes to sea. The Navy has used such rotations for its coastal patrol ships and some of its mine countermeasures ships. In the 2000s, the Navy conducted three multiple-crewing experiments—known as the Sea Swap—on Spruance and Arleigh Burke class destroyers. (Despite the project's name, however, the crews were swapped in port rather than at sea.) The experiments consisted of keeping one ship deployed overseas while rotating the crews of two or three other ships to that one.[18] The Navy concluded that the tests were a success, although the Government Accountability Office criticized their management, particularly concerning the collection of evaluation data.[19] The Navy plans to change its rotation for its newly deployed littoral combat ships from a dual-crew arrangement in which the U.S.-based crews swap overseas to what is known as the 3.2.1 concept: Three U.S.-based crews operate two ships, one of which is deployed overseas at all times.

In general, a rotation that involves more crews than ships will produce more forward presence than is possible with rotations that use equal numbers of crews and ships. Swapping the crews at overseas ports boosts the Navy's forward presence by reducing transit time to and from ports in the United States, but it requires appropriate infrastructure overseas to support crew exchanges and regular maintenance. Although the exact amount of additional presence depends on the method of crew rotation, CBO's analysis indicates that a dual- or multiple-crewed ship can provide between 1.4 times and 1.8 times the amount of presence that a single-crewed ship will provide and about half of what a ship with a home port overseas would provide.[20]

Nevertheless, crew rotation also poses several challenges. For much of its history, the Navy's culture has fostered strong identification of a crew with its ship: A single crew trains on, operates, maintains, and lives for significant periods on a single vessel. Crew members often take considerable pride in serving on and maintaining a ship, and some sense of ownership can be lost if a ship has more than one crew. One result could be a loss in efficiency in maintenance. If a repair is required close to the time of a switch, for example, the current crew could leave the work to the next crew to accomplish. If a ship has a single crew, its members have no such option, and they could be more motivated to complete the work in a timely manner.

Shifting from single to multiple crewing requires different procedures, additional personnel, and probably additional maintenance, and it could lead to a shorter service life for a ship. Training programs would need to account for the fact that more than one crew would operate a ship. Having additional crews would not only require the additional personnel to form the crew itself but would require additional trainers and recruiters as support personnel.

Maintenance and repair costs also would increase and service life could decrease as a result of longer periods of operation. For example, if nuclear-powered submarines were deployed for longer periods, their power plants and pressure hulls would wear out faster, those ships' normally fixed service lives could be shortened, and they would need to be replaced sooner than the Navy envisions under its current shipbuilding plans.

Table 6. The Navy's Continuing Operations and Past Experience with Crew Rotation, by Ship Class

	Number of Ships	Number of Crews	Rotation Type	Rotation Method
	Continuing Operations			
Ohio Ballistic Missile Submarines	14	28	Dual Crew	Two crews assigned to a single ship alternate on deployment; the submarine returns to a U.S. port for maintenance and a change of crew.
Ohio Guided Missile Submarines	4	8	Dual Crew	Similar to the rotation system for ballistic missile submarines, deployments are longer and some maintenance and crew changes occur at overseas ports.
Littoral Combat Ships	3	6	Dual or Multiple Crew	Initially, two crews alternate in operating the ship and crew changes occur at an overseas port. The ships will be converted to a system of three crews for a pair of ships to keep one ship deployed at all times. Crew members live in the United States.

Table 6. (Continued)

	Number of Ships	Number of Crews	Rotation Type	Rotation Method
	Past Experience			
Cyclone Coastal Patrol Ships	8	13	Multiple Crew	Before 2013, Bahrain was the home port for five ships; three were based in the United States. The 13 crews lived in the United States and rotated between deploying to the ships and Bahrain and training on the ships in the United States. In 2013, the ships were converted to single crews and all now have a home port in Bahrain, where the crews also live.
Avenger Mine Countermeasures Ships	9	9	Multiple Crew	Before 2013, Bahrain was home to four ships; five more were based in the United States.[a] The nine crews lived in the United States and rotated between deploying to the ships in Bahrain and training on the ships in the United States. The ships in Bahrain and the United States were converted to single crews in 2013 and have home ports with their crews in those two countries.

Source: Congressional Budget Office based on data from the Department of the Navy.

Note: With multiple crewing, several crews rotate among several ships. The number of crews and the ships may be the same or the number of crews may be larger.

[a] Four other ships, each with a single crew, are based in Japan.

The Navy also would need to change its support systems for ships and their crews by enhancing facilities and organizations to provide maintenance in short, high-intensity periods; by establishing training simulators and facilities to maintain crew proficiency; and by expanding organizations and facilities for recruitment and training of additional sailors. (The Navy accomplishes all of those tasks for its ballistic missile submarines.) The larger the ship, the greater those challenges are likely to be. Thus, crew rotation may not be a good choice for nuclear-powered aircraft carriers or large-deck amphibious assault ships, which have crews that number in the thousands and require significant shore-based infrastructure. (However, aircraft carriers and amphibious assault ships, which are among the most expensive ships in the Navy's fleet, could benefit from the efficiency offered by rotating crews.) For this report, CBO did not examine approaches that would use rotating crews on those ships.

Analysis of Approaches to Maintaining a Forward Presence

CBO examined two approaches that the Navy might pursue to maintain or increase its current forward presence with a smaller fleet under three targets for the shipbuilding budget—$16 billion, $14 billion, and $12 billion per year (see Table 1 on page 2):

- Under Approach 1, the Navy would either lengthen deployments or increase their frequency in an operating cycle so that smaller fleets matched the current forward presence in each of the main ship types (aircraft carrier, large surface combatant, attack submarine, and amphibious warfare ship). For this analysis, CBO assumed that there would be no difference from the Navy's current plans either in the number of ships based overseas or in the amount of rotational crewing used to staff certain ship classes.
- Under Approach 2, which would apply to the same four types of ships, there would be no deployments longer than six months, but more ships would be based overseas and more ships would use crew rotation.

Although it would be possible to blend various elements in any of several combinations, CBO structured its analysis to illustrate the trade-offs between long deployments and other methods of operation. The analysis shows that if the Navy lengthened deployments by 17 percent to 75 percent (depending on the ship type and the shipbuilding budget), it could maintain its current forward presence with fewer ships. Alternatively, by increasing the number of ships based overseas by 30 percent to 40 percent and by rotating crews on some or all of its large surface combatants, attack submarines, and amphibious warfare ships, the Navy could maintain the same amount of presence for each ship type without extending any deployments beyond six months.[21]

Each approach would involve greater operating costs for the ships and facilities affected by the changes in operating procedures. Those higher costs would offset some of the savings from reduced procurement budgets and from lower operation and support costs for a smaller fleet, and both approaches could pose drawbacks, including some involving recruitment and retention, as discussed earlier. Moreover, additional investment would be needed to build overseas bases and to establish dual or multiple crewing where it is not in use today. The introduction of rotating crews also could create new logistical and cultural challenges. Finally, although basing more ships overseas could provide assurance to U.S. allies and deter adversaries, it also might increase the fleet's vulnerability to attack.

Forward Presence under an Annual Shipbuilding Budget of $16 Billion

Restricting the Navy's shipbuilding budget to the 30-year historical average would produce a fleet of 251 ships by 2044, CBO estimates. The Navy could maintain a forward presence of 113 ships—slightly more than the fleet provides today—either by using longer deployments for its aircraft carriers, large surface combatants (cruisers and destroyers), attack submarines, and amphibious warfare ships (Approach 1) or by using more overseas basing and rotation of crews on those ships (Approach 2).[22]

Approach 1. This approach would have the Navy use longer deployments for aircraft carriers, large surface combatants, attack submarines, and amphibious warfare ships, as follows:

- U.S.-based aircraft carriers would be deployed for 10 months in each 36-month operating cycle instead of the deployments of 8 months as specified under the Navy's Optimized Fleet Response Plan (see Figure 3).
- All U.S.-based large surface combatants (roughly three-fourths of such vessels; by 2044, all of them will be destroyers) would be deployed routinely for 10 months out of 36, longer than normal since 2012 for large surface combatants and even longer than the Navy currently plans for the future.
- Eighteen of the Navy's 39 attack submarines would be deployed for 7 months out of a 24-month cycle. Over the past several years, most attack submarines' deployments have been 6 months or shorter.
- All U.S.-based amphibious warfare ships (accounting for 85 percent of such vessels) would be deployed for 8 months out of 27. Since 2008, only a few deployments have lasted that long or longer, although they have become more common in recent years.
- All of the Navy's small surface combatants would be littoral combat ships, which, according to the Navy's plan, would use rotating crews. CBO's analysis considered no changes in the deployment of those ships.
- The number of combat logistics and support ships would remain about the same under the $16 billion budget as it is for today's fleet. Each ship would spend about 70 percent of its time being operationally available, providing forward presence.
- The deployment cycles of all ships based overseas would remain unchanged.

Approach 2. Under this approach, the Navy could maintain the same forward presence as under Approach 1 by increasing the use of overseas basing and rotating crews, but limiting all deployments to six months (see Figure 4).

Additional ships based overseas would include an aircraft carrier, 4 large surface combatants (for a total of 19; the current plan calls for 15), 7 attack submarines (the current plan calls for 4; some of the additional submarines would go to Guam, others would be based with the second overseas carrier), and 2 amphibious warfare ships (for a total of 6). The number of ships using rotating crews also would increase. The attack submarine force would have 6 ships that adopted a modified version of the Navy's dual-crew system for ballistic missile submarines; all would continue to be based in the continental United States.[23] (Table A-1 in the appendix provides additional detail about the number of ships based overseas or having rotating crews at the end of 2013, under the Navy's 2015 plan, and under the two approaches discussed here.)

Forward Presence under an Annual Shipbuilding Budget of $14 Billion

If the Navy's shipbuilding budget was limited to the amounts that the service has spent over the past decade (and currently plans to spend over the next five years, on average, under the Department of Defense's 2015 Future Years Defense Program), by 2044, the fleet would number 230 ships, 51 fewer than it has today and 73 fewer than called for under its 2015 shipbuilding plan.[24] With a budget of $14 billion, the Navy could maintain a forward presence of 111 ships (which is greater than today's presence of about 100) by relying on longer deployments for aircraft carriers, large surface combatants, attack submarines, and amphibious warfare ships (under Approach 1). Alternatively, it could provide 112 ships by basing more ships overseas and using more crew rotation (Approach 2). But those approaches would have to be implemented more aggressively than would be required under a larger shipbuilding budget.

Approach 1. Under this approach, deployments would be longer or more frequent than if the annual shipbuilding budget was set for a $16 billion average (see Figure 3):

- The Navy would adopt a variant of its Enhanced Carrier Presence Plan (that it proposed in 2013) instead of its plan to conduct 8-month-long carrier deployments under the Optimized Fleet Response Plan (or 10-month deployments discussed above for the $16 billion shipbuilding budget).[25] Each U.S.-based aircraft carrier would be deployed for 12 months out of a 36-month operating cycle— twice for 6 months with an interval of 9 months between deployments (see Figure 2 on page 9).

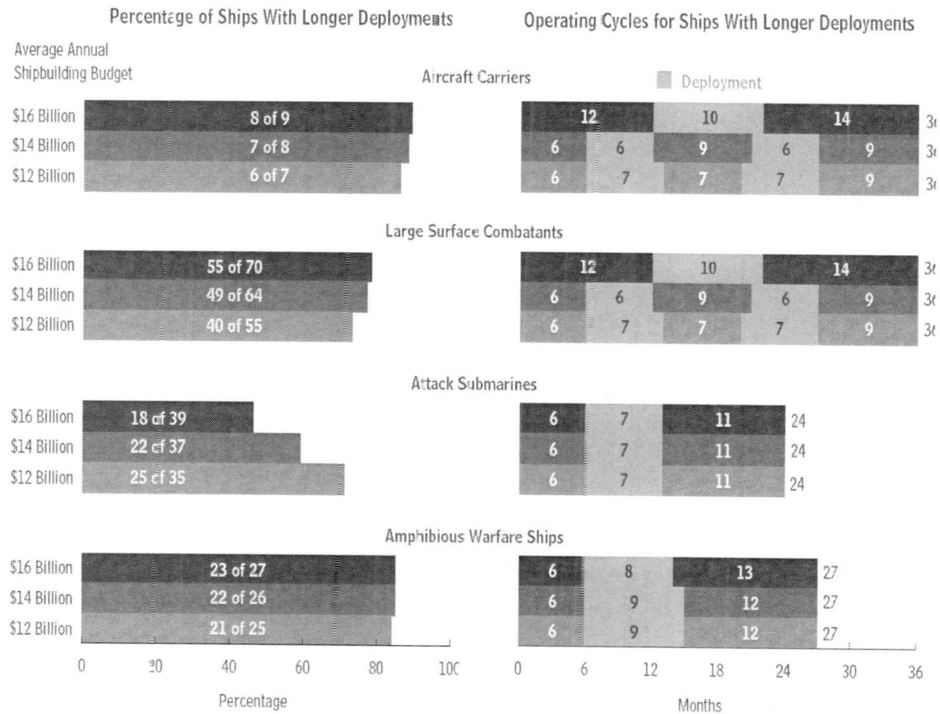

Source: Congressional Budget Office.

Notes: CBO calculated the percentage of ships with longer deployments by using the Navy's inventory of ships based in the United States and overseas.

Under the Navy's current plan for forward presence, the overseas-based forces after 2044 would include 1 aircraft carrier, 15 large surface combatants, 4 attack submarines, and 4 amphibious warfare ships.

The aircraft carriers, large surface combatants, and eventually amphibious warfare ships would have one 8-month deployment over 36 months; attack submarines would have one 6-month deployment over 24 months. CBO's analysis included the assumption that the 36-month cycle would apply to aircraft carriers and surface combatants but the existing 27-month cycle would be retained for amphibious warfare ships.

When ships are not deployed, they are undergoing maintenance, their crews are in training, or they are in sustainment and ready for deployment on short notice.

Figure 3. Deployments That Would Maintain the Same Amount of Forward Presence in 2044 as in 2013 With Smaller Fleets Than Under the Navy's Plan.

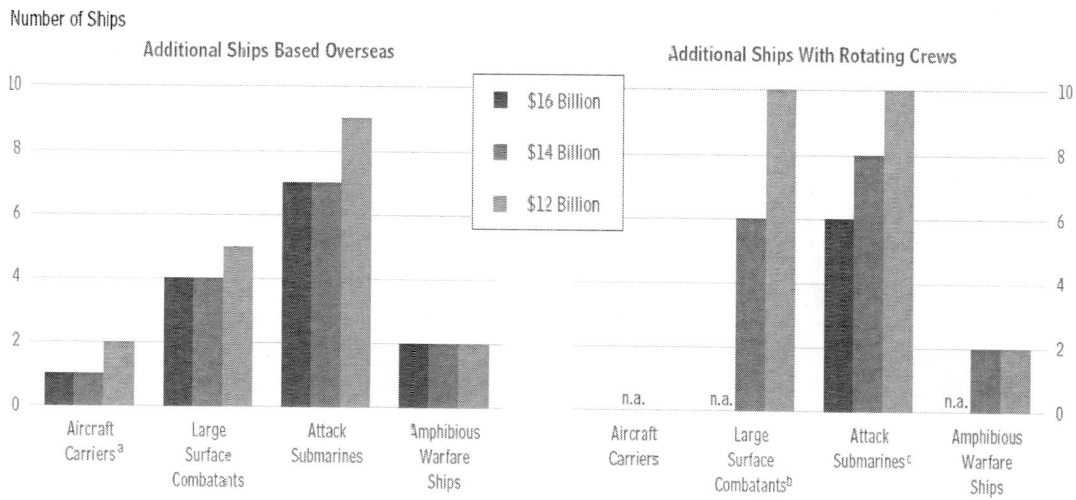

Source: Congressional Budget Office.

Notes: Ships based overseas are counted separately from those with rotating crews. At the end of 2013, the Navy based overseas 1 aircraft carrier, 9 surface combatants, 3 attack submarines, and 4 amphibious ships. It also based overseas 12 other ships of different types.

n.a. = not applicable.

[a] Under the $12 billion budget, another aircraft carrier would be transferred from the continental United States to Hawaii.

[b] Uses multiple crewing.

[c] Uses a dual-crew system modeled in part on the existing system for ballistic missile submarines.

Figure 4. Additional Ships Based Overseas and Additional Rotating Crews That Would Maintain the Same Amount of Forward Presence in 2044 as in 2013 With Smaller Fleets Than Under the Navy's Plan.

- All U.S.-based large surface combatants would follow the same 36-month deployment schedule as the aircraft carriers.
- Twenty-two U.S.-based attack submarines—four more than under the $16 billion budget—would routinely conduct 7-month deployments.
- All U.S.-based amphibious warfare ships would be deployed for 9 months out of a 27-month cycle.
- There would be no changes in the operation of littoral combat ships or any ships based overseas from the current plan. As is the case for the $16 billion budget, the number of support ships would remain about the same as it is for today's fleet.

Approach 2. Under this approach, the Navy could maintain a forward presence of 112 ships under an annual shipbuilding budget of $14 billion by increasing its use of overseas basing and crew rotation but still limiting all ship deployments to 6 months.

Overseas basing for the four ship types (aircraft carrier, large surface combatant, attack submarine, and amphibious warfare ship) would match that discussed above for a $16 billion annual budget (see Figure 4 on page 19).

This approach would put a second carrier overseas, increase the number of large surface combatants based overseas from today's planned 15 ships to 19, increase the number of attack submarines based overseas from a planned 4 to 11, and increase the number of amphibious warfare ships overseas from 4 to 6.

Approach 2 would have more ships using rotating crews than would be the case under a $16 billion budget. Six large surface combatants would use multiple crews: Two of those six would remain at a forward operating location and the crews of the remaining ships would rotate to those ships to increase the overall amount of presence provided by the group. That forward-based ship would return to the United States less frequently than it would under the regular operating cycle.

Two smaller amphibious warfare ships would have rotating crews; there are none in today's Navy and none are included under Approach 2 for a $16 billion budget. The attack submarine force would have eight ships with dual crews operating out of U.S. ports, two more than under the $16 billion budget.

Forward Presence under an Annual Shipbuilding Budget of $12 Billion

If the Navy received annual funding for shipbuilding that was equivalent to the amounts it spent in the 1990s, by 2044 its fleet of battle force ships would number 208. The Navy could maintain its forward presence at 108 to 110 ships by relying even more heavily on longer deployments or overseas basing and crew rotation than would be called for under a $14 billion annual budget.

Approach 1. Under this approach, the Navy would deploy most aircraft carriers and large surface combatants for longer periods than it would with a $14 billion budget (see Figure 3 on page 18):

- U.S.-based aircraft carriers would employ the Enhanced Carrier Presence Plan rather than the Optimized Fleet Response Plan. However, with one fewer carrier than under a $14 billion budget, the U.S.-based ships would conduct two 7-month deployments, with 7 months intervening, out of a 36-month operating cycle. The total period of deployment thus would be 2 months longer than under a $14 billion budget.
- The operating cycle for all U.S.-based large surface combatants would parallel that for the aircraft carriers.
- Twenty-five of the Navy's U.S.-based attack submarines—three more than under a $14 billion budget—would be deployed for 7 months out of a 24-month cycle.
- All U.S.-based amphibious warfare ships would be deployed for 9 months out of the 27-month cycle.
- There would be no changes from the current plan in the Navy's operation of its littoral combat ships.
- The number of support ships providing forward presence would remain about the same under a $12 billion budget as it is for today's fleet.

Approach 2. With a $12 billion average annual budget for shipbuilding, the Navy could maintain its forward presence by increasing the use of overseas basing and crew rotation and thereby limit all ship deployments to six months. The Navy would base two additional aircraft carriers overseas, while another carrier would be transferred from the continental United States to Hawaii (see

Figure 4 on page 19). Thus, with a force of seven aircraft carriers, only three would remain based in the continental United States.

The number of other ships based overseas also would increase. The fleet of large surface combatants with home ports in other countries would increase from 15 under today's plans to 20 under a $12 billion budget, the number of attack submarines would increase from 4 to 13, and the number of amphibious warfare ships would increase from 4 to 6.

Crew rotations would increase as well. The force of large surface combatants would consist of 10 ships and 2 amphibious warfare ships using multiple or dual crew rotation. The attack submarine force would have 10 ships using dual crews.

Cost Implications

Although the Navy would spend less money on ship construction and operations with smaller fleets (as well as saving on aircraft procurement and operations because of the need to buy and maintain fewer carrier air wings), those reductions would be partly offset by the additional costs of maintaining a forward presence. By CBO's estimate, the savings attributable to the smaller fleet would be offset by less than 5 percent to about 10 percent under a $16 billion annual budget for ship construction and by 23 percent to 45 percent under a $12 billion budget, depending on the approach taken. After factoring in those offsets, CBO estimates that the smaller fleets would result in net savings averaging $10 billion to $17 billion or more a year (see Table 7).

CBO's estimates of the savings in operation and support costs are based on the agency's assumption of roughly proportional cuts in the various ship forces within the fleet, initially without considering any adjustments needed to maintain the current forward presence.[26] Thus, the cost in 2044 to operate the 208-ship fleet under a $12 billion annual budget would be $30 billion—about two-thirds of the $43 billion cost in the same year to operate the 303-ship fleet anticipated in the Navy's 2015 shipbuilding plan. CBO relied on current operating costs to estimate costs for 2044, even though the design specifics of the ships of the future, and thus their costs, cannot be reliably estimated today. If the estimated reduction in operations spending is added to the assumed cuts in ship construction, total annual savings in 2044—out of a total annual cost of $64 billion estimated for that year under the Navy's 2015 plan—would be $11 billion under a $16 billion shipbuilding budget and $22 billion under a $12 billion budget (all measured in 2014 dollars).

Those savings would be partially offset by the cost of steps taken to maintain the Navy's forward presence. Although they are difficult to estimate precisely, CBO formulated some rough estimates of additional, recurring annual costs (including military pay and benefits, operations, and maintenance) and onetime costs (such as infrastructure construction) for each approach. To project recurring costs, CBO used information from the Future Years Defense Program, among other sources, and to estimate onetime costs it relied on several sources, but most heavily on a forthcoming RAND report.[27] In general, projected costs for Approach 2 are greater than those for Approach 1.

Net Savings Under Approach 1. Recurring costs from longer and more frequent deployments would include increased spending on ship maintenance, fuel, and sea pay. CBO increased its estimates of maintenance costs according to the proportion of maintenance days to at-sea days under the various ships' operating cycles. For example, if there is a 1-to-3 ratio of maintenance to at sea days for an amphibious warfare ship, a deployment of two additional months, resulting in 30 additional days at sea, would increase the ship's time in maintenance by 10 days.[28]

On that basis, CBO estimates that the additional costs for maintenance and fuel from longer deployments could amount to a few hundred million dollars per year under a $16 billion budget but would probably run to a few billion dollars per year under a $12 billion budget. Moreover, in the latter case, additional sea pay would add as much as several hundred million dollars per year to the Navy's operating budget. Overall, those recurring costs under Approach 1 would reduce annual procurement and operating savings from buying and operating smaller fleets by less than 5 percent under a $16 billion budget, but by as much as 20 percent under a $12 billion budget. Nevertheless, net annual savings would still range from roughly $11 billion to $17 billion for the three different-sized fleets considered in this analysis.

Other potential recurring costs that CBO did not include in its analysis are the differences in sea pay and retention bonuses that might be needed if longer deployments caused the Navy to regularly miss its retention goals. If such increases turned out to be necessary, Approach 1 would cost somewhat more, although not enough to offset the lower costs of building and operating a smaller fleet. That approach would not involve any additional onetime costs.

Table 7. Costs for and Savings From Maintaining Forward Presence Under Alternative Shipbuilding Budgets

	Navy's 2015 Plan ($21 Billion)	Average Annual Shipbuilding Budget		
		$16 Billion	$14 Billion	$12 Billion
Number of Battle Force Ships in 2044	303	251	230	208
Annual Operation and Support Costs for				
Battle Force Ships[a]	$43 billion	$37 billion[b]	$33 billion[b]	$30 billion[b]
		Additional Annual Operation and Support Costs by 2044		
Approach 1: Longer Deployments				
Ship maintenance and fuel	n.a.	A few hundred million dollars	Several hundred million dollars	A few billion dollars
Sea pay[c]	n.a.	About $100 million	A few hundred million dollars	Several hundred million dollars
Approach 2: More Overseas Basing and Crew Rotation				
Ship maintenance and fuel	n.a.	A few hundred million dollars	Several hundred million dollars	A few billion dollars
Additional crews, traning, and base operations	n.a.	Several hundred million dollars	A few billion dollars	Several billion dollars
		Net Average Annual Recurring Savings by 2044		
Approach 1: Longer Deployments	n.a.	$11 billion	$16 billion	$17 billion or more
Approach 2: More Overseas Basing and				
Crew Rotation	n.a.	$10 billion	$12 billion or more	$12 billion or more
		Additional Onetime Costs From 2015 Through 2044		
Approach 1: Longer Deployments	n.a.	0	0	0

	Navy's 2015 Plan ($21 Billion)	Average Annual Shipbuilding Budget		
		$16 Billion	$14 Billion	$12 Billion
Approach 2: More Overseas Basing and Crew Rotation				
Overseas bases	n.a.	$3 billion to $10 billion	$3 billion to $10 billion	$16 billion to $25 billion
U.S.-based infrastructure	n.a.	A few hundred million dollars	A few hundred million dollars	Several hundred million dollars

Source: Congressional Budget Office. Source: Congressional Budget Office.

Notes: Ships' operating costs are based on current amounts. n.a. = not applicable.

[a] Operation and support costs include the amounts paid from the Navy's military personnel appropriation for military pay and bonuses and those paid from the Navy's operation and maintenance appropriation for civilian salaries, military health care, daily operation of the Navy's units, maintenance of equipment, training, support contractors, and so on. CBO added the costs of operating carrier air wings to the costs of the aircraft carriers themselves. CBO's estimates are based on data for the 2015–2019 period as outlined in the Department of Defense's (DoD's) 2015 Future Years Defense Program. (In that five-year plan, DoD does not account for potential supplemental or emergency appropriations to fund ongoing operations.) CBO's estimates include a share of the Defense Health Program's costs that support sailors assigned to ships and air wings (and their families), although that would be paid for out of non-Navy accounts in DoD's budget. CBO also included the costs of recruiting and training sailors, which it estimated as a fraction of the recruitment and training budgets for sailors assigned to the ships and air wings considered for this report.

[b] Figures are for operation and support costs before adjustment using either Approach 1 or Approach 2.

[c] Sea pay does not include additional retention bonuses, which could be required to meet retention goals with longer deployments.

Net Savings Under Approach 2. The recurring costs for ship maintenance and fuel that arise from basing more ships overseas and using rotating crews would be roughly the same as those calculated for Approach 1. But the cost of paying, training, and housing the additional personnel that would be needed to maintain rotating crews plus the cost of operating new overseas carrier bases would amount to several hundred million dollars annually under a $16 billion shipbuilding budget—and several billion dollars a year under a $12 billion budget, mostly because of the large number of additional crews needed to maintain forward presence with such a small fleet.

All together, recurring costs under Approach 2 would offset 10 percent of the savings arising from buying and operating the smaller fleets under a $16 billion budget and as much as 45 percent of the savings under a $12 billion budget.

Net annual savings would amount roughly to $10 billion to $12 billion for the three different-sized fleets considered in this analysis. Moreover, some recurring costs could be shared by the host country—Japan and South Korea, for example, help defray expenses for U.S. forces stationed in those countries—but CBO did not account for that possibility in its analysis.

Unlike Approach 1, Approach 2 would result in significant onetime costs: Billions of dollars would be required to build new overseas bases, particularly for aircraft carriers. Although CBO has not formulated independent estimates, a report that was released in August 2012 by the Center for Strategic and International Studies proposed basing an aircraft carrier in Australia and estimated the costs of doing so.

The report stated that the cost of establishing an aircraft carrier base in Guam several years ago had been estimated at about $6.5 billion.[29] Unofficial Navy estimates put the onetime price of basing a carrier in Australia at about $10 billion. RAND's forthcoming report estimates fixed costs of about $1 billion to base a second carrier in Japan and $4 billion to $10 billion to base one in Guam.[30]

Although the RAND report did not examine the Australia option in detail, the costs would probably be comparable to those for Guam. For two additional carriers based overseas the costs would be higher. In addition, some small additional infrastructure costs (mostly for training facilities) would be required in the United States to support the new systems for rotating crews to large surface combatants, attack submarines, and amphibious warfare ships. CBO estimates onetime costs of $3 billion to $10 billion to provide forward presence under the $14 billion and $16 billion shipbuilding budgets and of $16 billion to $25 billion under the $12 billion budget. Those onetime costs would not exceed about two years of annual savings.

Costs Not Considered in CBO's Analysis. Additional costs that were not considered in this analysis would accrue after 2044 under either approach. Because more intensive use of nuclear-powered aircraft carriers and attack submarines would shorten the service lives of those weapon systems, replacement would occur sooner than is dictated by current schedules.

The service life of a dual-crewed attack submarine, at about 27 years, would be 18 percent shorter than the 33 years currently anticipated for a single-crewed submarine.[31]

An aircraft carrier operating under the Enhanced Carrier Presence Plan could have a service life of about 45 years, 10 percent shorter than the Navy's current plan of 50 years.

In contrast, more intensive use of surface ships (which are not nuclear powered) would not necessarily result in a shorter service life as long as the Navy's maintenance protocols compensated for the increased operational use.[32]

Even if the added costs of reduced service life were considered to be accrued during the period addressed in this analysis, they would not offset a substantial portion of the annual savings projected for the two approaches discussed here.

APPENDIX: COMPARISON OF DIFFERENT-SIZED FLEETS UNDER TWO APPROACHES TO MAINTAINING FORWARD PRESENCE

The Navy's 30-year shipbuilding plan envisions building a fleet of 306 ships (it would have 303 ships in 2044). The funding required to implement that plan, however, is considerably more than the amounts the Navy has received over the past 30 years.

The Congressional Budget Office projected the size of the Navy's fleet with annual funding of $16 billion, $14 billion, and $12 billion, and it examined two approaches for maintaining the Navy's forward presence with smaller fleets.

The first approach would emphasize longer deployments than under current practice; the second would emphasize more overseas basing and more crew rotation than is the case under current practice. Table A-1 is a summary of key data for comparing the three resulting fleets under the two approaches.

Table A-1. Number and Status of Ship Types, Deployment Lengths, and Basing and Crew Rotation Under Two Approaches and Several Alternative Shipbuilding Budgets, 2044

Ship Count

	2013 Inventory[a]	Navy's 2015 Plan ($21 Billion)	Approach 1: Longer Deployments			Approach 2: More Overseas Basing and Crew Rotation		
			$16 Billion	$14 Billion	$12 Billion	$16 Billion	$14 Billion	$12 Billion
Total Battle Force Ships	289	303	251	230	208	251	230	208
Ships Providing a Forward Presence at Any Given Time	103	130	113	111	108	113	112	110
	Aircraft Carriers							
Ships Conducting 6-Month Deployments	0	0	0	0	0	7	6	4
Ships Conducting 7- to 8-Month								
Deployments	7	9	0	0	0	0	0	0
Ships Conducting 8-Month or Longer								
Deployments	2	0	8	7 [b]	6 [b]	0	0	0
Ships Based Overseas	1	1	1	1	1	2	2	3
Ships With a Rotating Crew	0	0	0	0	0	0	0	0
Ship Inventory	10	10	9	8	7	9	8	7
	Large Surface Combatants							
Ships Conducting 6-Month Deployments	0	0	0	0	0	53	39	25
Ships Conducting 7- to 8-Month								
Deployments	63	83	0	0	0	0	0	0

	2013 Inventory[a]	Navy's 2015 Plan ($21 Billion)	Approach 1: Longer Deployments			Approach 2: More Overseas Basing and Crew Rotation		
			$16 Billion	$14 Billion	$12 Billion	$16 Billion	$14 Billion	$12 Billion
Ships Conducting 8-Month or Longer								
Deployments	12	0	57	49 [b]	40 [b]	0	0	0
Ships Based Overseas	9	15	15	15	15	19	19	20
Ships With a Rotating Crew	0	0	0	0	0	0	6 [c]	10 [c]
Ship Inventory	84	83	72	64	55	72	64	55
	Small Surface Combatants and Mine Countermeasures Ships							
Ships Conducting 6-Month Deployments	15	n.a.	n.a.	n.a.	n.a.	n.a.	n.a.	n.a.
Ships Conducting 7- to 8-Month								
Deployments	3	n.a.	n.a.	n.a.	n.a.	n.a.	n.a.	n.a.
Ships Conducting 8-Month or Longer								
Deployments	0	n.a.	n.a.	n.a.	n.a.	n.a.	n.a.	n.a.
Ships Based Overseas	8	16	16	16	16	16	16	16
Ships With a Rotating Crew	9	52	37	32	27	37	32	27
Ship Inventory	35	52 [d]	37 [d]	32 [d]	27 [d]	37 [d]	32 [d]	27 [d]
	Attack Submarines							
Ships Conducting 6-Month Deployments	43	48	17	11	6	22	18	12
Ships Conducting 7- to 8-Month Deployments	8	0	18	22	25	0	0	0

Table A-1. (Continued)

	2013 Inventory[a]	Navy's 2015 Plan ($21 Billion)	Approach 1: Longer Deployments			Approach 2: More Overseas Basing and Crew Rotation		
			$16 Billion	$14 Billion	$12 Billion	$16 Billion	$14 Billion	$12 Billion
Ships Conducting 8-Month or Longer Deployments	1	0	0	0	0	0	0	0
Ships Based Overseas	3	4	4	4	4	11	11	13
Ships With a Rotating Crew	0	0	0	0	0	6 [e]	8 [e]	10 [e]
Ship Inventory	55	52	39	37	35	39	37	35
	Amphibious Warfare Ships							
Ships Conducting 6-Month Deployments	0	0	0	0	0	21	18	17
Ships Conducting 7- to 8-Month Deployments	19	27	0	0	0	0	0	0
Ships Conducting 8-Month or Longer Deployments	8	0	23 [f]	22 [f]	21 [f]	0	0	0
Ships Based Overseas	4	4	4	4	4	6	6	6
Ships With a Rotating Crew	0	0	0	0	0	0	2	2
Ship Inventory	31	31	27	26	25	27	26	25
	Ballistic and Guided Missile Submarinesg							
Ship Inventory	18	12	10	8	6	10	8	6
	Combat Logistics and Support Shipsh							
Ship Inventory	56	63	59	55	53	59	55	53

Source: Congressional Budget Office.

Notes: Deployments for ships with rotating crews are longer than 9 months, although the crews are deployed for much shorter periods.

n.a. = not applicable.

[a] Ship counts refer to the entire operating cycle.

[b] All aircraft carrier and large surface combatant deployments would follow the Navy's enhanced carrier presence plan. Deployments might last 6 or 7 months, but two deployments would occur within a 21-month period and the 36-month operating cycle.

[c] Uses multiple crew rotation; ships are based in the United States.

[d] The small surface combatant and mine countermeasures inventory in the future will consist of littoral combat ships and therefore all will have rotating crews but not all will be based overseas.

[e] Uses a dual-crew system modeled in part on the existing system for ballistic missile submarines; submarines are based in the United States.

[f] All deployments are nearly 9 months long.

[g] All ballistic missile and guided missile submarines operate dual crews but are not counted in totals for a forward presence.

[h] Most combat logistics and support ships operate with civilian mariners and are available for forward presence 270 days of the year.

End Notes

[1] See Congressional Budget Office, *An Analysis of the Navy's Fiscal Year 2015 Shipbuilding Plan* (December 2014), www.cbo.gov/ publication/49818. All dollar amounts presented in this report are in 2014 dollars.

[2] See Department of the Navy, *Report to Congress on the Annual Long-Range Plan for Construction of Naval Vessels for FY2015* (July 2014), http://go.usa.gov/FYZR (PDF, 3.4 MB).

[3] See Department of the Navy, Chief of Naval Operations, *CNO's Sailing Directions* (accessed March 12, 2015), http://go.usa.gov/ feez (PDF, 163 KB).

[4] For more information, see Congressional Budget Office, *An Analysis of the Navy's Fiscal Year 2015 Shipbuilding Plan* (December 2014), www.cbo.gov/publication/49818, and *An Analysis of the Navy's Fiscal Year 2014 Shipbuilding Plan* (October 2013), www.cbo.gov/publication/44655. The 2014 and 2015 shipbuilding plans are similar, although the Navy changed the way it counts battle force ships for the 2015 plan. The changes affect a small number of ship classes designated as very small combatants or logistics and support ships. This report relies on the counting rules used for 2014 and earlier plans. CBO discusses the new rules on page 8 of its report on the 2015 plan. In the 2015 National Defense Authorization Act, the Congress directs the Navy to generally rely on the prior counting rules in formulating its future shipbuilding plans.

[5] That amount covers everything that the Navy pays for from its shipbuilding accounts, including construction of new ships, refueling of nuclear-powered aircraft carriers, ship conversions, construction of training ships, outfitting and postdelivery costs (which include the purchase of many smaller tools and pieces of equipment needed to operate a ship but not necessarily provided by the manufacturing shipyard), and other smaller items.

[6] Testimony of Jonathan Greenert, Chief of Naval Operations, U.S. Navy, before the Subcommittee on Defense of the Senate Committee on Appropriations, *FY 2016 Department of the Navy Posture* (March 4, 2015), http://go.usa.gov/3awCY.

[7] Department of the Navy, information supplied to CBO staff (April 23, 2013).

[8] According to a recent report, "Analysis predicts that extended and additional deployments will negatively impact personnel retention rates." See Office of the Chief of Naval Operations, *Naval Vessels and the Force Structure Assessment*, Report to Congress (July 2014), p. 7. Although that report does not discuss or cite the particular analysis, in communications with CBO, the Navy indicated that its assessment was based on information from a report that longer and more frequent deployments resulted in reenlistment rates that were between 1.2 and 1.9 percentage points below those otherwise observed. See Heidi L.W. Golding and Henry S. Griffis, *How Has PERSTEMPO's Effect on Reenlistments Changed Since the 1986 Navy Policy?* (CNA Corporation, July 2004), http://tinyurl.com/ lp2xonr.

[9] Bill Gortney, "Optimizing the Fleet Response Plan" (Navy briefing, January 14, 2014); Sam Fellman, "Navy's New Plan Aims to Lock in 8-Month Carrier Deployments," *Navy Times* (January 15, 2014), http://tinyurl.com/nh2ktwv; and Marcus Hitchcock, "Optimizing the Fleet Response Plan" (Navy briefing to CBO staff, February 7, 2013). The Navy has described the lengths of deployments under the Optimized Fleet Response Plan as lasting "up to 8 months"; CBO used that deployment period for this report. See Bill Gortney and Harry Harris, "Applied Readiness," *Proceedings Magazine*, vol. 140, no. 10, p. 1340 (October 2014), http://tinyurl.com/npxphma.

[10] Wm. Brent Boning, *Ship Depot Maintenance and Expected Service Life* (CNA Corporation, February 2013).

[11] Sailors assigned to ships *based* overseas may have their families accompany them; those assigned to ships *operated* overseas do not.

[12] See, for example, Congressional Budget Office, *An Analysis of the Navy's Amphibious Warfare Ships for Deploying Marines Overseas* (November 2011), Box 2, www.cbo.gov/publication/42716.

[13] Gaynor Dumat-ol Daleno, "4th Submarine to Be Deployed," *Pacific Daily News* (April 11, 2013), http://tinyurl.com/lpapbq4.

[14] See Rod McGuirk, "Australia Rejects Proposal to Base U.S. Carrier," *Navy Times* (August 2, 2012), http://tinyurl.com/ mug2c7y; and David J. Berteau and others, *U.S. Force Posture Strategy in the Asia Pacific Region: An Independent Assessment* (Center for Strategic and International Studies, August 2012), http://tinyurl.com/bbhapgh.

[15] Michael J. Lostumbo and others, *Overseas Basing of U.S. Military Forces: An Assessment of Relative Costs and Strategic Benefits* (RAND Corporation, 2013), pp. 143–149, www.rand.org/pubs/ research_reports/RR201.html.

[16] For a more detailed discussion, see Congressional Budget Office, *Crew Rotation in the Navy: The Long-Term Effect on Forward Presence* (October 2007), www.cbo.gov/publication /19283.

[17] Jessica Taylor, "USS *George Washington* (SSBN-598): The Nation's First Boomer," *Undersea Warfare* (Winter 2009), http://go.usa.gov/fA2x.

[18] See Congressional Budget Office, *Crew Rotation in the Navy: The Long-Term Effect on Forward Presence* (October 2007), pp. 5–9, www.cbo.gov/publication/19283.

[19] Government Accountability Office, *Ship Rotational Crewing Initiatives Would Benefit From Top-Level Leadership, Navy Wide Guidance, Comprehensive Analysis, and Improved Lessons-Learned Sharing,* GAO-08-418 (May 2008), www.gao.gov/products/ GAO-08-418.

[20] Congressional Budget Office, *Crew Rotation in the Navy: The Long-Term Effect on Forward Presence* (October 2007), www.cbo.gov/publication/19283; and *Increasing the Mission Capability of the Attack Submarine Force* (March 2002), www.cbo.gov/publication/13538.

[21] Ballistic missile submarines are counted in the fleet inventories and as ships employing rotating crews, but they were not counted in the forward-presence calculations because their number at sea at any time is classified.

[22] The increase in forward presence from today's amount represents the greater forward presence provided by the larger number of littoral combat ships that would be serving in the fleet by 2044; there were just four such ships in 2014.

[23] For a detailed discussion of how dual crews could be applied to attack submarines, see Congressional Budget Office, *Increasing the Mission Capability of the Attack Submarine Force* (March 2002), www.cbo.gov/publication/13538.

[24] See Congressional Budget Office, *An Analysis of the Navy's Fiscal Year 2015 Shipbuilding Plan* (December 2014), www.cbo.gov/ publication/49818.

[25] Before it adopted the Optimized Fleet Response Plan, the Navy considered another approach, the Enhanced Carrier Presence Plan, for its aircraft carriers. That plan called for an operating cycle of two 7-month deployments out of 36 months, with a 7-month interval between them—compared with the previous cycle of 6 to 7 months out of 32 and possibly an additional 2- or 3-month deployment. The Enhanced Carrier Presence Plan would have provided an additional carrier deployed overseas. Specifically, the Navy estimated that, for a cost increase of 20 percent for carrier operations (including the air wing), average global carrier presence would increase by 40 percent. The drawback was that crews would have spent more time at sea over the 36-month operating cycle than they would under the normal

operating cycle. Spending caps imposed by the Budget Control Act of 2011 led the Navy to forgo the plan. See Jason Kelly, "Enhanced Carrier Presence—What Do I Need to Know...Why Should I Care?" *Navy Live* (blog entry, April 22, 2013), http://go.usa.gov/fAEj.

[26] Operation and support costs include the amounts paid from the Navy's military personnel appropriation for military pay and bonuses and those paid from the Navy's operation and maintenance appropriation for civilian salaries, military health care, daily operation of the Navy's units, maintenance of equipment, training, support contractors, and so on. CBO added the costs of operating carrier air wings to the costs of the aircraft carriers themselves but did not include any savings that might come from purchasing fewer aircraft for those wings. CBO's estimates are based on data for the 2015–2019 period as outlined in the Department of Defense's (DoD's) 2015 Future Years Defense Program. (In that five-year plan, DoD does not account for potential supplemental or emergency appropriations to fund ongoing operations.) CBO's estimates include a share of the Defense Health Program's costs that support sailors assigned to ships and air wings (and their families) but that would be paid for out of non-Navy accounts in DoD's budget. CBO also included the costs of recruiting and training sailors, which it estimated as a fraction of the recruitment and training budgets for sailors assigned to the ships and air wings considered for this report.

[27] Michael McMahon and Roland Yardley, *Alternatives to Increase Carrier Strike Group (CSG) Forward Posture* (RAND Corporation, forthcoming).

[28] The Navy's budget calls for 45 days at sea for every 90 days when a ship is deployed—or one-half the time. When the ship is not deployed, the budget calls for 20 days at sea out of every 90.

[29] David J. Berteau and others, *U.S. Force Posture Strategy in the Asia Pacific Region: An Independent Assessment* (Center for Strategic and International Studies, August 2012), p. 74, http://tinyurl.com/ bbhapgh.

[30] Michael McMahon and Roland Yardley, *Alternatives to Increase Carrier Strike Group (CSG) Forward Posture* (RAND Corporation, forthcoming). Most of the uncertainty in RAND's cost analysis for Guam lies in the investment needed to improve the land-based airfield on the island that would support the carrier's air wing when the ship is in port. Further study of that issue would be necessary if the Guam option was chosen.

[31] See Congressional Budget Office, *Increasing the Mission Capability of the Attack Submarine Force* (March 2002), www.cbo.gov/ publication/13538.

[32] Wm. Brent Boning, *Ship Depot Maintenance and Expected Service Life* (CNA Corporation, February 2013).

In: U.S. Navy Force Structure ...
Editor: Agnes S. Jennings

ISBN: 978-1-63482-939-7

Chapter 3

AN ANALYSIS OF THE NAVY'S FISCAL YEAR 2015 SHIPBUILDING PLAN*

Eric Labs

NOTES

Unless otherwise indicated, all dollar amounts in this report reflect budget authority in 2014 dollars, and all years are federal fiscal years (which run from October to September).

Numbers in the text and tables may not add up to totals because of rounding.

SUMMARY

The Department of Defense (DoD) submitted the Navy's 2015 shipbuilding plan, which covers fiscal years 2015 to 2044, to the Congress in July 2014.[1] The total costs of carrying out the 2015 plan—an average of about $21 billion in 2014 dollars per year over the next 30 years— would be one-third higher than the funding amounts that the Navy has received in recent decades, the Congressional Budget Office (CBO) estimates. The Navy's 2015

---

* This is an edited, reformatted and augmented version of a report issued by the Congressional Budget Office, December 2014.

shipbuilding plan is very similar, but not identical, to its 2014 plan with respect to the Navy's total inventory goal for battle force ships, the number and types of ships the Navy would purchase, and the proposed funding to implement the plans.

The Navy Plans to Buy 264 Ships over the Next 30 Years

The Navy's 2015 shipbuilding plan states that the service's overall inventory goal (in military parlance, its requirement) is 306 battle force ships. The Navy's shipbuilding plan falls short of meeting the service's inventory goals for some types of ships in some years, although generally the shortfalls are smaller than in previous years' plans.

Under the 2015 plan, the Navy would buy a total of 264 ships over the 2015–2044 period: 218 combat ships and 46 combat logistics and support ships (see the top panel of Table 1). Given the rate at which the Navy plans to retire ships from the fleet, that construction plan would not achieve a fleet equal to the inventory goal of 306 ships until 2019 under new rules for counting ships that the Navy implemented this year or until 2022 under the old counting rules.

CBO Estimates the New-Ship Construction Costs in the Navy's Plan At About $19 Billion per Year

The Navy estimates that buying the new ships specified in the 2015 plan would cost $500 billion over 30 years, or an average of $16.7 billion per year—slightly less than the costs of the 2014 plan (see the bottom panel of Table 1). (Unless otherwise indicated, all dollar amounts in this report reflect budget authority in 2014 dollars.) Those figures apply solely to the construction of new ships—the only type of costs reported in the Navy's 30-year shipbuilding plan. Other activities typically funded from the Navy's budget accounts for ship construction—such as refueling nuclear-powered aircraft carriers and outfitting new ships with various small pieces of equipment after the ships have been built and delivered—would, in CBO's estimation, add $1.9 billion to the Navy's average annual shipbuilding costs under the 2015 plan. (Between 2009 and 2014, the cost of those other activities averaged $1.9 billion per year.) Including those extra costs would increase the average annual cost of the Navy's 2015 plan to $18.6 billion, slightly less than the cost of the 2014 plan.

Using its own models and assumptions, CBO estimates that the cost of new-ship construction in the Navy's 2015 plan will total $566 billion over 30 years, or an average of $18.9 billion per year. Including the costs of refueling aircraft carriers and other items, such as outfitting new ships, raises the overall average cost of the Navy's plan to $20.7 billion per year, CBO estimates. That figure is slightly less than CBO's estimate of the average annual cost of the Navy's 2014 plan.

CBO's estimate of the cost of new-ship construction in the Navy's 2015 shipbuilding plan is $66 billion, or 13 percent, higher over the next 30 years than the Navy's estimate. CBO's estimate is 6 percent higher than the Navy's for the first 10 years of the plan, 14 percent higher for the following decade, and 20 percent higher for the final 10 years (see Figure 1). The difference widens over time in part because the Navy, in its constant-dollar estimates and in contrast with CBO, does not appear to have accounted for the fact that costs of labor and materials have traditionally grown faster in the shipbuilding industry than in the economy as a whole. Also, the Navy and CBO used different estimating methods and assumptions regarding the designs and capabilities of future ships. CBO's estimate of the total cost of the Navy's plan over the next 30 years, including all ship construction activities, is 11 percent higher than the Navy's estimate.

Table 1. The Navy's 2014 and 2015 Shipbuilding Plans

	2014 Plan (2014–2043)	**2015 Plan (2015–2044)**	**Change From 2014 to 2015**
Combat Ships	**Number of Ships Purchased Over 30 Years**		
Aircraft carriers	6	6	0
Ballistic missile submarines	12	12	0
Attack submarines	47	48	1
Destroyers	70	65	5
Littoral combat ships	66 a	66 a	0
Amphibious warfare ships	19	21	2
Subtotal	220	218	2
Combat Logistics and Support Ships	46	46	0
Total	266	264	-2

Table 1. (Continued)

	2014 Plan (2014–2043)	2015 Plan (2015–2044)	Change From 2014 to 2015
	Costs of New-Ship Construction[b] (Billions of 2014 dollars)		
Total Cost Over 30 Years			
Navy's estimate	518	500	-18
CBO's estimate	596	566	-30
Average Annual Cost			
Navy's estimate	17.3	16.7	-0.6
CBO's estimate	19.9	18.9	-1.0
Average Cost per Ship			
Navy's estimate	1.9	1.9	0
CBO's estimate	2.2	2.1	-0.1
Memorandum:			
Average Annual Costs of All Activities			
Typically Funded From Budget			
Accounts for Ship Construction			
Navy's estimate	19.2	18.6	-0.6
CBO's estimate	21.8	20.7	-1.1

Source: Congressional Budget Office based on data from the Department of the Navy.

[a] Under the 2014 and 2015 plans, the Navy will have 52 littoral combat ships in service after 2029. However, because each of those ships is expected to be in service for 25 years, the Navy will begin buying replacements in 2030.

[b] Costs of new-ship construction exclude funds for some activities that are typically funded in the Navy's shipbuilding accounts, such as refueling of nuclear-powered aircraft carriers, ship conversions, construction of ships that are not part of the Navy's battle force (oceanographic survey ships, for instance), training ships, outfitting and postdelivery (which include the purchase of many smaller tools and pieces of equipment that are needed to operate a ship but are not necessarily provided by the manufacturing shipyard as part of ship construction), and smaller items. Costs for the mission packages for littoral combat ships, which are not funded in the Navy's shipbuilding accounts, also are not included.

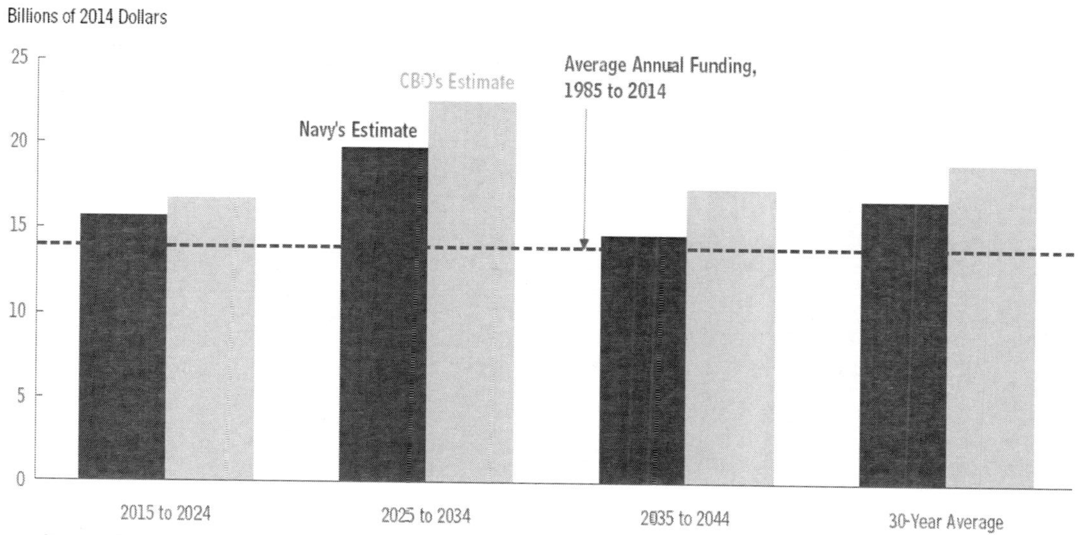

Source: Congressional Budget Office based on data from the Department of the Navy.

Note: Costs of new-ship construction exclude funds for some activities that are typically funded in the Navy's shipbuilding accounts, such as refueling of nuclear-powered aircraft carriers, ship conversions, construction of ships that are not part of the Navy's battle force (oceanographic survey ships, for instance), training ships, outfitting and postdelivery (which include the purchase of many smaller tools and pieces of equipment that are needed to operate a ship but are not necessarily provided by the manufacturing shipyard as part of ship construction), and smaller items. Costs for the mission packages for littoral combat ships, which are not funded in the Navy's shipbuilding accounts, also are not included.

Figure 1. Average Annual Costs of New-Ship Construction Under the Navy's 2015 Plan.

CBO's Estimate of Costs Over the Next 30 Years Is One-Third Higher Than What the Navy Has Spent Over the Past 30 Years

If the Navy receives the same amount of funding (in constant dollars) for new-ship construction in each of the next 30 years that it has on average over the past three decades, it will not be able to afford its 2015 plan. GBO's estimate of $18.9 billion per year for new-ship construction in the Navy's 2015 shipbuilding plan is 36 percent above the historical average annual funding of $13.9 billion.

And GBO's estimate of $20.7 billion per year for the full cost of the plan is 32 percent higher than the $15.7 billion the Navy has spent on average per year for all items in its shipbuilding accounts over the past 30 years.

The Navy Would Probably Need to Purchase Substantially Fewer Ships to Comply with Caps on Defense Funding

The shipbuilding plan, at least for 2015 through 2019, is based on an assumption of funding at the President's requested level—a level that exceeds the amounts scheduled under current law, which caps discretionary funding through 2021.

In submitting its report, the Navy described the plan as "difficult to execute" under current fiscal constraints, and it separately identified changes it would make to the plan if funding for defense equals the amounts scheduled under current law: The Navy would buy 8 fewer ships, including 3 fewer destroyers and 1 fewer attack submarine, between 2015 and 2019; it would charter and lease 3 fleet oilers rather than buy them; and it would put 6 destroyers in a reduced status.[2]

However, the identified changes suggest that the Navy would try to cut shipbuilding less than other activities, because if the Navy were to reduce its shipbuilding spending proportionally with the rest of its spending and lower total spending by enough to meet the caps, the service would probably need to cut roughly twice as many ships.

Table 2. The Navy's Goals for Its Force Structure

	Goals for a 313-Ship Fleet in the Navy's 2005 Force Structure Assessment	Goals for a 313-Ship Fleet in the Navy's 2010 Force Structure Assessment	Goals for a 306-Ship Fleet in the Navy's 2012 Force Structure Assessment
Aircraft Carriers	11	11	11
Submarines			
Ballistic missile	14	12	12
Attack	48	48	48
Guided missile	4	4	0
Large Surface Combatants	88	94	88
Small Surface Combatants and Mine Countermeasures Ships[a]	55	55	52
Amphibious Warfare Ships	31	33	33
MPF(F) Ships	12	0	0
Combat Logistics Ships	30	30	29
Support Ships Joint high speed vessels	3	10	10
Other[b]	17	16	23
Total	**313**	**313**	**306**

Source: Congressional Budget Office based on data from the Department of the Navy.
Note: MPF(F) = Maritime Prepositioning Force (Future).

[a] Includes littoral combat ships, Oliver Hazard Perry FFG-7 frigates, and Avenger class mine countermeasures ships.

[b] Includes command ships, salvage ships, ocean tugs, ocean surveillance ships, and tenders.

SHIP PURCHASES AND INVENTORIES UNDER THE 2015 PLAN

The Navy's 2015 shipbuilding plan, submitted to the Congress by the Deputy Secretary of Defense on July 1, 2014, reflects the Navy's goal of 306 battle force ships. That goal, first described by the Navy in a report to the Congress in January 2013, was based on a force structure assessment conducted by the Navy in 2012.[3] It replaced the 313-ship goal developed in the 2005 force structure assessment and updated in a 2010 force structure assessment (see Table 2).

This report does not evaluate the validity of the goals identified by the Navy, such as the fleet's ability to fulfill its missions in the national military strategy. Rather, the report assesses the costs of the Navy's 2015 shipbuilding plan, the effects of that plan on the force structure, and the extent to which the plan would satisfy the Navy's goals for major components of the U.S. fleet. (For a discussion of the major types of ships in the Navy's fleet and the roles they play, see Box 1.)

Total Ship Purchases and Inventories

The Navy intends to buy 7 ships in 2015 and a total of 44 ships between 2015 and 2019—the period covered by DoD's 2015 Future Years Defense Program, a five-year funding plan that DoD updates annually (see Figures 2 and 3). Thereafter, the Navy would buy an additional 220 ships through 2044, for a total of 264 ships over 30 years, or an average of about 9 per year. The pace of shipbuilding would be slightly faster, on average, in the near term than later on. The Navy plans to purchase an average of about 10 ships annually between 2015 and 2024, a little less than 9 ships per year between 2025 and 2034, and 8 ships per year between 2035 and 2044.

<table>
<tr><th colspan="2">Box 1. The Roles of Major Types of Ships in the Navy's Battle Force Fleet</th></tr>
<tr><td>
Nimitz Class
Aircraft Carrier</td><td>The Navy's 10 aircraft carriers are the heart of the battle force. Each carries an air wing of about 60 aircraft, which can attack hundreds of targets per day for up to a month before needing to be rested. Carriers are by far the largest ships in the fleet, with a weight (displacement) of about 100,000 tons. All 10 current carriers belong to the Nimitz class.</td></tr>
</table>

 Ohio Class Ballistic Missile Submarine	Strategic ballistic missile submarines carry one of the major parts of the U.S. nuclear deterrent, up to 24 Trident missiles with one to eight nuclear warheads apiece. The Navy has 14 Ohio class ballistic missile submarines, each of which displaces about 19,000 tons when submerged, in that strategic role. In addition, the Navy has converted 4 submarines of that class to a conventional guided missile (SSGN) configuration. Those SSGNs carry up to 154 Tomahawk missiles as well as special-operations forces.
 Los Angeles Class Attack Submarine	Attack submarines are the Navy's premier undersea warfare and antisubmarine weapons. Since the end of the Cold War, however, they have mainly performed covert intelligence-gathering missions. They have also been used to launch Tomahawk missiles at inland targets in the early stages of conflicts. The Navy has 55 attack submarines, 41 of which belong to the Los Angeles class. At 7,000 tons, they are less than half the size of ballistic missile submarines.
 Arleigh Burke Class Destroyer	Large surface combatants, which include cruisers and destroyers, are the workhorses of the fleet. They provide ballistic missile defense for the fleet and for regional areas overseas. They defend the Navy's aircraft carriers and amphibious warfare ships against other surface ships, aircraft, and submarines. They also perform many day-to-day missions, such as patrolling sea lanes, providing an overseas presence, and conducting exercises with allies. In addition, they are capable of striking land targets with Tomahawk missiles. Most of the Navy's surface combatants displace about 9,000 to 10,000 tons.

(Continued)

 Freedom Class Littoral Combat Ship	Small surface combatants include frigates and littoral combat ships. Frigates today are used to perform many of the same day-to-day missions as large surface combatants. Littoral combat ships are intended to counter mines, small boats, and diesel electric submarines in the world's coastal regions. More routinely, they also patrol sea lanes, provide an overseas presence, and conduct exercises with allies. They range in size from 3,000 to 4,000 tons. The Navy plans to retire all of its remaining frigates in 2015.
 Wasp Class Amphibious Assault Ship  San Antonio Class Amphibious Transport Dock	The Navy has six classes of amphibious warfare ships. Three classes, referred to as amphibious assault ships (also known as large-deck amphibious ships or helicopter carriers), are the second-largest types of ships in the fleet at 40,000 to 45,000 tons. They form the centerpiece of amphibious ready groups, and each can carry about half the troops and equipment of a Marine expeditionary unit. In addition, they can carry as many as 30 helicopters and 6 fixed-wing Harrier jump jets; alternatively, they can carry up to 20 Harriers or short take-off and landing versions of the Joint Strike Fighter. The other three classes are divided into two types: amphibious transport docks and dock landing ships. Two of those ships together provide the remaining transport capacity for a Marine expeditionary unit in an amphibious ready group. They range in size from 16,000 to 25,000 tons.

 Supply Class Fast Combat Support Ship	The many combat logistics and support ships in the Navy's fleet provide the means to resupply, repair, salvage, or tow combat ships. The most prominent of those vessels are fast combat support ships, which operate with carrier strike groups to resupply them with fuel, dry cargo (such as food), and ammunition. Logistics and support ships can be as small as 2,000 tons for an oceangoing tug or as large as 50,000 tons for a fully loaded fast combat support ship.

Source: Congressional Budget Office.
Note: Ship silhouettes are not to scale.

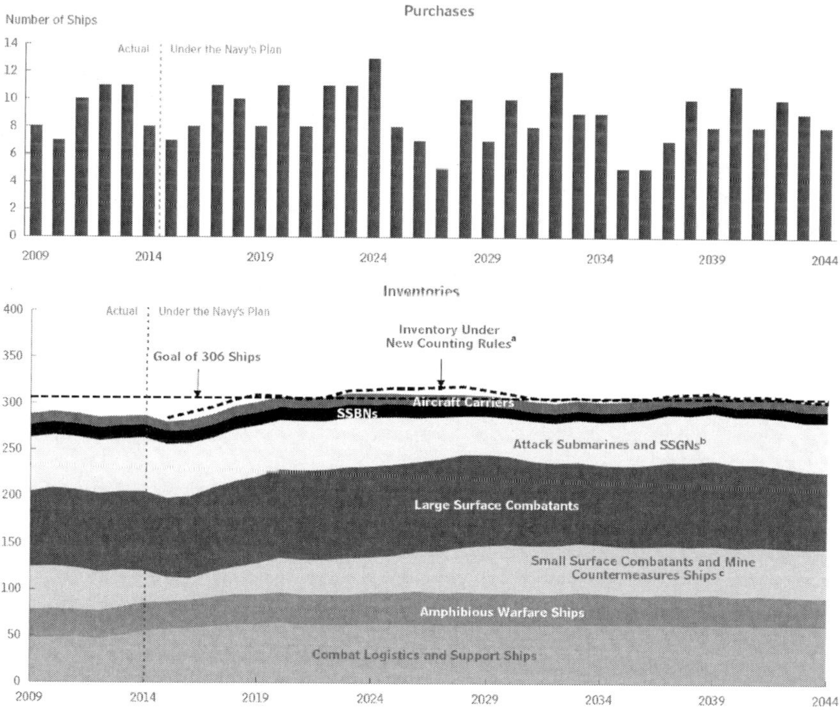

Source: Congressional Budget Office based on data from the Department of the Navy.
Notes: The colored parts of the chart reflect the Navy's old counting rules.

SSBNs = ballistic missile submarines; SSGNs = guided missile submarines.

[a] Effective with the 2015 President's budget and shipbuilding plan, the Navy is modifying its method for counting battle force ships. The changes affect a small number of ship classes designated as (very) small combatants or logistics and support ships. Specifically, the Navy will now count Cyclone class patrol combatants that are based overseas (in the theater of operations) but not those that are based in the United States. It will treat Avenger class mine countermeasures ships the same way. The Navy will now also include the 2 hospital ships operated by the Military Sealift Command in the battle force. Patrol combatants and hospital ships did not count under the old rules, whereas all mine countermeasures ships did count, not just those in-theater.

[b] Although the Navy does not plan to build more SSGNs, four will be in service through the mid-2020s.

[c] Small surface combatants and mine countermeasures ships include littoral combat ships, Oliver Hazard Perry FFG-7 frigates, and Avenger class mine countermeasures ships.

Figure 2. Annual Ship Purchases and Inventories Under the Navy's 2015 Plan.

Effective with the President's 2015 budget and the 2015 shipbuilding plan, the Navy has modified which ships are counted as battle force ships. The changes in the counting rules involve a small number of ship classes designated as (very) small combatants or logistics and support ships. The Navy is now counting as battle force ships Cyclone class patrol combatants that are based overseas (in the theater of operations), although it is not counting those that are based in the United States. It will treat Avenger class mine countermeasures ships the same way. The Navy is also now including in the battle force the 2 hospital ships operated by the Military Sealift Command. Under the old rules, patrol combatants and hospital ships did not count in the battle force, whereas all mine countermeasures (not just those that are in-theater) did count in the battle force. The Navy projects that, at the end of 2015, it will have 284 ships in the fleet under the new counting rules and 274 ships under the old rules. The patrol combatants and the mine countermeasures ships are slated to retire from service in the 2020s, and the 2 hospital ships will retire in 2035. The 2015 shipbuilding plan does not replace those vessels. Thus, by 2036 and beyond, the size of the battle force is planned to be the same under either set of counting rules.

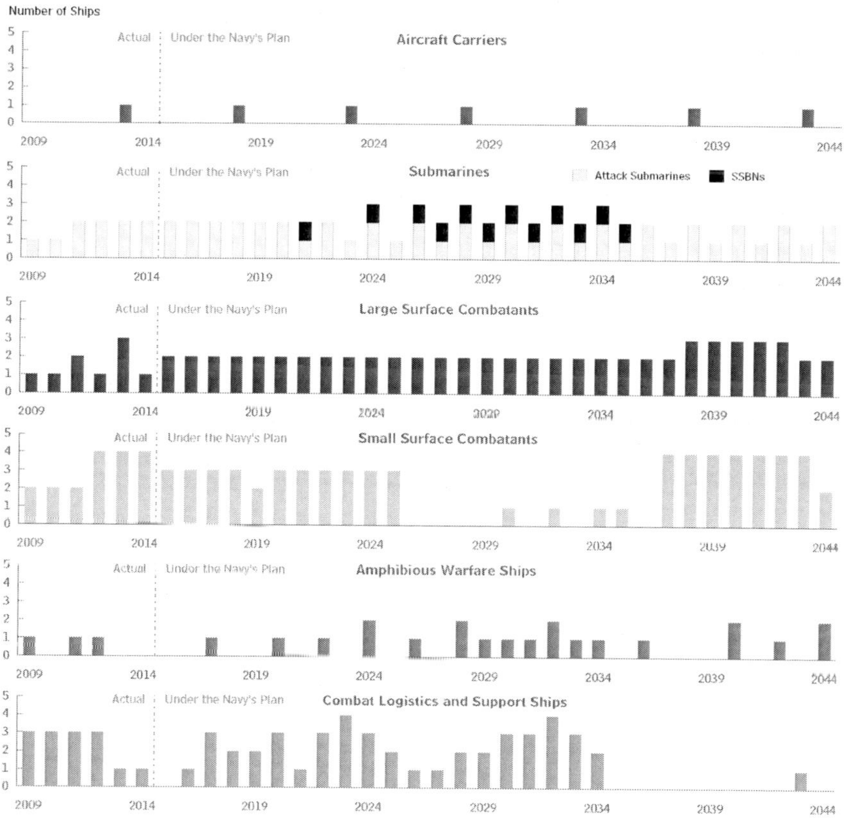

Source: Congressional Budget Office based on data from the Department of the Navy.
Note: SSBNs = ballistic missile submarines.

Figure 3. Annual Ship Purchases, by Category, Under the Navy's 2015 Plan.

The 2015 plan would not achieve the intended force of 306 ships until 2019 under the Navy's new counting rules or 2022 under the old rules. The Navy would meet its overall goal of 306 ships for 21 years of the 30-year plan under the new counting rules and for 16 years under the old rules. Under the new rules, the shortfall is never more than 1 to 3 ships, except for the 2015–2017 period (see the bottom panel of Figure 2). The Navy achieves its force structure goal much sooner under the 2015 plan than under the 2014 plan, which would not have reached the goal of 306 ships until 2037. The Navy's goal for battle force ships would be realized more quickly under the 2015 plan partly because of the change in counting rules, but largely because the Navy now intends to retain in its inventory 7 cruisers and 2 amphibious ships that it proposed to retire in 2014 under the 2014 plan. The Congress opposed the early retirement of those ships.

All together, the Navy would buy 2 fewer ships over 30 years under the 2015 plan than it would have under the 2014 plan. The composition of ship purchases—particularly the mix of combat ships and logistics and support vessels—is virtually the same under the 2014 and 2015 plans.

Combat Ships

Under the 2015 plan, the Navy envisions buying 218 combat ships—aircraft carriers, submarines, large and small surface combatants, and amphibious warfare ships—between 2015 and 2044. That total is 2 fewer than specified in the 2014 plan for 2014 through 2043. Those purchases would still leave the Navy short of its inventory objectives for ballistic missile and attack submarines for significant parts of the 2015–2044 period (see Figure 4). In contrast, there are essentially no projected shortfalls in large surface combatants or amphibious warfare ships (which represents an improvement from the 2014 plan). For aircraft carriers, the Navy would meet or exceed its goal of 11 ships throughout the 2014– 2044 time frame, except for brief periods from 2015 to 2016 and 2040 to 2044. For small surface combatants, the Navy plans to replace its frigates and mine countermeasures ships with littoral combat ships (LCSs); it would not reach its objective of having 52 LCSs in the fleet until 2028, one year earlier than in the 2014 plan. (The Navy has stated that any future plans designed to increase the survivability and lethality of its small surface combatants would not change its inventory goal for those ships.)

Ballistic Missile Submarines. The 2015 shipbuilding plan calls for buying the first replacement for the Ohio class ballistic missile submarines in 2021 and for purchasing 12 such submarines, also known as SSBN(X)s, in total (see Figure 3); those boats would begin to enter the fleet in 2028. (The Navy estimates that the lead submarine will take about seven years to build and that an additional two to three years will be needed to complete testing before it is ready for regular operations.) However, the retirement of Ohio class submarines as they reach the end of their 42-year service life means that the Navy's inventory of ballistic missile submarines (SSBNs) would fall below the stated goal of 12 by 1 or 2 submarines between 2030 and 2041 (see Figure 4). In particular, between 2032 and 2040, the Navy would have 10 SSBNs.

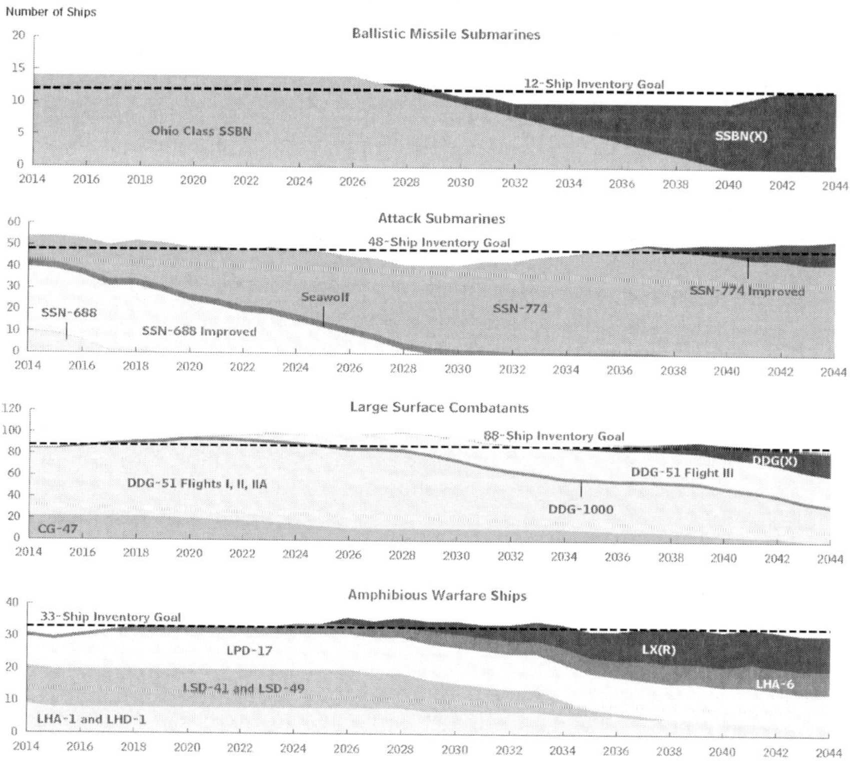

Source: Congressional Budget Office.

Note: SSBN = ballistic missile submarine; SSN = attack submarine; DDG = guided missile destroyer; CG = guided missile cruiser; LSD = dock landing ship; LHA and LHD = amphibious assault ship; LPD = amphibious transport dock; LX(R) = amphibious ship replacement.

Figure 4. Annual Inventories Versus Goals for Selected Categories of Ships Under the Navy's 2015 Plan.

Attack Submarines. Under the 2015 plan, the Navy would purchase 48 attack submarines (SSNs) through 2044, which would not be enough to keep that force at the stated goal of 48 throughout the next 30 years. The number of attack submarines would decline from 48 in 2024 to a low of 41 in the 2028–2030 period and then would increase to 51 or more after 2039. The decline would result because, in 2014, the Navy began retiring Los Angeles class attack submarines (SSN-688s), which were generally built at rates of 3 or 4 per year during the 1970s and 1980s, as they reached the end of their service life. The Navy would replace those submarines with Virginia class attack submarines (SSN-774s) and their successors at rates of generally 1 or 2 per year.

Large Surface Combatants. The 2015 shipbuilding plan calls for buying 65 destroyers—5 fewer than in the 2014 plan—based on the existing Arleigh Burke class destroyer (DDG-51) design (see Table 1 on page 2). Those purchases, along with the Navy's plan for modernizing its cruiser force (and several amphibious ships), would allow the Navy's inventory of large surface combatants to meet or exceed the goal of 88 ships for most years over the next 30. (For a discussion of the Navy's modernization plan for cruisers and amphibious warfare ships, see Box 2.) Specifically, the number of such ships would meet or exceed the goal in each year through 2033 (with the exception of 2015) and fall short only in the 2034–2035 and 2042–2044 periods.

The Navy's assumptions about the service lives of its large surface combatants remain the same under the 2015 plan as under the 2014 plan. The 2014 plan incorporated an assumption that all 34 Arleigh Burke class destroyers commissioned after 2000 would have a service life of 40 years and that the 28 destroyers of that class commissioned in 2000 and earlier would remain in the fleet for 35 years. Historically, very few cruisers or destroyers have served in the fleet longer than 30 years.[4] If the Navy's large surface combatants serve for 30 years instead of the longer intended lives, and if the Navy's acquisition of such ships matches the pace of the 2015 plan, then the Navy will experience a substantial shortfall of those ships relative to its goal.[5]

Amphibious Warfare Ships. The current shipbuilding plan calls for buying 21 amphibious warfare ships through 2044—2 more than specified in the 2014 plan—which would increase the amphibious force from 31 ships today to the goal of 33 by 2018. The force would stay at that size or greater through 2044—except for 2035 to 2036, when the force would fall to 32 ships, and 2040, 2042, 2043, and 2044, when the force would have 32, 32, 31, and 31 ships, respectively. The Navy assumes that it will keep its LHD class amphibious assault ships in the fleet for 43 to 45 years.

Combat Logistics and Support Ships

In its 2015 plan, the Navy envisions buying 46 combat logistics and support ships in the next three decades—the same number as in the 2014 plan. Combat logistics ships include T-AKE dry cargo ships, T-AO oilers, and AOE fast combat support ships; they operate with or directly resupply combat ships that are on deployment. Those planned purchases include 17 new oilers (which provide fuel and a few other supplies to ships at sea) at a rate of 1 per year through the 2020s; that program would conclude in 2033. The plan also includes the purchase of 1 replacement T-AKE dry cargo and ammunition ship in 2043.

Support ship purchases in the Navy's plan include 10 joint high-speed vessels (JHSVs), 4 salvage ships, 5 surveillance ships, 2 tenders, 4 fleet tugs, 2 command ships to replace those in the existing fleet that will retire over the next 30 years, and 1 new afloat forward staging base, a variant of the Navy's mobile landing platform ships.[6] H.R. 83, the Consolidated and Further Continuing Appropriations Act, 2015, which cleared the Congress on December 13, 2014, added funding for 1 JHSV. If signed into law, that legislation will increase the Navy's inventory by one, barring other changes; the effects of that change are not reflected in this analysis.

The only significant change from the Navy's 2014 plan in this category is the decision to retire 2 salvage ships and 2 fleet tugs nine years and four years earlier, respectively, than called for in the previous plan. According to the Navy, the decision to retire those ships earlier was made in order to reduce costs. That action would leave the Navy with 2 salvage ships and 2 fleet tugs in its inventory until 2023 and 2019, respectively, when replacements enter the fleet. The decision to retire those ships early (even though they are not very expensive to operate) and the consequent gaps in the inventory raise the question of whether the Navy needs 4 ships of each type to support fleet operations. The Navy states in the plan that "if mission workload requires additional ships," it would use leased vessels.[7]

Box 2. The Navy's Modernization Plan for Cruisers and Amphibious Ships

The Navy's 2015 plan largely meets the service's inventory goals for large surface combatants and amphibious ships, which the 2014 plan did not. The difference arises primarily from a new proposal for modernizing 11 CG-47 Ticonderoga class cruisers and 3 amphibious dock landing ships.

Previously, the Navy had proposed retiring 7 cruisers and 2 amphibious ships (largely as a means to save money), but the Congress rejected those proposals and instead provided funding for operating and modernizing the ships in a special account called the Ship Modernization, Operations, and Sustainment Fund (SMOSF).

In the President's 2015 budget submission, the Navy proposes to lay up (to put in a reduced status for maintenance and modernization) 11 cruisers, which is half the force, and 3 amphibious ships. The ships would be minimally manned while in that reduced status and, as the other 11 active cruisers reach the end of their service life, cruisers in lay-up would be modernized and returned to operational status. Using that approach, the Navy would be able to maintain at least 11 operationally active cruisers (1 for each of the Navy's planned 11 carrier strike groups) through 2034, with the last cruiser retiring in 2044. (The Navy's 2015 shipbuilding plan does not include replacements for the Ticonderoga class cruisers, but the midsized surface combatants planned for the 2030s and 2040s could be designed to perform the same missions as the current cruisers.) The 3 amphibious ships would be put in a reduced status sequentially, so that all 3 would be modernized but only 1 would be in lay-up at a time.

All 22 cruisers would be counted toward the Navy's inventory of battle force ships in each year. The Navy's justification for including the 11 cruisers in lay-up in its inventory is that the cruisers could be brought out of reduced operating status and returned to the fleet within a year's time; cruisers and destroyers that are currently undergoing long-term maintenance of a year or more are also counted as part of the battle force.

If the modernization plan is not implemented and the Navy's cruisers and amphibious ships remain in fully operational status, then all of those ships would probably be retired from the fleet by 2028 (which reflects the retirement schedule under the 2014 plan). The result would be to create larger shortfalls relative to the Navy's inventory goals in later years. If the Navy is able to implement its plan for cruisers and amphibious ships, the service estimates that it will save about $8 billion through 2026.

H.R. 83, the Consolidated and Further Continuing Appropriations Act, 2015, which cleared the Congress on December 13, 2014, rejects the Navy's cruiser and amphibious ship modernization plan. Instead, if signed into law, the legislation will give the Navy authority to lay up and modernize 2 cruisers in 2016, using the funds provided in the SMOSF. It stipulates that no more than 6 cruisers may be in lay-up at any given time.

It is not clear how that legislation would affect the long-term inventory of large surface combatants. The legislation did not specify the approach the Navy should take for amphibious ships.

SHIPBUILDING COSTS UNDER THE 2015 PLAN

According to the Navy's estimates, carrying out its planned purchases of new ships would cost an average of $16.7 billion per year through 2044—3 percent less than the $17.3 billion average under its 2014 plan (in 2014 dollars). In making its estimates, the Navy divided the time frame of the 2015 plan into three periods: the near term (2015 to 2024), the midterm (2025 to 2034), and the far term (2035 to 2044). CBO also estimated the costs of the Navy's 2015 plan; to price the Navy's ships, it used its own cost models and assumptions, which are explained in detail later in this report. CBO's estimates are $2.2 billion per year, or 13 percent, higher than the Navy's over the next 30 years as a whole, but the differences are smaller for the near term, larger for the midterm, and larger still for the far term (see Figure 5). Including other items that the Navy would need to fund from its budget accounts for ship construction would raise both the Navy's estimates and CBO's estimates by $1.9 billion per year; CBO's estimates of that full cost are 11 percent above the Navy's corresponding figures.[8]

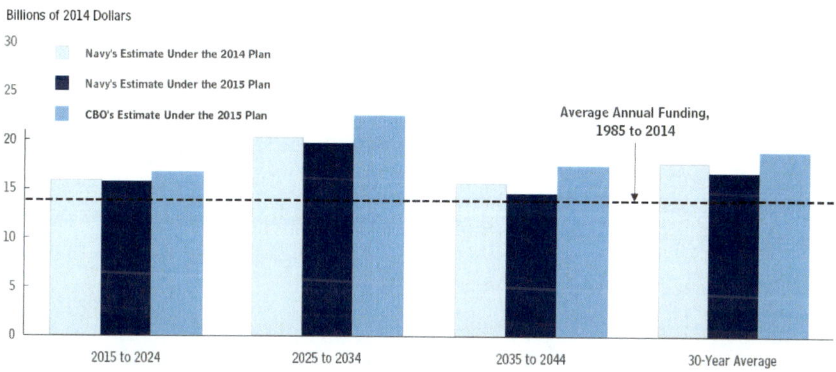

Source: Congressional Budget Office based on data from the Department of the Navy.

Note: Costs of new-ship construction exclude funds for some activities that are typically funded in the Navy's shipbuilding accounts, such as refueling of nuclear-powered aircraft carriers, ship conversions, construction of ships that are not part of the Navy's battle force (oceanographic survey ships, for instance), training ships, outfitting and postdelivery (which include the purchase of many smaller tools and pieces of equipment that are needed to operate a ship but are not necessarily provided by the manufacturing shipyard as part of ship construction), and smaller items. Costs for the mission packages for littoral combat ships, which are not funded in the Navy's shipbuilding accounts, also are not included.

Figure 5. Average Annual Costs of New-Ship Construction Under the Navy's 2014 and 2015 Plans.

The Navy's Estimates

The Navy's 2015 report offers a frank discussion of the difficulties in estimating the capabilities that the Navy will want ships to have—and thus the cost of those ships—over the three planning periods. For the near term, the report explains, "The projections in the period are based on our most accurate understanding of required combat capabilities, future defense budget top-lines, and shipbuilding costs based on actual procurements in progress. The cost estimates for this period are the most accurate of the three planning periods." For the midterm, "The accuracy of plan cost estimates diminishes." And for the far term, "Since the strategic environment and state of technology 20–30 years hence are both sure to be much different than they are today, the precision and accuracy of the ship types required and cost projections in this period are much more speculative."[9]

New-Ship Construction Costs. According to this year's plan, in the near term, building new ships will cost an average of $15.7 billion per year (see the top row of Table 3). That number excludes $1.4 billion in cost overruns and sequestration shortfalls for ships that were funded before 2015, which will require additional funds to be paid out in 2015 and 2016. In the midterm, replacing the Navy's current Ohio class ballistic missile submarines drives up the average cost of new-ship construction to $19.7 billion per year. According to the Navy's estimates, building the SSBN(X) will cost $5.5 billion per year in the middle decade of the plan. In the far term, the Navy's estimated costs fall to an average of $14.6 billion annually.

Although the Navy's shipbuilding plan suggests that the midterm will be its most challenging fiscal period, the latter half of the near term (2020 to 2024) will require shipbuilding budgets that are substantially larger than those in the first half of the first decade (2015 to 2019). According to the Navy's estimates, the average budget for new-ship construction rises from $13.7 billion per year for the 2015–2019 period to $17.8 billion per year for the 2020–2024 period (see Figure 6).

Total Shipbuilding Costs. As in previous shipbuilding plans, the Navy's latest estimates exclude other costs that it would have to pay out of its budget accounts for ship construction. Specifically:

- Costs of refueling nuclear-powered aircraft carriers, whose reactors are replaced midway through the ships' service lives,[10] and
- Other costs, such as those for ship conversions, construction of ships that are not part of the Navy's battle force (oceanographic survey ships, for instance), training ships, outfitting and postdelivery (which include the purchase of many smaller tools and pieces of equipment that are needed to operate a ship but are not necessarily provided by the shipyard when the ship is built), and smaller items.

Including the costs of refueling carriers, as estimated by CBO, would increase the Navy's estimate for the cost of the 2015 shipbuilding plan by $1 billion per year to an average of $17.7 billion a year through 2044.

Adding the $1.4 billion in cost-to-complete funding that will be spent in 2015 and 2016, along with the costs of the other items described above, would boost the Navy's estimate for the full cost of the 2015 shipbuilding plan to $18.6 billion per year, or $1.9 billion more than the Navy's estimate for new-ship construction alone. That figure is 18 percent higher than the average funding for total shipbuilding the Navy has received in the past three decades—$15.7 billion per year.

CBO's Estimates

In CBO's estimation, the full annual cost of the 2015 shipbuilding plan would average $20.7 billion over the 2015–2044 period—32 percent more than the average annual funding the Navy has received in the past three decades. The estimated costs have a fair amount of yearly variation but trend upward for the first two decades of the plan (see Figure 7 on page 16). Looking at the 30-year period as a whole, CBO estimates that:

- Costs for new-ship construction alone would average $18.9 billion per year, 13 percent more than the Navy's figure of $16.7 billion (see Table 3);

- New-ship construction plus refueling of nuclear-powered aircraft carriers would cost an average of $19.9 billion per year, 12 percent more than the Navy's figure of $17.7 billion; and
- All other items would add annual costs of about $900 million, raising CBO's estimate to an average of $20.7 billion per year through 2044, 11 percent more than the Navy's figure of $18.6 billion.

CBO's estimates of the full cost of the plan are only 4 percent higher than the Navy's for the first 10 years but 18 percent higher for the final 10 years. For the near term, CBO's and the Navy's cost estimates are similar because most of the ships that the Navy plans to buy are already under construction and their costs are reasonably well known. For the midterm and far term, however, CBO and the Navy made different assumptions about the size and capabilities of future ships that led to different cost estimates. Generally, CBO estimates the cost of a future ship on the basis of the relationship between the weight and cost of analogous ships. The resulting figure is then adjusted for factors such as production efficiencies that occur as more ships of the same type are built at a given shipyard simultaneously and additional efficiencies that occur as more ships are built (and learning takes place) over the duration of a production run. CBO also incorporated into its estimates (which are in constant 2014 dollars) a projection that costs for labor and materials would probably continue to grow faster in the shipbuilding industry than in the economy as a whole, as they have for the past several decades; the Navy's estimates do not reflect such faster growth (see Box 3 on page 18). That difference in estimates is much more pronounced in the last decade of the plan, after 20 or more years of compounded growth, than in the early years. (For more information on how much of the overall difference between the Navy's estimates and CBO's estimates can be attributed to individual ship programs, see Table A-1 in the appendix.)

Table 3. Average Annual Shipbuilding Costs under the Navy's 2015 Plan, by Decade

	Near Term (2015–2024)	Midterm (2025–2034)	Far Term (2035–2044)	Total (2015–2044)
	Navy's Estimates (Billions of 2014 dollars)			
New-Ship Construction	15.7	19.7	14.6	16.7
New-Ship Construction and Refueling of Nuclear-Powered Aircraft Carriers[a]	17.1	20.7	15.2	17.7

	Near Term (2015–2024)	Midterm (2025–2034)	Far Term (2035–2044)	Total (2015–2044)
New-Ship Construction, Refueling of Nuclear-Powered Aircraft Carriers, and Other Items[b]	18.4	21.4	15.8	18.6
	CBO's Estimates (Billions of 2014 dollars)			
New-Ship Construction	16.7	22.5	17.5	18.9
New-Ship Construction and Refueling of Nuclear-Powered Aircraft Carriers	18.0	23.5	18.1	19.9
New-Ship Construction, Refueling of Nuclear-Powered Aircraft Carriers, and Other Items	19.2	24.2	18.7	20.7
	Percentage Difference Between the Navy's and CBO's Estimates			
New-Ship Construction	6	14	20	13
New-Ship Construction and Refueling of Nuclear-Powered Aircraft Carriers	6	13	19	12
New-Ship Construction, Refueling of Nuclear-Powered Aircraft Carriers, and Other Items	4	13	18	11
Memorandum (Billions of 2014 dollars):				
CBO's Estimate of the Costs of New-Ship Construction Needed to Meet Nearly All All Inventory Goals in Each Year	19.0	22.6	17.6	19.7
Costs of Mission Packages for Littoral Combat Ships	0.4	0.1	0.3	0.3

Source: Congressional Budget Office based on data from the Department of the Navy.

Note: Other items include ship conversions, construction of ships that are not part of the Navy's battle force (oceanographic survey ships, for instance), training ships, outfitting and postdelivery costs (which include the purchase of many smaller tools and pieces of equipment needed to operate a ship but not necessarily provided by the manufacturing shipyard as part of ship construction), and smaller items. Actual costs for the Navy's shipbuilding accounts over the past 30 years averaged about $16 billion per year for all items.

[a] These numbers represent the Navy's estimate for new-ship construction and CBO's estimate for the refueling of nuclear-powered aircraft carriers.

[b] These numbers represent the Navy's estimates for both new-ship construction and cost-to-complete funding for ships purchased in prior years, and CBO's estimates for the refueling of nuclear-powered aircraft carriers and other items.

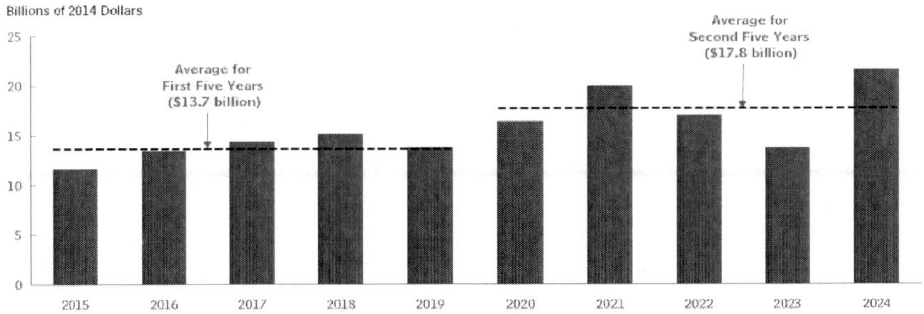

Source: Congressional Budget Office based on data from the Department of the Navy.

Note: Costs of new-ship construction exclude funds for some activities that are typically funded in the Navy's shipbuilding accounts, such as refueling of nuclear-powered aircraft carriers, ship conversions, construction of ships that are not part of the Navy's battle force (oceanographic survey ships, for instance), training ships, outfitting and postdelivery (which include the purchase of many smaller tools and pieces of equipment that are needed to operate a ship but are not necessarily provided by the manufacturing shipyard as part of ship construction), and smaller items. Costs for the mission packages for littoral combat ships, which are not funded in the Navy's shipbuilding accounts, also are not included.

Figure 6. The Navy's Estimates of the Costs of New-Ship Construction, 2015 to 2024.

COSTS OF MEETING NEARLY ALL INVENTORY GOALS IN EACH YEAR

Under its 2015 shipbuilding plan, the Navy would not build enough ships at the right times to meet the service's inventory goal of 306 battle force ships until 2019 under the Navy's new counting rules and 2022 under the old rules. In particular, the plan would lead to temporary shortfalls relative to the Navy's goals for ballistic missile submarines and attack submarines and, in the far term, for aircraft carriers as well.

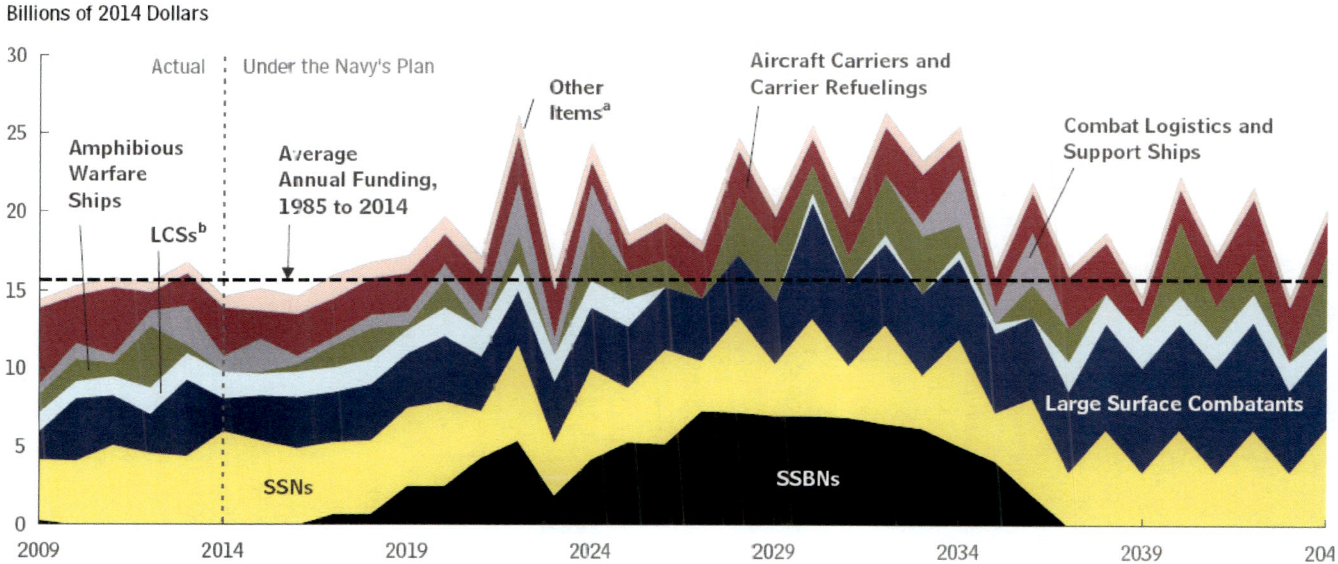

Source: Congressional Budget Office based on data from the Department of the Navy.

Note: LCSs = littoral combat ships; SSNs = attack submarines; SSBNs = ballistic missile submarines.

a. Other items include funds for ship conversions, construction of ships that are not part of the Navy's battle force (oceanographic survey ships, for instance), training ships, outfitting and postdelivery (which include the purchase of many smaller tools and pieces of equipment needed to operate a ship but not necessarily provided by the manufacturing shipyard as part of ship construction), and smaller items.

b. Costs for the mission packages for littoral combat ships, which are not funded in the Navy's shipbuilding accounts, are not included.

Figure 7. CBO's Estimates of Annual Shipbuilding Costs Under the Navy's 2015 Plan.

However, there would be only small and short-lived shortfalls for large surface combatants and amphibious warfare ships (see Figure 4 on page 9).

The Navy does not believe it can prevent the shortfall in ballistic missile submarines. The service life of existing Ohio class submarines cannot be extended because of technical reasons relating to the ships' material condition (particularly the hull) and reactor life.[11] And building the new class of ballistic missile submarines faster, the Navy argues, would introduce technical risks that would outweigh the risks of having 10—rather than the preferred 12—SSBNs that are deployable for a decade.

Other shortfalls, however, could be avoided or reduced by accelerating or increasing ship purchases relative to those specified in the 2015 shipbuilding plan. To meet most of its existing goals, the Navy could make the following changes to the current shipbuilding plan:

- To prevent the attack submarine force from falling below the inventory goal of 48 submarines, the Navy could accelerate the purchase of 7 submarines. Specifically, it could purchase 7 additional submarines from 2017 through 2023, increasing the production rate to 3 submarines per year for most of those years. If that increase occurred, the Navy could buy 7 fewer attack submarines between 2025 and 2034 than are called for under the 2015 plan and still maintain the desired inventory.
- To prevent the carrier force from declining in the 2040s to 10 ships, 1 short of its inventory goal of 11, the Navy could accelerate carrier purchases after 2018 to 1 every four years, rather than 1 every five years.
- To meet its goal of 88 large surface combatants in the last years of the plan, the Navy could purchase 5 additional destroyers between 2028 and 2037, increasing the production rate to 3 ships per year for five more years. That change would restore the reduction of 5 destroyers that occurred between the 2014 and 2015 plans.
- To prevent small shortfalls in later years of the plan, the Navy could purchase 2 additional amphibious warfare ships by 2030. That course of action would allow the Navy to meet its inventory goal of 33 ships in each year after 2017. However, the Navy cannot prevent a shortfall in amphibious warfare ships relative to the Navy's goal in the next few years, because ships of that sort take four to five years to build.

According to CBO's estimates, incorporating the changes described above into the Navy's 2015 plan would raise costs significantly in the first decade of the plan and by very small amounts in the second and third decades. The annual cost of new-ship construction would average $19.0 billion between 2015 and 2024 (instead of $16.7 billion, as in CBO's estimate of the Navy's plan), $22.6 billion between 2025 and 2034 (instead of $22.5 billion), and $17.6 billion between 2035 and 2044 (instead of $17.5 billion). Over the entire 30-year period, new-ship construction would average $19.7 billion per year, compared with $18.9 billion per year for the Navy's plan.

Other approaches to prevent falling short of the Navy's inventory goals could have different costs. For example, if the Navy was able to extend the service life of some existing ships, it would need fewer new ships, thus reducing procurement costs but possibly increasing operation and maintenance costs because older ships tend to be more expensive to operate than newer ships of the same class. Such an approach would not be effective in preventing a shortfall of all types of ships, however. In particular, the Navy's plan already reflects an assumption that most destroyers will be in service for 40 years, although historically very few have served longer than 30 years. Consequently, CBO does not expect that those ships could serve for an even longer period to prevent the shortfall in large surface combatants. By contrast, extending service life for amphibious warfare ships seems more plausible because those ships are already serving for 40 years and the Navy is planning to keep some beyond 40 years. Thus, the Navy could prevent the minor shortfalls in amphibious warfare ships after 2035 by not retiring existing ships and extending their service life by a few years in several cases.

Shipbuilding Given Historical Average Funding

CBO's estimate of $20.7 billion per year for the full cost of the Navy's 2015 shipbuilding plan is 32 percent higher than the $15.7 billion the Navy has spent on average per year for all items in its shipbuilding accounts over the past 30 years. If the Navy's future funding for shipbuilding is in line with its past funding, the Navy will need to reduce substantially its new-ship purchases relative to the number called for in its 2015 plan.[12]

To illustrate how much smaller the fleet of battle force ships would be under that scenario, CBO constructed an alternative shipbuilding plan to meet two criteria. First, the purchase of specific types of ships would be reduced relative to the 2015 plan in rough proportion, with the exception of ballistic missile submarines. The Navy's most senior officials have described replacing the current Ohio class submarines as the service's top priority; CBO assumed, therefore, that the Navy would purchase all 12 submarines included in its 2015 plan. With the nearly proportional reduction in purchases of other types of ships, the distribution of the fleet in 2044 among types of ships would be about the same as that specified in the 2015 plan, although the number of ships of each type would be smaller. Second, spending would be fairly similar (in inflation-adjusted dollars) during the near-term, midterm, and far-term periods. That alternative plan is not a recommendation by CBO but simply an illustration of the possible consequences of continuing funding for shipbuilding at its historical average amount rather than increasing it, as would be required under the Navy's 2015 plan.[13]

Purchases under that alternative plan would number 195 ships (versus 264 in the Navy's plan) and would consist of the following:

- 4 aircraft carriers (compared with 6 in the Navy's plan),
- 12 ballistic missile submarines (there also are 12 in the Navy's plan),
- 31 attack submarines (compared with 48 in the Navy's plan),
- 45 destroyers (compared with 65 in the Navy's plan),
- 47 littoral combat ships (compared with 66 in the Navy's plan),
- 15 amphibious ships (compared with 21 in the Navy's plan), and
- 41 combat logistics and support ships (compared with 46 in the Navy's plan).

Box 3. Inflation in Shipbuilding

The costs of building future ships depend on the sizes and capabilities of those ships, as well as on the evolution of the cost of building a ship of any given size and capability. The differences between the Navy's and the Congressional Budget Office's (CBO's) estimates of the cost of the Navy's shipbuilding plans arise in part because of differences in the projected future cost of building a ship of any given size and capability.

The Navy provided CBO with an index of shipbuilding costs between 1960 and 2013, which measures the historical growth in the costs of labor and materials used in shipbuilding. To project the increase in those costs for 2014 through 2020, the service extrapolated from that historical experience and also incorporated information from advance pricing agreements, vendor surveys, and projections of the cost of materials from the Bureau of Labor Statistics.

For those years, the Navy projects that the index of shipbuilding costs will increase at an average annual rate of 2.9 percent. By comparison, CBO projects that the gross domestic product (GDP) price index, which measures the prices of all final goods and services produced in the economy, will increase at an average annual rate of 1.9 percent during those years. Thus, CBO estimates that the cost of building a given ship (as projected by the Navy's index) will increase between 2014 and 2020 at a rate that is 1.0 percentage point faster per year, on average, than inflation for the economy as a whole. That difference in projected inflation rates is larger than the 0.9 percentage-point difference that CBO found in its analysis of the Navy's 2014 plan. Since 1984, the difference between the rate of increase in the Navy's shipbuilding cost index and the GDP price index has averaged about 1.3 percentage points per year (see the figure).

The Navy incorporated that projected increase of 2.9 percent per year in shipbuilding costs into its budget request for 2015 and into the associated Future Years Defense Program; both of those documents express costs in nominal dollars. In projecting the constant-dollar costs for its 2015 shipbuilding plan, the Navy converted those nominal dollars to inflation-adjusted dollars using the shipbuilding price index rather than the GDP price index. That is, the 2015 shipbuilding plan incorporates the view that a ship that costs $2.5 billion to build in 2014 will cost the same (in 2014 dollars) to build in 2035.

In contrast, CBO converted the costs of ships from nominal dollars to inflation-adjusted dollars using the GDP price index, thereby reflecting the expectation that inflation in shipbuilding will exceed overall inflation. As noted, cost growth in the shipbuilding industry has exceeded general inflation for most of the past three decades, and CBO lacks an analytic basis for determining when and to what extent the difference between the two growth rates might narrow. Therefore, CBO projects that shipbuilding inflation will outpace inflation as measured by the GDP price index by 1.0 percentage point per year between 2014 and 2020 and by 1.3 percentage points per year—the 30-year historical average—thereafter.

Under that alternative plan, the battle force fleet in 2023 would be about the same size as in the Navy's plan but by 2044 would number 242 ships, as opposed to the 303 ships in the Navy's plan. The inventory in 2044 would consist of the following ships:

- 8 aircraft carriers (compared with 10 in the Navy's plan),
- 12 ballistic missile submarines (there also are 12 in the Navy's plan),
- 41 attack submarines (compared with 52 in the Navy's plan),
- 69 destroyers (compared with 83 in the Navy's plan),
- 33 littoral combat ships (compared with 52 in the Navy's plan),
- 27 amphibious ships (compared with 31 in the Navy's plan), and
- 52 combat logistics and support ships (compared with 63 in the Navy's plan).[14]

Box 3. Inflation in Shipbuilding

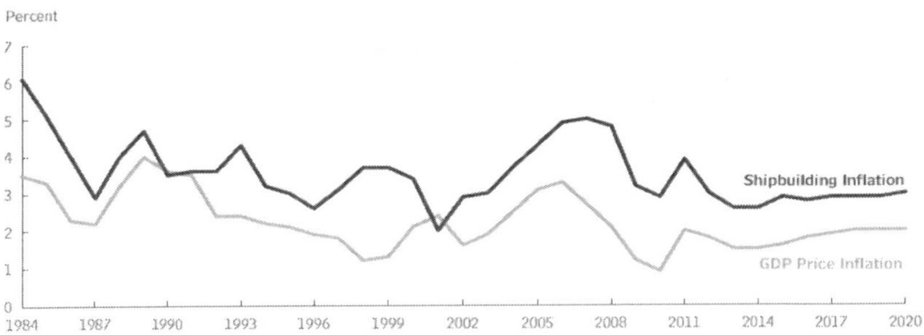

Sources: Congressional Budget Office; Department of the Navy. Note: GDP = gross domestic product.

Annual Rates of Shipbuilding Inflation and GDP Price Inflation

The difference between shipbuilding inflation and overall inflation represents projected growth in the cost of a future ship of any given size and capability relative to the average cost of goods and services in the economy. For example, CBO estimates that a ship costing $2.5 billion to build in 2014 will cost $3.3 billion (in 2014 dollars) to build in 2035. Thus, CBO's constant-dollar estimates reflect the increased costs of ships in comparison to an average increase for other goods and services that might be purchased with discretionary funding. Nevertheless, shipbuilding costs cannot continue indefinitely to grow faster than the costs of goods and services in the economy as a whole. If that were to happen, the price of ships would eventually outstrip the Navy's ability to pay for even a very small number of them.

Other approaches to staying within historical funding would have different results. If the Navy reduced the number of larger and more expensive ships more sharply than in the alternative plan described above, then the overall fleet would be larger. Conversely, if the Navy preserved the programs of more expensive ships, then the overall fleet would be smaller. Ultimately, decisions about which ships to build would depend on the priorities that policymakers established for certain naval missions relative to others.

SHIPBUILDING UNDER THE BUDGET CONTROL ACT OF 2011

Given the caps on defense funding from 2015 to 2021 that stem from the Budget Control Act of 2011 as amended by the American Taxpayer Relief Act of 2012 and the Bipartisan Budget Agreement of 2013, DoD will receive funding for its base budget—which excludes the cost of overseas contingency operations, such as the war in Afghanistan—that is substantially lower after adjusting for inflation than the funding it received in 2010, when such funding reached its peak. Specifically, after adjusting for inflation, DoD's base budget fell in 2014 to about the same amount that the department received in 2007, and it will remain essentially flat through 2021.[15] Consequently, under current law, DoD faces a choice between implementing the Navy's 2015 shipbuilding plan and exerting strong pressures on other parts of the defense budget, scaling back that plan, or some combination of those two actions.

If the Navy receives the same percentage of DoD's budget during the coming decade and devotes the same percentage of its budget to ship construction that it has historically, the shipbuilding budget would be a little less than $13 billion per year from 2015 through 2021. In comparison, the Navy's 2015 shipbuilding plan would require spending a little more than $17 billion on all shipbuilding activities over the same period, CBO estimates. (During the past 15 years, the Department of the Navy has received about 30 percent of DoD's base budget and has devoted about 10 percent of its funding to shipbuilding.) That amount would be $5.5 billion per year—or 30 percent—below CBO's estimate of the amount required to execute the Navy's 2015 shipbuilding plan. If all shipbuilding programs were cut proportionally, a reduction of that magnitude would require the Navy to purchase 16 fewer ships over the 2015–2021 period than the 63 ships it would purchase under its 2015 plan.

So far, the Navy has not canceled any ship purchases because of insufficient funding, although it has proposed to retire a number of ships early because of fiscal constraints. However, the cuts in funding in 2013 triggered under the Budget Control Act led the Navy to slow or otherwise alter elements of its shipbuilding programs. Funding in 2014 and 2015 would largely, if not completely, make up for the funding lost in 2013.

In an April 2014 report, DoD identified the changes it would make to the Navy's shipbuilding plan and ship operations, along with the resulting inventory, if the current caps on defense funding are left in place.[16] Specifically, the Navy would:

- Buy 8 fewer ships between 2015 and 2021, including 3 fewer destroyers and 1 fewer attack submarine;
- Charter and lease 3 fleet oilers rather than buy them;
- Not refuel the U.S.S. *George Washington*, thereby reducing its inventory of aircraft carriers by 1 and disestablishing its associated air wing (although the Navy later announced that it would plan to refuel the aircraft carrier as part of its 2016 budget request);[17] and
- Put 6 destroyers in a reduced status (in addition to the cruisers and amphibious ships that the Navy intends to put in a reduced status under its own plans).[18]

Those identified changes suggest that the Navy would try to cut shipbuilding less than its other activities, because if the Navy reduced its shipbuilding spending proportionally with the rest of its spending and cut total spending by enough to meet the caps, the service would probably need to cut roughly twice as many ships.

OUTLOOK FOR SPECIFIC SHIP PROGRAMS

To estimate the costs of implementing the Navy's 2015 shipbuilding plan, CBO calculated the cost of each of the 264 ships that the Navy intends to purchase from 2015 through 2044. For ships under construction, the estimates were based in part on data for actual costs from the Navy. For ships yet to be built, the estimates were based primarily on relationships between the cost and weight of similar ships in the past. Specifically, CBO used the cost per thousand tons of lightship displacement—the weight of the ship itself without its crew, materiel, weapons, or fuel.

CBO then adjusted its estimates to incorporate the effects of "rate" (the reduction in average overhead costs that occurs when a shipyard builds more than one of the same type of ship at a time) and "learning" (the efficiencies that shipyards gain as they produce additional units of a given type of ship). The effects of rate and learning were applied to the estimated cost of the first ship of a class (the lead ship) to determine the estimated costs for all subsequent ships of that class.

Thus, CBO's estimate of the cost of the lead ship in a class drove its estimate of the costs of subsequent ships of that class. To estimate the costs of ships for which the Navy has yet to develop even notional designs, CBO had to make assumptions about the size and capabilities of those ships. All costs of individual ships described in this section exclude outfitting and postdelivery costs, which typically add about 3 percent to the cost of a ship.

Aircraft Carriers

The 2015 shipbuilding plan states that the Navy's goal is to have 11 aircraft carriers. The Navy intends to buy 6 CVN-78 Gerald R. Ford class aircraft carriers over the 2015–2044 period. Building 1 carrier every five years (referred to as five-year centers) would enable the Navy to have a force of at least 11 carriers almost continuously through 2044, with two exceptions. One exception would be from 2015 to 2016, when the number of carriers would be 10. That temporary decline occurs because the *Enterprise* (CVN-65) was retired in early 2013 after 52 years of service, and the next new carrier, the *Gerald R. Ford* (CVN-78), will not be commissioned until 2016. Any delays in completing that new carrier would extend the period during which the Navy has only 10 carriers.

The other exception would be from 2040 to 2044 and beyond. If carriers continued to be built every five years and to serve for 50 years, the Navy's carrier force would fall to 10 in 2040 and remain at that level.[19]

The Navy currently projects that the total cost of the lead ship of the CVN-78 class will be $12.9 billion in nominal dollars over the period from 2001 to 2016, an amount equal to the Congressional cost cap.[20] Using the Navy's inflation index for naval shipbuilding, CBO converted that figure to $14.3 billion in 2014 dollars.[21] That amount is 23 percent more than the amount requested in the President's budget when the ship was first authorized in 2008.

The Navy's estimate does not include $4.7 billion in research and development costs that apply to the entire class.

CBO estimates that the total cost of the lead ship of the CVN-78 class will be $13.5 billion in nominal dollars and $14.8 billion in 2014 dollars. To generate that estimate, CBO used the actual costs of the previous carrier—the CVN-77—and adjusted them for the higher costs of government-furnished equipment in the newer configuration and for more than $3 billion in costs for nonrecurring engineering and detail design (the plans, drawings, and other one-time items associated with the first ship of a new class). Subsequent ships of the CVN-78 class will not require as much funding for onetime items, although they will incur the same costs for government-furnished equipment. All together, CBO estimates the average cost of the 6 carriers in the 2015 plan at $12.8 billion, compared with the Navy's estimate of $12.5 billion (see Table 4).

The final cost of the CVN-78 could be higher or lower than CBO's estimate. Possible reasons for a higher cost include the following:

- The costs of many lead ships built in the past 20 years have increased by more than 30 percent from the original budgeted estimates. CBO's estimate of the cost of the CVN-78 incorporates an amount of growth that falls within the range of historical cost growth for lead ships, and the costs reported for the roughly 80 percent of construction completed to date are consistent with that estimate—but costs have tended to rise more in the latter stages of ship construction, when systems are being installed and integrated. For example, the test program for the carrier could reveal one or more major and possibly expensive problems.
- The Navy has stated that there is a 50 percent probability that the cost of the CVN-78 will exceed its estimate. Specifically, in its most recent selected acquisition report, the Navy stated that it has budgeted an amount for the CVN-78 that covers up to the 50th percentile of possible cost outcomes.

Table 4. Comparison of the Navy's and CBO's Estimates for the Construction of Major New Ships under the Navy's 2015 Plan

Billions of 2014 Dollars							
		2015–2044 Period Total Costs per Class Over the 2015–2044 Period		Ship Over the Average Costs per 2015–2044 Period		Memorandum: Average Costs per Ship Under the 2014 Plan	
	Number of Ships Purchased Under the 2015 Plan	Navy's Estimates	Estimates CBO's	Navy's Estimates	CBO's Estimates	Navy's Estimates	CBO's Estimates
CVN-78 Gerald R. Ford Class Aircraft Carriers	6	74 a	76 a	12.5 a	12.8 a	12.5	12.9
Ohio Replacement Ballistic Missile Submarines	12	79	92	6.6	7.7	6.5	7.4
Virginia Class Attack Submarines	31	88	90	2.8	2.9	2.8	2.8
Improved Virginia Class Attack Submarines							
(Replacements for Virginia class)	17	49	54	2.9	3.2	3.3	3.2
DDG-51 Arleigh Burke Class Destroyers							
Flight IIA	3	4	4	1.4	1.4	1.6	1.6
Flight III	27	44	51	1.6	1.9	1.8	2.0
DDG(X) Destroyers (Replacements for Arleigh Burke class)	35	63	88	1.8	2.5	2.0	3.4
Littoral Combat Ships							
Flight 0	12	b	6	b	0.5	0.5	0.5
Flight 1	20	b	12	b	0.6	n.a.	n.a.
Total	32	15	18	0.5 c	n.a.		

Table 4. (Continued)

Billions of 2014 Dollars							
		2015–2044 Period Total Costs per Class Over the 2015–2044 Period		Ship Over the Average Costs per 2015–2044 Period		Memorandum: Average Costs per Ship Under the 2014 Plan	
	Number of Ships Purchased Under the 2015 Plan	Navy's Estimates	Estimates CBO's	Navy's Estimates	CBO's Estimates	Navy's Estimates	CBO's Estimates
LCS(X)s (Replacements for littoral combat ships)	34	16	16	0.5 c	0.5	0.4	0.6
LX(R)s (Replacements for amphibious dock landing ships)	11	16	19	1.4	1.8	1.4	1.8
LHA-6 Amphibious Assault Ships	7	24 d	26 d	3.7 d	4.0 d	3.7	4.5
LPD-17 Replacements	3	7	8	2.2	2.6	e	e
T-AO(X) Oilers	17	8	8	0.5	0.5	0.5	0.5

Source: Congressional Budget Office based on data from the Department of the Navy. Notes: The costs in this table exclude funding for research and development for these ships. Relative to Table 1, this table excludes 29 support ships of various types.

n.a. = not applicable.

[a] In CBO's and the Navy's estimates for aircraft carriers, total costs per class include remaining funds for the CVN-78 and CVN-79, but exclude that part of the funding for the carrier the Navy plans to purchase in 2043 that would be budgeted after 2044. CBO's and the Navy's estimates of the average cost per ship exclude the remaining funding for the CVN-78 and CVN-79 but include all of the funding for the carrier slated for purchase in 2043.

[b] The Navy did not make a distinction between the existing design for littoral combat ships (LCSs) and an improved LCS design that may be required as a result of the proposal for building a small combatant that is more capable of surviving attacks and more lethal to adversaries. CBO's estimates include some additional funding, roughly estimated, for improving 20 of the LCSs in those ways.

[c] The Navy's estimate for the LCSs is $464 million per ship, and its estimate for the LCS(X)—the replacement ship—is $473 million. Those costs exclude the cost of LCS mission packages, which CBO also excluded from its estimates.

[d] In CBO's and the Navy's estimates for amphibious assault ships, total costs per class exclude half the funding for the ship that would be purchased in 2044 because that money would be budgeted for 2045. CBO's and the Navy's estimates of the average cost per ship include all of the funding for the ship scheduled for purchase in 2044.

[e] CBO did not report these data in its analysis of the Navy's 2014 plan.

Possible reasons for a lower cost than CBO's estimate include the following:

- The Navy and the builder of the CVN-78 recognize that cost growth for lead ships is a significant concern, and they are actively managing the CVN-78 program to restrain costs.
- All of the materials for the CVN-78 have been purchased, and much of the equipment for the vessel is being purchased under fixed-price contracts; those factors essentially eliminate the risk of further cost growth for about half of the projected cost of the carrier.
- The test program might reveal only minor problems. In that case, the cost of the ship would probably be less than CBO's estimate, although it might still exceed the Navy's estimate.

The next carrier following the CVN-78 will be the CVN-79, the *John F. Kennedy*. Funding for that ship began in 2007, the Congress officially authorized its construction in 2013, and appropriations for it are expected to be complete by 2018. The Navy estimates that the ship will cost $11.5 billion in nominal dollars ($160 million more than the estimate under the President's 2014 budget) and $10.6 billion in 2014 dollars. In its selected acquisition report on the CVN-79, the Navy describes its cost estimate as an "aggressive but achievable target." In contrast, CBO estimates that the cost of the ship will be $12.6 billion in nominal dollars and $11.5 billion in 2014 dollars, about 8 percent more than the Navy's estimate.

Submarines

Under the 2015 shipbuilding plan, submarines would overtake surface combatants as the largest source of demand for shipbuilding funds over the next 20 years (see Table 5). The Navy currently operates 14 Ohio class ballistic missile submarines (SSBNs), 4 Ohio class guided missile submarines (SSGNs) modified from the SSBN version, and 55 attack submarines (SSNs) of several classes. Over the next three decades, the Navy plans to buy 12 new SSBNs starting in 2021; 48 new SSNs, including 31 Virginia class submarines (mostly at an average rate of 1.5 per year through 2033); and 17 submarines based on a redesign and improvement of the Virginia class, with production scheduled to begin in 2034. The Navy does not plan to replace its 4 SSGNs when they are retired in the mid- to late 2020s.

Ohio Replacement Ballistic Missile Submarines. SSBNs carry Trident ballistic missiles and are the sea-based leg of the United States' strategic triad for delivering nuclear weapons. (The other two legs are land-based intercontinental ballistic missiles and manned strategic bombers.) The design, cost, and capabilities of the Ohio Replacement submarine class are among the most significant uncertainties in the Navy's and CBO's analyses of the cost of future shipbuilding. Under the 2015 plan, the first Ohio Replacement submarine—sometimes called the SSBN(X)—would be purchased in 2021, although advance procurement funds would be needed starting in 2016 for items with long lead times. The second submarine would be purchased in 2024, followed by 1 per year from 2026 to 2035 (see Figure 3 on page 7). [22]

The Navy currently estimates the cost of the first Ohio Replacement submarine at $12.4 billion in 2014 dollars. The estimated average cost of follow-on ships is now $6.0 billion, which implies a total cost for 12 submarines of $79 billion, or an average of $6.6 billion each. However, the Navy has stated an objective of reducing that $6.0 billion figure to $5.5 billion.[23]

The Navy's estimate represents considerable improvement in the cost per thousand tons of the first Ohio Replacement submarine compared with the first Virginia submarine—an improvement that would affect costs for the entire new class of ballistic missile submarines. The main reason for those improved costs by weight for the Ohio Replacement is that the Navy will recycle, to the extent possible, the design, technology, and parts used for the Virginia class. Furthermore, because ballistic missile submarines (like the Ohio Replacements) tend to be larger and less dense ships than attack submarines (like the Virginia class), they will be easier to build and therefore less expensive on a weight basis, the Navy argues.

Yet the historical record for the lead ships of new classes of submarines in the 1970s and 1980s provides little reason to believe that ballistic missile submarines are cheaper by weight to build than attack submarines (see Figure 8). The first Ohio class submarine was more expensive to build than the lead ships of the two classes of attack submarines built during the same period—the Los Angeles and the Improved Los Angeles (which made design changes to the Los Angeles that included the addition of 12 vertical launch system cells). In addition, the average costs by weight of the first 12 or 13 ships of the Ohio, Los Angeles, and Improved Los Angeles classes were virtually identical. By the 1990s, the costs of lead ships for submarines had grown substantially, with both the first Seawolf submarine and first Virginia submarine costing about the same by weight—even though the Seawolf is 20 percent larger and was built nine years earlier than the first Virginia.

Table 5. Total Shipbuilding Costs, by Major Category, 1985 to 2044

		Historical			CBO's Estimates Under the Navy's 2015 Plan			
	1985-1994	1995-2004	2005-2014	1985-2014	2015-2024	2025-2034	2035-2044	2015-2044
New-Ship Construction			Average Annual Costs (Billions of 2014 dollars)					
Aircraft carriers	1.5	1.8	1.8	1.7	2.4	2.4	2.7	2.5
Submarines	6.1	2.6	4.1	4.3	7.1	11.2	5.3	7.9
Surface combatants	7.4	4.7	4.2	5.4	5.2	5.2	7.5	6.0
Amphibious ships	1.4	1.5	1.7	1.5	1.1	2.3	1.8	1.8
Logistics and support ships	1.7	0.4	0.8	1.0	0.9	1.4	0.1	0.8
Subtotal	18.2	10.9	12.5	13.9	16.7	22.5	17.5	18.9
Carrier and Submarine								
Refuelings[a]	0.4	0.9	1.3	0.9	1.4	1.0	0.6	1.0
Other Items	1.1	1.2	0.6	1.0	1.2	0.7	0.6	0.8
Total	**19.6**	**13.0**	**14.5**	**15.7**	**19.2**	**24.2**	**18.7**	**20.7**
			Percentage of Average Annual Costs					
New-Ship Construction								
Aircraft carriers	9	16	14	12	12	10	15	12
Submarines	34	24	32	31	37	46	29	38
Surface combatants	41	43	33	39	27	21	40	29
Amphibious ships	8	14	14	11	6	10	10	8
Logistics and support ships	9	3	6	7	4	6	0	4
Subtotal	92	84	87	88	87	93	94	91
Carrier and Submarine								
Refuelings[a]	2	7	9	5	7	4	3	5
Other Items	6	9	4	6	6	3	3	4
Total	**100**	**100**	**100**	**100**	**100**	**100**	**100**	**100**

Source: Congressional Budget Office.

Note: Costs of new-ship construction exclude funds for some activities that are typically funded in the Navy's shipbuilding accounts, such as refueling of nuclear-powered aircraft carriers, ship conversions, construction of ships that are not part of the Navy's battle force (oceanographic survey ships, for instance), training ships, outfitting and postdelivery (which include the purchase of many smaller tools and pieces of equipment that are needed to operate a ship but are not necessarily provided by the manufacturing shipyard as part of ship construction), and smaller items. Costs for the mission packages for littoral combat ships, which are not funded in the Navy's shipbuilding accounts, also are not included.

[a] CBO's estimates under the Navy's 2015 plan reflect only the costs of refueling aircraft carriers. Historically, the refueling of nuclear-powered submarines was also included in the Navy's shipbuilding accounts. In 2010, however, the Navy transferred the funding for those refuelings to other accounts.

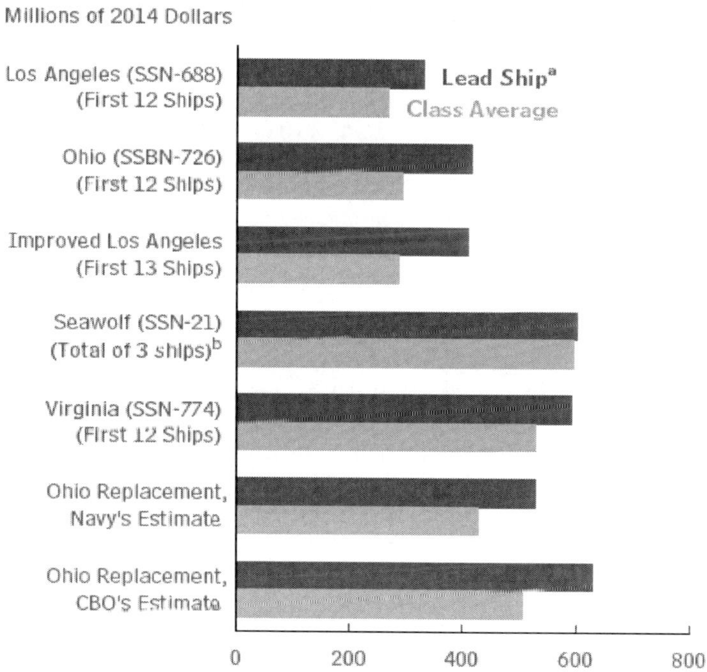

Source: Congressional Budget Office based on data from the Department of the Navy.

Note: Cost per thousand tons of Condition A-1 displacement (the weight of the submarine without its crew, materiel, weapons, or fuel), which is analogous to lightship displacement for surface ships.

[a] Data exclude costs for plans, which comprise nonrecurring engineering and detail design.

[b] Although 29 Seawolf class submarines were planned, only 3 were built.

Figure 8. Cost per Thousand Tons of Various Classes of Submarine, Lead Ship and Class Average.

Using data from the Virginia class submarine program, CBO estimates that the first Ohio Replacement submarine will cost $13.8 billion in 2014 dollars. Estimating the cost of the first submarine of a class with an entirely new design is particularly difficult because of uncertainty about how much the Navy will spend on nonrecurring engineering and detail design. All told, 12 Ohio Replacement submarines would cost $92 billion in CBO's estimation, or an average of $7.7 billion each—$1.1 billion more per boat than the Navy's estimate. That average includes the $13.8 billion estimated cost of the lead submarine and a $7.1 billion average estimated cost for the 2nd through 12th submarines. Research and development would cost an additional $10 billion to $15 billion, for a total program cost of $102 billion to $107 billion, CBO estimates.

Overall, the Navy expects a 19 percent improvement in the cost-to-weight relationship of the Ohio Replacement class compared with the first 12 of the Virginia class. CBO estimates a 4 percent improvement, which is based in part on savings that will probably be achieved because of projected concurrent production of the Ohio Replacement and Virginia class submarines.

Attack Submarines. Under the 2015 plan, the Navy would buy 31 Virginia class attack submarines. Between 2015 and 2033, those purchases would occur mostly at a rate alternating between 1 and 2 per year. In 2034, the Navy would switch to an improved Virginia class but maintain the same build rate of 1 or 2 per year. With such a procurement schedule, the attack submarine force would remain at or above the Navy's goal of 48 submarines through 2024 but would then fall to between 41 and 47 submarines between 2025 and 2034 before reaching or exceeding 48 submarines again beginning in 2035 (see Figure 4 on page 9).

Senior Navy leaders have stated that Virginia class SSNs would have to cost $2.8 billion or less apiece for the Navy to be able to afford 2 per year.[24] The President's 2015 budget indicates a current cost of those vessels of $2.6 billion each. For the entirety of the Virginia class under the 2015 shipbuilding plan, the Navy's and CBO's estimates are virtually the same: The Navy estimates that the total cost for all 31 of the Virginia class submarines purchased between 2015 and 2044 would be about $88 billion, and CBO estimates that cost at $90 billion.

The Navy expects to begin purchasing the improved Virginia class submarine in 2034. The service's recent shipbuilding plans call for the continuing evolution of the current submarine—as a new class of submarine—to incorporate significant technological upgrades in systems and capabilities. CBO similarly assumed that the improved Virginias would incorporate changes that were sufficiently important to make the submarines a new class, although not with a wholly new design. On the basis of that assumption, CBO estimated, the average submarine would cost $3.2 billion, whereas the Navy's estimate was $2.9 billion under the 2015 plan. For reasons that are not clear, the Navy's estimate is a reduction from an average cost of $3.3 billion under the 2014 plan.

Although the Navy's plan does not include submarines to replace the existing SSGNs when they retire in the 2020s, the service expects to lengthen the hull of future Virginia class submarines to insert the Virginia Payload Module (VPM). The VPM would contain four large-diameter payload tubes, each of which could carry seven Tomahawk missiles. That change would increase the submerged displacement of the submarine by nearly 30 percent and would raise the number of the Virginia class's vertical-launch weapons from 12 to 40 (in addition to the 27 weapons in the torpedo room). The Navy estimates that 20 Virginia class submarines equipped with the additional payload modules would provide a "near equivalent" to the strike capability of the existing force of 4 SSGNs. The President's 2015 budget proposed spending $700 million between 2015 and 2019 for research and development on the payload module and for modifying the design of the Virginia class. The Navy's 2015 plan, in contrast to earlier plans, now includes building Virginia class submarines with the VPM beginning in 2021. Both the Navy's and CBO's estimates of costs reflect that change. Neither the Navy nor CBO assumes that the improved Virginia class will include the module.

Large Surface Combatants

The Navy's 2015 plan incorporates the purchase of the same types of destroyers as the 2014 plan. The service restarted production of DDG-51 Flight IIA destroyers in 2010 and purchased 8 ships through 2014 (in addition to the 62 ships that had been purchased when production was initially stopped in 2005). The Navy plans to purchase 3 more DDG-51 Flight IIAs through 2016. Beginning in 2016 and continuing through 2029, the Navy plans to purchase 27 DDG-51s with an upgraded design, a configuration known as

Flight III. In 2030, the Navy would start buying 33 DDG(X)s, a not-yet-designed destroyer intended to replace the DDG-51 class.

The Navy is also pursuing two other strategies to boost its inventory of large surface combatants. One is to modernize 11 of its Ticonderoga class cruisers and thereby extend their service in the fleet through 2043. If the Navy does not modernize those ships, all of the Navy's cruisers would be retired by 2028 (see Box 2 on page 11). The other critical strategy is to keep all DDG-51 Flight IIAs and subsequent destroyers serving in the fleet for 40 years. The class was originally designed to serve for 30 years, but the Navy has gradually increased the planned service life—first to 35 years and then, in the 2009 shipbuilding plan, to 40 years—of Flight IIA and Flight III ships. Of the last 13 classes of destroyers and cruisers, 12 have been retired after serving for 30 years or less. Indeed, in recent years, Spruance class destroyers and some Ticonderoga class cruisers have been retired after serving 25 years or less. The Navy retired those destroyers for various reasons: They reached the end of their useful service lives, they became too expensive to maintain in the waning years of their service lives, or they no longer had the combat capabilities needed to meet existing threats and modernization was not considered cost-effective.[25] If the DDG-51 class met the same fate, then additional ship purchases would be needed to achieve the Navy's inventory goal.

Taken together, the intended ship purchases, cruiser modernization, and extended service lives for destroyers would allow the Navy to meet or exceed its inventory goal of 88 large surface combatants in most years through 2044 (see Figure 4 on page 9).

DDG-51 Flight IIAs. The Navy's existing force of 62 DDG-51 destroyers was built in three primary configurations. The first 28 ships, designated Flight I or II, did not include a hangar for embarking helicopters—which play important roles in countering enemy submarines, attacks by small boats, and, to a lesser degree, mines. The next 34 ships, designated Flight IIA, included a hangar and were therefore able to carry two helicopters or several ship-launched unmanned aerial vehicles.[26] In the Navy's 2015 plan, 3 new DDG-51s purchased through 2016 (in addition to 8 purchased between 2010 and 2014 but not yet in the fleet) would use the Flight IIA configuration but would also incorporate the latest ballistic missile defense capabilities.[27] Those ships would have an average cost of $1.4 billion, in CBO's estimation.

DDG-51 Flight IIIs. The Navy's strategy to meet combatant commanders' demands for greater ballistic missile defense capabilities than is provided by existing DDG-51s—and to replace 11 Ticonderoga class cruisers when they are retired in the 2020s—is to modify the design of the DDG-51

Flight IIA destroyer substantially, creating a Flight III configuration.[28] That configuration would incorporate the new Air and Missile Defense Radar (AMDR), now under development, which is larger and more powerful than the radar on earlier DDG-51s. The effective operation of the AMDR in the new Flight III configuration, however, will require increasing the amount of electrical power and cooling available on a Flight III.[29]

With those changes and associated increases in the ship's displacement, a DDG-51 Flight III destroyer would cost about $300 million—or about 20 percent—more than a new Flight IIA destroyer, CBO estimates.[30] Thus, CBO expects that the average cost per ship over the entire production run would be $1.9 billion, or about 19 percent more than the Navy's estimate of $1.6 billion.

CBO's estimate of the costs of the DDG Flight IIA and Flight III ships to be purchased in the future is a little less than it was last year. Most of the decrease for the Flight III can be attributed to updated information on the cost of incorporating the AMDR into the Flight III configuration. The cost of the AMDR itself, according to the Navy, has declined steadily through the development program, and DoD's Cost Analysis and Program Evaluation (CAPE) office concurs with the reduced estimate. The Navy decreased its estimate for the average price of a DDG-51 Flight III ship from $1.8 billion in the 2014 plan to $1.6 billion in the 2015 plan, primarily as a result of continued reductions in the estimate of the cost of the AMDR. Considerable uncertainty remains in the DDG-51 Flight III program, however. Costs could be higher or lower than CBO's estimate, depending on the eventual cost and complexity of the AMDR, along with associated changes in the ship's design to integrate the new radar.

DDG(X) Future Guided Missile Destroyers. Like the Navy's 2014 shipbuilding plan, the current plan includes a future class of destroyers intended to replace the DDG-51 Flight I and II ships when they retire in the late 2020s and 2030s.[31] The Navy's 2015 plan describes the ship as a "mid-sized future surface combatant" but does not provide further specification.[32] CBO has adopted a generic DDG(X) designation, implying an unknown design.

Under the 2015 plan, production of the DDG(X) would start in 2030, which would make it a successor to the DDG-51 Flight III program. The Navy says that it would buy 35 DDG(X)s at an average cost of $1.8 billion, or about $200 million more than the cost of DDG-51 Flight III ships. Those cost estimates imply that the DDG(X)'s capabilities would represent a relatively modest improvement over those of the DDG-51 Flight III or (if capabilities were significantly improved) the DDG(X) would be a smaller ship than the DDG-51 Flight III.

CBO expects that the DDG(X) will have a largely new design but will be about the same size as the DDG-51 Flight III—consistent with the concept of a midsized surface combatant. CBO projects the average cost of the DDG(X) at $2.5 billion, roughly 40 percent higher than the Navy's projection. Over the 2015–2044 period, CBO estimates, the Navy would have to spend $88 billion for the DDG(X) portion of the shipbuilding program— $25 billion more than the Navy's estimate of $63 billion. That difference represents nearly 40 percent of the overall difference of $66 billion between the Navy's and CBO's estimates of the cost of the 2015 shipbuilding plan as a whole.

CBO's current estimate of a $2.5 billion average cost for the DDG(X) is substantially lower than its estimate of $3.4 billion last year. The downward revision reflects CBO's assumption that the DDG(X) would be similar in size to the DDG-51 Flight III, rather than significantly larger as CBO assumed in its estimate of the 2014 plan. The large amount of uncertainty about the ultimate size and capabilities of the DDG(X) suggests that the true cost could be substantially different from either the Navy's or CBO's estimate.

Littoral Combat Ships

In the 2015 plan, the Navy envisions building a force of 52 small surface combatants called littoral combat ships by 2025. The first LCS was authorized in 2005, and the Navy already has 20 of those ships either in its fleet or under construction—10 each of two different designs being built by two different contractors. Because those ships are assumed to have a service life of 25 years, the Navy would need to begin procuring their replacements in 2030. Therefore, the Navy plans to purchase 32 more LCSs through 2025 to complete its initial force of 52 ships and then to purchase 34 next-generation ships, called LCS(X)s, between 2030 and 2044 to replace the first-generation LCSs as they retire.

The LCS differs from past and present U.S. warships in that its production program is divided into two components—the sea frame (the ship itself) and mission packages (the main combat systems). The sea frame is being designed and built so that mission packages can be switched on a given ship over time as the ship's mission changes. Currently, the Navy expects to use three types of mission packages—one each for countering mines, submarines, and surface ships. It also expects that the LCS will be able to perform maritime security operations (such as sanctions enforcement, counterpiracy operations, and engagement with friendly navies) while equipped with any of those mission packages. In all, the service plans to buy 64 mission packages for the 52 ships by 2025.[33] In time, the Navy may also develop and purchase other types of mission packages.[34]

Of the 32 additional LCSs that the Navy intends to purchase, 4 are planned to be purchased in 2015 and 2016— completing the 10-ship purchase agreements with the two existing shipbuilders—and an additional 8 in 2016 through 2018, under contractual arrangements that have not yet been announced.[35] Therefore, the Navy expects to have 32 LCSs in the fleet or under construction by the end of 2018 and plans to purchase 20 more between 2019 and 2025.

However, the Navy's plans for the LCS were called into question earlier this year by the Secretary of Defense. On February 24, 2014, the Secretary expressed concerns that the LCS and its associated mission packages, as currently designed, were not survivable enough and lacked offensive firepower to operate independently and effectively against potential future adversaries that employ the most advanced antiship technologies and weapon systems.[36] He ordered the Navy not to contract for more than 32 ships until it studied those issues and made proposals to "procure a capable and lethal small surface combatant, generally consistent with the capabilities of a frigate" by considering "a completely new design, existing ship designs (including the LCS), and a modified LCS." The proposals were to be submitted in sufficient time to inform the President's 2016 budget submission.

On December 11, 2014, the Secretary of the Defense announced the results of that study: He has decided that the last 20 ships will be modified from the two existing LCS designs to include additional offensive weapons and survivability features. Those changes would begin with the ships planned for purchase in 2019. The Navy's 2015 shipbuilding program does not incorporate any additional costs that may be incurred as a result of the recent decision. In its December 2014 announcement, DoD estimated that its proposed changes would increase the cost of an LCS by a little less than 20 percent.

In the 2015 Future Years Defense Program, the Navy estimates the average cost of the LCS at about $420 million per ship over the next five years, including the 10 ships to be purchased from 2016 through 2019, after the end of the two 10-ship contracts. That figure is well below the Congressionally mandated cost cap for the LCS program of $515 million per ship (adjusted for inflation).[37] Overall, the Navy estimates that the 32 LCSs to be purchased by 2025—designated by the Navy as Flight 0—would cost about $464 million per ship, on average, which does not include any additional costs to make the LCS more capable of surviving attacks or more lethal to adversaries.

Since its analysis of the Navy's 2012 shipbuilding plan, CBO has lowered its estimate for the cost of the LCSs purchased between 2010 and 2015 to reflect the prices and terms to which the Navy and the two shipyards agreed. However, CBO expects that the Navy will pay slightly higher prices for the ships purchased after 2015, in part because the annual procurement quantities planned for those years are lower than in previous years.

In addition, CBO anticipated that changes in the design of the LCS in response to the Secretary's directive would add 15 percent to the cost of the last 20 LCSs, which CBO calls the Flight 1 ships but the Navy calls small surface combatants. Based on that assumption, CBO expects that those ships would cost an average of $600 million each. (CBO completed its analysis before the Secretary of Defense announced his decision about the configuration of those last ships, which DoD anticipates will add a little less than 20 percent to their cost. CBO will reexamine that issue in its analysis of the 2016 shipbuilding plan.)

Under the 2015 plan, the Navy would also buy 34 next-generation littoral combat ships—called LCS(X)s—beginning in 2030. Both the Navy and CBO assumed that the LCS(X)s would have the capabilities of the Flight 0 ships they would be replacing rather than those of the later Flight 1 ships. The Navy's cost estimate for an LCS(X) is $473 million, just slightly more (after adjusting for inflation) than the expected average cost of an LCS Flight 0. CBO estimates the average cost of the LCS(X) would be a little higher, about $500 million per ship. CBO's current estimate is less than its estimate last year, when CBO assumed that the LCS(X) would look more like the proposed Flight 1. If the LCX(X) were designed to meet or exceed the capabilities of the LCS Flight 1, then its cost would probably be higher than the Navy and CBO now estimate.

Amphibious Warfare Ships

The Navy's inventory goal for amphibious warfare ships is 33. The proposed force would consist of 11 LHA or LHD amphibious assault ships, 11 LPD amphibious transport docks, and 11 replacements for the Navy's LSD dock landing ships. In pursuit of that force, the 2015 plan calls for buying 7

LHA-6s, at a rate of 1 every four or seven years, to replace LHD-1 class amphibious assault ships as they are retired.[38] The plan envisions buying 11 LX(R)s (the replacement for LSDs), 1 every other year between 2020 and 2028 and then 1 per year until 2034, to replace existing dock landing ships in the LSD-41 and LSD-49 classes. Under the 2015 plan, the LX(R) would enter the fleet one year later than under the 2014 plan. (This is the third consecutive shipbuilding plan in which the Navy has delayed the start of the LSD replacement class by one year.) The 2015 plan would also start replacing the LPD-17 class with a new class in the early 2040s, buying 1 ship each in 2040, 2042, and 2044.

The Navy also intends to keep the existing class of LHD-1 amphibious assault ships in service for 43 to 45 years. That expectation, which was also stated in the 2013 and 2014 plans, represents an increase relative to the 40-year service life incorporated in the 2012 plan.

With that procurement schedule and those intended service lives, the total number of amphibious warfare ships would be at or above the goal of 33 ships for about two-thirds of the 30-year period covered by the plan (see Figure 4 on page 9). After 2015, the number of such ships would never fall short of the goal by more than 2 ships.

The Navy estimates that the LHA 6 class amphibious assault ships will cost $3.7 billion apiece. CBO's estimate for those ships is slightly higher: an average of $4.0 billion per ship. Both CBO and the Navy assumed that the LHA-6 class ship authorized for 2016 and all subsequent amphibious assault ships would include well decks, necessitating some redesign of the LHA 6 class—and therefore additional costs. (Well decks are large floodable areas in the sterns of most amphibious warfare ships that allow amphibious vehicles and craft to be launched directly from the ships.) Those costs are included in both the Navy's and CBO's estimates.

For the LX(R), the Navy estimates an average cost of $1.4 billion per ship. Since the publication of the Navy's 2015 plan, press reports have indicated that the service wants the LX(R) to be based on the hull of the LPD-17, which is much larger than existing LSDs. An LPD-17 ordered today would cost about $2.1 billion. Therefore, to meet its estimate for the cost of the LX(R), the Navy would need to make significant changes to the ships and the manner in which it buys them. First, the LX(R) variant of the LPD-17 would need to have substantially less capability than the LPD-17 class. The Navy has not yet released any specifications or details about the capabilities it intends to include in the LX(R).

Second, the Navy would need to adopt a competitive process for procurement and probably also ask the Congress to give it multiyear, or "block buy," authority to purchase ships— or at least their materials—in batches of 5 to 10. Such authority would be similar to the multiyear contracts the Navy employs for the Arleigh Burke class destroyers and to the block buy contracts the Navy uses for Virginia class attack submarines and littoral combat ships. If the Navy did open the LX(R) to competition, the shipyards bidding for the right to build the ships would probably incorporate the benefits of those types of contracts into their bids.

Based on the limited information available now, CBO estimates the cost of the LX(R) at an average of $1.8 billion per ship. CBO used the existing LPD-17 hull as the starting point for its estimate and then adjusted the ship's size to reflect the reduced capability it expects for the LX(R). CBO's estimate also accounts for the use of multiyear or block buy procurement authority in a potentially competitive environment. Various factors could cause the actual cost to be above or below the estimate. For example, it is not clear that the Navy would be able to conduct a full and open competition for the LX(R) in light of the fact that the yard currently building the LPD-17 class, Ingalls of Huntington-Ingalls Industries, would presumably enter the bidding with a significant advantage. The Navy might also have a limited ability to benefit from competition for the LX(R) if the Congress directed the Navy to ensure that all of the shipyards building the Navy's ships received enough business to remain profitable.

In contrast, if the Navy designs and builds the LX(R) in ways that are substantially different from the methods used for the LPD-17, then the cost of the new ships could be less than CBO estimates.

APPENDIX: COMPARISON OF CBO'S AND THE NAVY'S COST ESTIMATES FOR INDIVIDUAL SHIP PROGRAMS

Each year the Navy provides estimates of the costs of building each class of ship in its 30-year shipbuilding plan. The Congressional Budget Office also produces annual estimates. Table A-1 presents a comparison of the two sets of figures for the past four 30-year plans.

Table A-1. Difference Between CBO's and the Navy's Cost Estimates for Individual Ship Programs

Percentage of Total Cost Difference **Ship Program**	**2012 Plan**	**2013 Plan**	**2014 Plan**	**2015 Plan**
CVN-78 Gerald R. Ford Class Aircraft Carriers	18	13	3	3
Ohio Replacement Ballistic Missile Submarines	15	13	12	20
Virginia Class Attack Submarines	1	1	-1	3
Improved Virginia Class Attack Submarines				
(Replacements for Virginia class)	3	4	-3	8
DDG-51 Arleigh Burke Class Destroyers				
Flight IIA	3	0	0	0
Flight III	-7	11	7	11
DDG(X) Destroyers (Replacements for Arleigh Burke class)	41	34	58	38
Littoral Combat Ships	1	3	4	5
LCS(X)s (Replacements for littoral combat ships)	5	4	7	0
LX(R)s (Replacements for amphibious dock landing ships)	5	4	4	5
LHA-6 Amphibious Assault Ships	7	5	5	3
T-AO(X) Oilers	0	0	1	1
Other	8	7	4	4
Total	**100**	**100**	**100**	**100**
Memorandum:				
Difference in Billions of Dollars[a]	74	94	76	66

Source: Congressional Budget Office.

Note: Numbers reflect the percentage of the total cost difference between CBO's and the Navy's estimates for each plan: Positive values indicate instances in which CBO's estimate is higher; negative values, instances in which the Navy's is higher.

[a] For each plan, the difference is expressed in constant dollars from the preceding year. For instance, the value for the 2012 plan is expressed in 2011 dollars; for the 2013 plan, in 2012 dollars; and so on.

End Notes

[1] Department of the Navy, *Report to Congress on the Annual Long-Range Plan for Construction of Naval Vessels for FY 2015* (June 2014), http://go.usa.gov/FYZR (PDF, 3.4 MB).

[2] In a reduced status, the ships would not be operated and would have only caretaker crews. Because they would not be retired, though, they could be restored to full operational status in a year's time.

[3] Department of the Navy, *Report to Congress: Navy Combatant Vessel Force Structure Requirement* (January 2013), http://tinyurl.com/kvhspjs. Battle force ships comprise aircraft carriers, submarines, surface combatants, amphibious warfare ships, and combat logistics and some support ships. For a more extensive discussion of the history of the Navy's force structure goals, see Ronald O'Rourke, *Navy Force Structure and Shipbuilding Plans: Background and Issues for Congress*, Report for Congress RL32665 (Congressional Research Service, August 1, 2014).

[4] See Congressional Budget Office, *Resource Implications of the Navy's Fiscal Year 2009 Shipbuilding Plan* (June 9, 2008), p. 25, www.cbo.gov/publication/41703.

[5] See Congressional Budget Office, *An Analysis of the Navy's Fiscal Year 2014 Shipbuilding Plan* (October 2013), p. 26, www.cbo.gov/publication/44655.

[6] The afloat forward staging base is a ship designed to remain on station overseas for long periods of time, providing support to other naval forces, such as special operations units, patrol craft, or minesweepers.

[7] Department of the Navy, *Report to Congress on the Annual Long-Range Plan for Construction of Naval Vessels for FY 2015* (June 2014), p. 13, http://go.usa.gov/FYZR (PDF, 3.4 MB).

[8] The Navy has funded shipbuilding through two accounts: Shipbuilding and Conversion, Navy (commonly called the SCN account) and the National Defense Sealift Fund (NDSF), which includes, among other things, funding for the procurement of some types of logistics ships. With the 2015 budget, the Navy proposes disestablishing the NDSF and funding all ships through the SCN account.

[9] Department of the Navy, *Report to Congress on the Annual Long-Range Plan for Construction of Naval Vessels for FY 2015* (June 2014), p. 10, http://go.usa.gov/FYZR (PDF, 3.4 MB).

[10] In 2010, the Navy transferred funding for refueling nuclear-powered submarines to other accounts (Other Procurement, Navy; Operation and Maintenance, Navy; and Weapons Procurement, Navy) that are not used to purchase ships. Therefore, CBO did not include the refueling costs for submarines in its estimates of future shipbuilding costs.

[11] The service life of submarines is determined by many factors; two major ones are the condition of their hulls and the energy remaining in their reactor cores. Submarines can only "cycle"—that is, submerge and surface a limited number of times before they need to be retired. In addition, after a nuclear reactor has produced a certain amount of energy, it needs to be retired. Some nuclear submarines can be refueled if the hull has remaining life, but those submarines with "life of the ship" reactor plants cannot be refueled.

[12] For a broader discussion of historical cost trends in Navy shipbuilding, see the testimony of Eric J. Labs, Senior Analyst for Naval Forces and Weapons, Congressional Budget Office, before the Subcommittee on Seapower and Expeditionary Forces of the House Committee on Armed Services, *The Long-Term Outlook for the U.S. Navy's Fleet* (January 20, 2010), www.cbo.gov/ publication/41886.

[13] In its report accompanying the 2014 National Defense Authorization Act, the House Committee on Armed Services directed the Navy to provide to the Congress a similar

illustration of a shipbuilding plan (starting in 2015) that conforms to historical funding levels. The Navy has not yet responded to that Congressional directive.

[14] The alternative plan would also fund one fewer carrier refueling.

[15] For a more thorough discussion of the Budget Control Act and its effect on the Department of Defense, see Congressional Budget Office, *Approaches for Scaling Back the Defense Department's Budget Plans* (March 2013), www.cbo.gov/publication/43997.

[16.] Department of Defense, *Estimated Impacts of Sequestration-Level Funding: United States Department of Defense Fiscal Year 2015 Budget Request* (April 2014), pp. 3-3, 4-7 to 4-9, http://go.usa.gov/sZkJ (PDF, 2.2 MB).

[17] Sam Langrone, "Stackley: Navy Plans to Refuel Carrier *George Washington*," *USNI News* (July 10, 2014), http://tinyurl.com/ mwoodta.

[18] To lower costs, the President's 2015 budget proposed putting in a reduced status ("laying up") 11 cruisers and 1 amphibious ship. (The Navy actually proposed laying up 3 amphibious ships, but it would do so sequentially, so there would be only 1 amphibious ship in a reduced status at any point in time.) The budget also proposed modernizing those ships to extend their service life.

[19] In addition, if the Navy ultimately does not refuel the U.S.S. *George Washington*, the carrier force would fall to 9 through early 2016 and then remain at 10 until 2023.

[20] In its 2015 budget request, the Navy asked for an extra $787 million in nominal dollars in 2015 and 2016 to cover cost growth and additional tooling and vendor services, most of which was anticipated in the 2014 budget request. That amount is included in the Navy's estimate of the total cost to complete the ship.

[21] Using a different method, the Navy estimated that the $12.9 billion cost in nominal dollars for the lead ship would equate to just over $15 billion in 2014 dollars. The Navy's calculation is based on a unique method that is not comparable to CBO's method for estimating costs in constant dollars and is not used by the Navy to estimate costs in constant dollars for any other shipbuilding program. If CBO used the Navy's unique method to convert its own estimate for the carrier program (which involves using different carrier-specific inflation indexes for different cost components of the ship) from nominal dollars to constant dollars, CBO's estimate for the cost of the CVN 78 would still be about $600 million more than the Navy's.

[22] For more information, see Ronald O'Rourke, *Navy SSBN(X) Ballistic Missile Submarine Program: Background and Issues for Congress,* Report for Congress R41129 (Congressional Research Service, July 31, 2014); and the testimony of Eric J. Labs, Senior Analyst for Naval Forces and Weapons, Congressional Budget Office, before the Subcommittee on Seapower and Expeditionary Forces of the House Committee on Armed Services, *The Long-Term Outlook for the U.S. Navy's Fleet* (January 20, 2010), www.cbo.gov/publication/41886.

[23] Briefing by the Navy to the staff of the House Committee on Armed Services, CBO, and the Congressional Research Service, February 28, 2011. The Navy's numbers in that briefing, expressed in 2010 dollars, were $5.6 billion for the average follow-on submarine, with an objective of reducing that cost to $4.9 billion. Although the Navy's 2015 plan does not yet reflect it, the Navy's Ohio Replacement Program Office currently estimates that it has already reduced the cost to $5.4 billion in 2010 dollars.

[24] Specifically, the Navy has said that to purchase 2 Virginia class submarines a year, the cost would have to decline to $2.0 billion each in 2005 dollars, which is equivalent to $2.8 billion in 2014 dollars.

[25] See the testimony of Eric J. Labs, Senior Analyst, Congressional Budget Office, before the Subcommittee on Seapower and Expeditionary Forces of the House Committee on Armed Services, *The Navy's Surface Combatant Programs* (July 31, 2008), www.cbo.gov /publication/20065.

[26] For a detailed discussion of the differences between the DDG-51 flights, see Norman Polmar, *The Naval Institute Guide to the Ships and Aircraft of the U.S. Fleet,* 19th ed. (Naval Institute Press, 2013), pp. 140–145.

[27] The Navy has announced that all existing DDG-51s will eventually be equipped with improved ballistic missile defenses; up to 33 of those upgrades were funded by the end of fiscal year 2014. For more about the Navy's plans for the DDG-51 program, see Ronald O'Rourke, *Navy DDG-51 and DDG-1000 Destroyer Programs: Background and Issues for Congress,* Report for Congress RL32109 (Congressional Research Service, July 31, 2014).

[28] Combatant commanders—the four-star generals or admirals who head the regional commands—are responsible for all U.S. military operations within their geographic areas.

[29] See Ronald O'Rourke, *Navy Aegis Ballistic Missile Defense (BMD) Program: Background and Issues for Congress,* Report for Congress RL33745 (Congressional Research Service, November 7, 2014), and *Navy DDG-51 and DDG-1000 Destroyer Programs: Background and Issues for Congress,* Report for Congress RL32109 (Congressional Research Service, July 31, 2014). Press reports indicate that some Navy officials do not agree with the DDG-51 Flight III strategy and would prefer to build Flight IIAs a little longer while designing an entirely new destroyer that would allow for greater growth potential in all respects. See Christopher P. Cavas, "U.S. Navy Weighs Halving LCS Order," *Defense News* (March 17, 2013), http://tinyurl.com/kbey7qp.

[30] As a point of comparison, the Navy's first Flight IIA ship—the DDG-79, which incorporated such changes as a helicopter hangar and a larger displacement—cost about 20 percent more than the DDG-78. The transition from the Flight IIA to Flight III ships is expected to involve more extensive changes than the transition from the Flight I/II to Flight IIA ships.

[31] That retirement date is based on the Navy's assumption that all DDG-51 Flight IIAs will be modernized midway through their service life and will operate for 40 years.

[32] Department of the Navy, *Report to Congress on the Annual Long-Range Plan for Construction of Naval Vessels for FY 2015* (June 2014), p. 15, http://go.usa.gov/FYZR (PDF, 3.4 MB). This description did not appear in previous shipbuilding plans.

[33] Department of the Navy, *Report to Congress: Littoral Combat Ship Mission Packages* (May 2009).

[34] For more detail on the LCS program, see Ronald O'Rourke, *Navy Littoral Combat Ship (LCS) Program: Background and Issues for Congress*, Report for Congress RL33741 (Congressional Research Service, August 4, 2014).

[35] Although the Navy already has 20 LCSs in its fleet or under construction, 4 of those ships were purchased between 2005 and 2009 prior to the two 10-ship contracts. Thus, the Navy needs to purchase 4 more ships to complete those contracts.

[36] Secretary of Defense Chuck Hagel, memorandum to the Secretary of the Navy and Chief of Naval Operations on the Littoral Combat Ship Program (February 24, 2014).

[37] The National Defense Authorization Act for Fiscal Year 2010, which set the LCS cost cap that would apply to ships purchased in fiscal year 2010 and beyond, gave the Secretary of the Navy authority to waive compliance with the cap if doing so was considered in "the best interest of the United States," if the ship was "affordable, within the context of the annual naval vessel construction plan," or in other specific circumstances.

[38] There is a seven-year gap between the ship purchased in 2017 and the next one purchased in 2024. After that, however, the LHA class is purchased at a rate of 1 every four years.

In: U.S. Navy Force Structure ...
Editor: Agnes S. Jennings

ISBN: 978-1-63482-939-7

Chapter 4

CREW ROTATION IN THE NAVY: THE LONG-TERM EFFECT ON FORWARD PRESENCE*

Eric Labs

PREFACE

The Navy today deploys most of its ships with single crews. Thus, when a ship goes on deployment, the crew that takes it out of port is the same crew that brings it back, normally six months later. For some ships, however, the Navy employs a variety of dual-crew or multi-crew concepts to increase the amount of time that those ships can spend on-station in their operating areas overseas. In some cases, such as with ballistic missile submarines, crew rotation means that two crews alternate taking a single ship out for relatively short deployments from its home port (usually for less than three months). In other cases, three or more crews successively rotate to a ship while it is deployed overseas so the ship can stay on-station for longer periods and thus provide more "forward presence." In the past few years, the Navy has experimented with the latter approach by rotating crews to large surface combatants in order to increase the amount of forward presence they provide.

The John Warner National Defense Authorization Act for Fiscal Year 2007 directed the Congressional Budget Office (CBO) to prepare a report examining different approaches to crew rotation, the amount of forward

* This is an edited, reformatted and augmented version of a report issued by the Congressional Budget Office, October 2007.

presence that the Navy's future fleet could provide with and without greater use of crew rotation, and the advantages and disadvantages of such a change. This paper responds to that directive. In keeping with CBO's mandate to provide objective, impartial analysis, it contains no recommendations.

Peter R. Orszag
Director

SUMMARY

Crew rotation—the practice of using more than one crew to operate a single ship—has attracted growing attention in the Navy in recent years. Under conventional crewing concepts, one crew is assigned to each naval vessel and operates it on all deployments and training cruises. (Individual personnel join or leave the crew as part of their normal career rotations.) On a small number of ships, however, the Navy employs rotation systems in which two or more crews take turns manning a particular ship. The purpose of crew rotation is to increase the amount of time that a ship spends operating overseas— providing "forward presence"—compared with conventional single crewing.

The Navy currently uses crew rotation on ballistic missile submarines, mine-countermeasures ships, and coastal patrol craft. According to the service, that approach has worked well. Between 2002 and 2006, the Navy experimented with rotating crews to individual Spruance class or Arleigh Burke class destroyers while those ships were deployed overseas. The Navy concluded that those experiments were a success. Nonetheless, the Navy does not plan to employ crew rotation on large numbers of those types of ships in the foreseeable future because it says it does not need to. The Navy expects to have enough cruisers and destroyers in its inventory over the next 30 years to meet its requirements for forward presence by using single-crewed ships. However, the service plans to use rotating crews on the new class of littoral combat ships (LCSs) that it has begun building, in order to meet the forward-presence requirement that the Department of Defense (DoD) has set for those ships.

This report describes the different approaches to crew rotation that the Navy uses today, has experimented with, or plans to employ. It also analyzes the forward-presence and force-structure implications of using or not using crew rotation on the Navy's surface combat ships. That analysis suggests the following conclusions:

- If the Navy employs crew rotation on its planned new classes of cruisers and destroyers, it would probably be able to provide substantially more overseas presence than it can today using single crews.
- If the Navy's plan to use rotating crews on littoral combat ships does not prove viable, the service will need to buy an additional 30 LCSs to meet DoD's current forward-presence requirement for those ships.
- If the Navy cannot fully execute its latest long-term shipbuilding plan because of fiscal constraints—resulting in a smaller fleet of cruisers and destroyers—using rotating crews on some of those ships may allow the Navy to meet its current and projected forward-presence requirements for large surface combatants despite having fewer ships.

Crew rotation has several potential drawbacks, however. Depending on the type of rotation scheme used, crews may have less familiarity with the ship they are going to operate and thus a reduced sense of "ownership" about it. Crew rotation is also more complex to administer than single crewing—although the success of rotational crewing on the Navy's strategic submarines suggests that once the transition to crew rotation is complete, administering the practice becomes routine. Finally, crew proficiency, morale, and retention are not necessarily as high as they would be on single-crewed ships. The extent of those problems may depend on the size of the ship (and thus of the crew), the nature of the ship's mission, and the amount of time that a particular crew rotation concept has been in use. Long-standing rotation practices work better than more-recent or experimental ones.

In addition, the costs or savings of crew rotation (compared with the costs of equivalent single-crewed ships) vary by type of rotation scheme. Dual-crew concepts, such as those used on ballistic missile submarines—in which two crews take turns operating a single ship—can entail increased one-time and recurring costs. One time costs can be higher because of the need to spend more on designing and building a class of ships for dual-crew use and the need for more-elaborate training and maintenance facilities. Recurring costs can be higher because there are twice as many personnel per ship and because more maintenance is necessary when ships are at sea for longer periods. In return, dual-crewed ships spend far more time on-station in their areas of operations than their single-crewed counterparts do.

Other versions of crew rotation—in which ships are divided into groups of three or four and their crews take turns operating one of the ships, which is kept deployed overseas for a long time—may actually save money, principally from reduced fuel consumption. However, the amount of additional time that such ships spend on-station is much less than under the dual-crew model used for submarines. So far, the Navy has limited such multi-crewing concepts to small surface combatants and its three recent experiments with destroyers.

Crew Rotation in the Navy Today

Although most U.S. naval vessels are operated by a single crew that stays with a ship whether it is in its home port or at sea, the Navy employs crew rotation schemes on some of its ships and submarines. Those rotation systems, which take various forms, have the same goal: to increase the time a ship can spend away from home providing forward presence in its area of operations.

The longest running and most formal crew rotation scheme in the Navy is the dual-crew system that has been used on ballistic missile submarines (SSBNs) since they were first deployed in 1960. The Navy is converting four of its SSBNs to a guided missile configuration; it plans to continue using a dual-crew system on those submarines as well. In recent years, the Navy has begun routinely using multiple, rotating crews on its Cyclone class patrol craft and Avenger class mine-countermeasures ships. In addition, dual crews—modeled on the SSBN system— are used on the Navy's single high-speed ferry ship, the *Swift* (also known as HSV-2).

The Navy has looked into extending crew rotation to parts of its fleet of surface combatants. Between 2002 and 2006, it conducted three experiments that involved rotating crews to forward-deployed destroyers. The Navy also plans to deploy the first of its new littoral combat ships (LCSs)—small vessels designed to operate in coastal waters—with a yet-to-be-defined dual-crewing system, at least initially. (As more LCSs are commissioned, the Navy may use multiple, rotating crews on those ships.) Moreover, when the Navy unveiled its fiscal year 2007 plan for a 313-ship fleet, it told the Congressional Budget Office (CBO) that it would adopt a crew rotation scheme for the new DDG-1000 Zumwalt class destroyers, which it began ordering this year. However, in updating its 313- ship plan for fiscal year 2008, the Navy said in a briefing to CBO and the Congressional Research Service that it intends to use single crews on those destroyers.

The Blue/Gold System for Ballistic Missile and Guided Missile Submarines

Since the first patrol of the first ballistic missile submarine, the *George Washington,* each SSBN has been assigned two full, alternating crews: the blue crew and the gold crew. The nuclear missiles that those George Washington class submarines carried had relatively short ranges, and to be an effective deterrent, the submarines had to operate relatively close to the Soviet Union. To reduce time spent going back and forth from the continental United States, the SSBNs operated out of forward bases in Holy Loch, Scotland; Rota, Spain; and the Pacific island of Guam. Crew exchanges took place there, as did lower-level maintenance on the submarines (with the support of a submarine tender). More-substantial maintenance work, such as that requiring a dry dock, was performed in the United States.

The purpose of the dual crewing and forward basing was to increase the time that those SSBNs—which were seen as better able to survive attack than any other U.S. system for delivering nuclear weapons—could spend deployed on-station. Those practices allowed more than half of the SSBN force to be at sea and operational at any given time. (The equivalent figure for the Navy's surface combatant force is about one-fifth.)

Changes to Facilitate Dual Crewing on Current-Generation SSBNs. In the 1970s, when the Navy decided to replace the George Washington class SSBNs, it developed a new generation of ballistic missile submarine (the Ohio class) and a new submarine-launched nuclear ballistic missile (the Trident) specifically with dual crewing in mind. The development program incorporated a number of features to make maintenance and training easier, thus allowing the submarines to spend less time in port.

First, whereas the early George Washington class SSBNs were attack submarines that had been modified to carry ballistic missiles, the Ohio class submarines were specifically designed and engineered for that role.[1] They include features intended to speed up maintenance, such as an extra-large hatch (called a logistics escape trunk) and removable decks to facilitate the quick replacement of large pieces of equipment. (Removing large items from an attack submarine, by contrast, may require dismantling them onboard the sub, which takes time, or cutting a hole in the hull to remove them.)

Second, the Navy instituted the Trident Planned Equipment Replacement Program for conducting periodic, large-scale equipment changes to ensure that Trident- carrying submarines operate with "like-new" equipment during each deployment. Rather than wait for equipment to fail and be replaced as needed, the Navy replaces equipment on those submarines on a regular schedule. The maintenance facilities at the Trident submarine bases in Kings Bay, Georgia, and Bangor, Washington, include large dry docks, rail-mobile pier-side cranes to quickly remove or insert big pieces of equipment in the submarines, and advanced machine shops. In addition, those facilities are given enough resources to ensure a readily available supply of parts. In those ways, the shore infrastructure for the SSBNs is designed to maximize their availability for deployment.

Third, the Trident Training Facility at each submarine base is more extensive than the training facilities for other Navy ships. Crews that are not on deployment train onshore in facilities that appear virtually identical to those they will use on the submarines at sea.

How the Dual-Crew System Works for Submarines. The Navy operates Trident SSBNs on a 224-day cycle (see Figure 1). One of a submarine's two crews takes the submarine to sea for 77 days and then returns it to its home port. Both crews then perform maintenance on the submarine for a 35-day period, after which the second crew takes the submarine to sea for 77 days before returning it to the home port for further maintenance. After that, the cycle begins again.

Because the principal mission of an SSBN is to provide deterrent patrols with strategic weapons, and because the Trident D-5 missile has a range of about 7,000 miles, an SSBN is effectively considered on-station soon after it leaves its home port in the continental United States. As a result, Trident SSBNs spend a majority of their service life at sea on-station, compared with about 20 percent of the time for a single-crewed attack submarine or surface combatant.[2]

The four SSBNs that the Navy is converting into guided missile submarines (SSGNs) will use a modified blue/ gold crewing system that has the same advantages for maintenance and training as the system for SSBNs. However, their different missions and weaponry mean that those guided missile submarines will follow a much longer operating cycle: 461 days (see Figure 1). SSGNs are armed with cruise missiles that have roughly one-seventh the range of Trident D-5 missiles, and they are intended to perform land-attack or special-operations missions (as well as providing forward presence in peacetime). For those reasons, SSGNs need to operate much farther away from the continental United States than ballistic missile submarines do.

In the Navy's planned deployment cycle for SSGNs, one crew will take a submarine on deployment for 73 days. After that, the SSGN will spend 23 days at an overseas port, during which time the second crew will arrive and both crews will perform maintenance on the submarine, probably with the support of a submarine tender. The first crew will then fly back to the United States—where it will train at onshore facilities—and the second crew will take the SSGN to sea for 73 more days. That part of the cycle is repeated once, and then the submarine returns to the United States for 100 days of maintenance in its home port.

Unlike a ballistic missile submarine, an SSGN is generally not considered on-station for the entire time it is deployed. Of the 361 days it is away from its home port, 56 are spent going to and from the theater of operations, loading and unloading equipment from the submarine's dry-deck shelter, and undergoing the certifications and inspections that are required as part of the crew-exchange process. Consequently, the SSGN provides forward presence for 305 days of its 461-day cycle, or about the same percentage of time that an SSBN spends performing its mission.

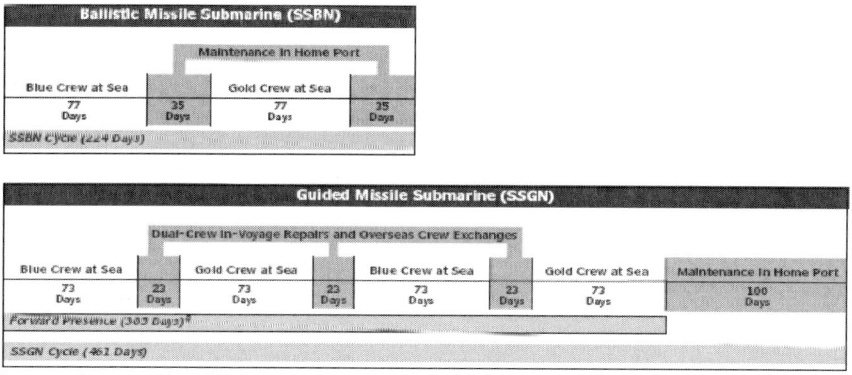

Source: Congressional Budget Office based on data from the Navy.

[a] Of the 361 days the SSGN is on deployment, 56 days are used for transit to and from the theater of operations, loading and unloading of equipment, and certifications and inspections following crew exchanges. Those 56 days do not count as forward presence.

Figure 1. Deployment Cycles of Ballistic Missile and Guided Missile Submarines.

THE BLUE/GOLD SYSTEM FOR THE *U.S.S. SWIFT*

The *Swift* (also known by its designation HSV-2, for high-speed vessel) is a small, fast catamaran that the Navy has leased from a private contractor since 2003. The ship is used to test new technologies and concepts for mine warfare, logistical support, and other missions, as well as to support humanitarian operations and exercises with U.S. allies.

From the time the Navy acquired the *Swift,* it has operated the ship with a blue/gold crewing system modeled on that of ballistic missile submarines. The blue crew is based in Ingleside, Texas, and the gold crew in Little Creek, Virginia. Each crew operates the ship for about 117 days, with crew exchanges occurring wherever the ship happens to be at the end of that period. (In the past, those exchanges have taken place in the continental United States, Hawaii, Guam, Bahrain, Cyprus, and other locations.) As a result, since the Navy began operating it, the *Swift* has been out of its home port and available for missions more than 80 percent of the time.

Because the *Swift* is leased and is unique in the Navy, its maintenance is handled differently than that of SSBNs. Minor repairs are done by the individual crews, but more-substantial maintenance is performed by a contractor through the Military Sealift Command (the agency that provides, operates, and maintains most of the transport and support ships of the Department of Defense).

Table 1. Navy Ships That Have Used Crew Rotation

	Displacement When Fully Loaded (Long tons)	Crew Size
Ohio Class Ballistic Missile		
Submarines	18,400	160
Swift High-Speed Ferry	1,700	40
Cyclone Class Coastal Patrol Ships	331	28
Avenger Class Mine-Countermeasures Ships	1,300	83
Spruance Class Destroyers	9,300	346
Arleigh Burke Class Destroyers	9,200	340

Source: Congressional Budget Office based on Norman Polmar, The Naval Institute Guide to the Ships and Aircraft of the U.S. Fleet, 18th ed. (Annapolis, Md.: Naval Institute Press, 2005).

The *Swift* is relatively simple to operate, so the Navy does not maintain dedicated training facilities for the shore-based crew. Instead, at the beginning of a crew exchange, the incoming sailors conduct a series of tests and drills to ensure that they are proficient in running the ship.

MULTICREWING ON COASTAL PATROL SHIPS

The Navy's fleet includes eight Cyclone class coastal patrol ships, three of which have their home port in Little Creek, Virginia, and five in Bahrain. Those vessels, which are just one-fifth the size of the *Swift,* are among the smallest ships operated by the Navy (see Table 1). To support them, the Navy uses 13 crews that rotate back and forth from Bahrain. Five crews deploy to the five ships homeported in Bahrain for six months at a time. The other eight crews stay in Virginia with the three remaining patrol ships for eight to nine months, after which they rotate to one of the overseas vessels. Six of those eight crews are assigned to the three Virginia-based Cyclones (two crews per ship) for training. The two crews not assigned to a ship use onshore facilities for additional training courses. During the training phase, crews may change ships, and during the deployment phase, they may return to a different ship than they operated during their previous deployment.

In essence, that system is a hybrid of the Navy's practices of having some ships and crews homeported overseas and having other ships and crews homeported in the United States that then go on routine deployments. Navy ships normally deploy for six months if they are stationed in the United States. Likewise, Cyclone crews go on six-month deployments, although their ships remain based either in Bahrain or Virginia. That system allows the Navy to count five of the eight patrol ships as being forward deployed 100 percent of the time—resulting in a deployment rate for the force of 62 percent, only slightly less than that of the SSBN force.[3] Maintenance on the patrol boats is performed by the crew and contractors in the ships' home ports.

According to the Navy, that multicrewing approach has several advantages. It allows for a high level of forward presence with the five ships stationed in Bahrain, while requiring crew members to be deployed only about 40 percent of the time over a five-year period. In addition, it saves the Navy from having to get the patrol ships overseas, which would be costly if the Cyclones were transported on larger, ship-carrying vessels or would cause wear and tear on the Cyclones if they made the transoceanic voyages themselves.

DUAL CREWING AND MULTICREWING ON MINE-COUNTERMEASURES SHIPS

The Navy operates 14 Avenger class ships, which are designed to find and destroy mines at sea. Two of the ships are based in Japan, where they are operated by single crews. Four others are based permanently in Bahrain, and the remaining eight are stationed in Ingleside, Texas. Those 12 ships are operated by 12 crews using a rotation system.

Eight crews, divided into four blue/gold pairs, are assigned to the four ships in Bahrain and to four ships in Texas. While a blue crew is operating its ship in Bahrain, its gold counterpart is operating a ship in Texas and training to go on deployment to relieve the blue crew. Four other crews, designated silver, operate the four remaining Texas-based Avengers. Those crews train on and maintain their own ships and also take custody of other Texas-based ships when a blue or gold crew leaves for a crew exchange in Bahrain.

The sailors assigned to the blue or gold crews spend about half of their time deployed (alternating four months in Bahrain with four months in Texas). The silver crews are not part of the overseas deployment rotation; instead, they serve in a logistical and support function for the crews that do deploy. As in the case of Cyclone patrol ships, the families of the Avenger crews remain stationed in Texas.

The advantages of that crewing arrangement are similar to those of the system for coastal patrol craft. The Navy uses three ships to keep one providing overseas presence full time. In addition, as with the Cyclones, the Navy forgoes the wear and tear on the ships' hulls associated with deploying from the United States or the expense involved in transporting the ships overseas. According to the Navy, the crews generally like that schedule because they are not deployed overseas for more than four months at a time. When they are deployed, they maintain a high level of operational availability for the theater commanders who assign them missions.

THE NAVY'S SEA SWAP EXPERIMENTS WITH DESTROYERS

Between 2002 and 2006, the Navy conducted three experiments with extending multiple crewing to destroyers, the workhorses of the surface combatant fleet. Those experiments, called Sea Swap, aimed to determine whether the Navy could effectively keep a destroyer overseas longer by rotating crews to the ship, thus providing more forward presence than if the destroyer repeatedly deployed from the United States. The first two experiments were conducted by the Navy's Pacific Fleet Command using Spruance and Arleigh Burke class destroyers. A third experiment was conducted by Fleet Forces Command (FFC)—the Navy's principal entity for organizing, training, and equipping forces for assignment to regional combatant commanders—to refine and improve the Sea Swap concept.

Overall, the Navy was pleased with the results of those experiments. The destroyers that used rotating crews were able to provide significantly more forward presence over a given period than similar ships crewed the traditional way, with few significant negative side-effects for the ships or their crews. The cost implications of using rotational crewing on those ships are not yet clear, however.

The Traditional Single-Crew Concept for Deploying Surface Combatants

Under the Navy's normal crewing concept for surface combatants, one crew operates one ship. The crew spends 12 to 18 months training and performing maintenance on the ship to prepare it for deployment. At the end of that period, the crew takes the ship on a six-month deployment, after which the crew and the ship return to their home port, and the cycle begins again. Most of the Navy's surface combatants are based in San Diego, California, or Norfolk, Virginia—the main naval bases on the West and East Coasts of the United States.

Unlike a Trident submarine, which is on-station almost from the time it leaves its home port, a surface combatant does not arrive on-station until it reaches its area of operations overseas. How long that takes depends on whether the ship is leaving from the East or West Coast and whether it is assigned to European Command, Pacific Command, or Central Command (which has responsibility for the Middle East, the Horn of Africa, Central Asia, and parts of the Indian Ocean). That amount of time also depends on how fast the ship sails and on the number and duration of stops it makes along the way. (An important perk of deploying overseas on a Navy ship is the opportunity to visit "liberty ports" where sailors can go ashore for several days to enjoy the sights, sounds, and foods of other countries.) In a routine deployment, a Navy ship can take between three and six weeks to arrive on-station.[4]

With that traditional single-crewing concept, the Navy needs a force of six surface combatants to keep one on-station at all times in Central Command—or a rotation ratio of 6 to 1. For European Command or Pacific Command, the analogous ratio is 4.5 to 1. The goal of the Sea Swap experiments was to try to reduce those ratios by gaining more forward presence from a given group of ships.

Pacific Command's Sea Swap Experiment with Spruance Class Destroyers

The first experiment began in 2002 and included four Spruance class destroyers: the *Fletcher,* the *Kinkaid,* the *Oldendorf,* and the *Elliott.* All of those ships were slated to be retired within two years. The *Fletcher* deployed to the western Pacific and Indian Ocean areas of operation in August 2002 and remained on-station for almost two years, with a crew from one of the other three ships rotating to it every six months. Those other destroyers remained in the United States, where their crews performed the usual routine of training and preparing to deploy with their ships. But when a crew's turn came to rotate to the *Fletcher,* its regular ship was decommissioned. Crew exchanges took place in Australia, Singapore, and the United Arab Emirates. At the end of the *Fletcher*'s two-year deployment, the last crew brought her back to the United States and the ship was retired.

That crewing experiment produced a significant increase in the amount of forward presence provided by the Sea.

Swap ships compared with an equivalent number of traditionally deployed ships (see Figure 2). A single-crewed Spruance class destroyer deploying from the West Coast to the western Pacific would provide 100 days of forward presence per 180-day deployment (with the rest of the time spent in transit, at liberty ports, or in training). Thus, four of those ships would provide a total of 400 days of presence. In comparison, the four ships and crews involved in the first Sea Swap experiment provided 509 days of forward presence, or an average of 127 days per ship—a 27 percent improvement over traditional deployments.

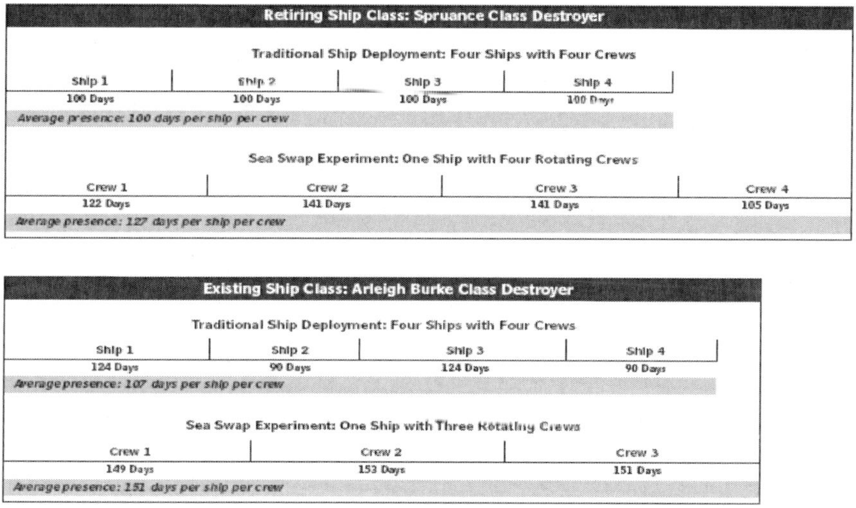

Source: Congressional Budget Office based on data from the Navy.

Notes: The numbers shown here are for operations in the U.S. Central Command's area of responsibility (which includes the Indian Ocean, the Persian Gulf, and the Red Sea).

The Spruance class experiment was conducted by Pacific Command and thus used only Pacific Fleet destroyers for the comparison group. The Arleigh Burke class experiment was conducted by Fleet Forces Command and used a mix of Pacific Fleet and Atlantic Fleet destroyers for the comparison group.

The entire deployment for any destroyer or (in the case of the Sea Swap experiments) destroyer crew was 180 days. The difference between that figure and the number of days of forward presence a ship actually provided reflects time spent sailing to and from the theater of operations. Some additional time may have been spent at a liberty port outside the theater of operations.

Figure 2. Overseas Presence Provided by Sea Swap Experiments Compared with Traditional Ship Deployments.

Beginning in late 2002, Pacific Command conducted a second Sea Swap trial using Arleigh Burke class destroyers. That experiment is not discussed here, however, because it was similar in concept and results to the third Sea Swap test (by Fleet Forces Command using Arleigh Burke class destroyers), which is described in detail below. In addition, the Navy collected much more data for the FFC experiment than it did for the Pacific Command experiments.

What Pacific Command wanted from its Sea Swap tests was to prove that more presence could be provided by rotating crews to a forward-deployed ship. On that basis, Pacific Command deemed Sea Swap a success. Because of that emphasis, the data that the Navy collected in the experiment focused on how the crew exchanges worked, the readiness of the crews when the exchanges took place, and what shore-based infrastructure was needed to support crew rotation. The Navy did not collect data on the costs of the experiment or compare the material condition of the multicrewed ships with that of traditionally operating ships.

From the Navy's perspective, a principal advantage of the Spruance class experiment (aside from providing more forward presence) was that the Navy did not have to spend as much money on ship maintenance. The Navy aims to send its ships overseas in very good material condition. However, since the *Kinkaid,* the *Oldendorf,* and the *Elliott* were being decommissioned rather than deployed, the Navy did not provide the normal amount of maintenance needed to send those ships overseas. For that reason, the Navy concluded that rotational crewing works especially well with classes of ships that are being retired.[5] However, the Navy did not document how much it might save in maintenance costs because of crew rotation because it already planned to retire the ships used in that experiment and thus did not evaluate them to determine how much maintenance they would have needed to be fit for deployment.

In a report released in late 2004, the Government Accountability Office (GAO) criticized the first two Sea Swap experiments as insufficiently rigorous and lacking in appropriate oversight and guidance from the Navy.[6] Specifically, GAO stated that the lack of an analytic framework—which would have included formal measurable goals, objectives, and metrics to determine the effects of crew rotation on operational requirements, costs, ship condition, and crew morale—prevented the Navy from effectively evaluating the Sea Swap concept. The Navy did not provide guidance for crew-exchange procedures or for documenting a ship's condition when an exchange took place. In particular, the Navy did not collect enough information to properly evaluate the effect that such a long deployment had on the amount of maintenance that the ship needed overseas or on its return home. Although the Navy intended to retire the *Fletcher,* failure to evaluate whether it was in worse condition as a result of its long deployment prevented a proper cost-effectiveness analysis of Sea Swap, according to GAO.[7]

Partly in response to GAO's criticisms, the Navy conducted a third Sea Swap experiment, this time carried out by Fleet Forces Command. The trial focused on providing a more rigorous experiment and collecting more data, particularly about costs and maintenance.

FFC's Sea Swap Experiment with Arleigh Burke Class Destroyers

The third Sea Swap experiment began in early 2005 and employed three Arleigh Burke class destroyers: the *Gonzalez,* the *Laboon,* and the *Stout.* The *Gonzalez* deployed to Central Command's area of responsibility for 18 months, three times longer than the traditional deployment of a surface combatant with a single crew. Every six months, the crew of one of the other two destroyers rotated to the *Gonzalez,* with the exchanges taking place in Bahrain. Shore personnel in Norfolk, Virginia—where the three destroyers are based—acted as caretakers for the other ships while the crew exchanges were occurring. During the course of its deployment, the *Gonzalez* operated with five expeditionary strike groups (task forces that comprise three amphibious ships and three surface combatants), three of which deployed from the Atlantic Fleet and two from the Pacific Fleet.

This crew rotation experiment provided much more forward presence than either traditional ship deployments or the test with Spruance class destroyers (see Figure 2 on page 6). The control group in the experiment consisted of four Arleigh Burke class destroyers with single crews on six-month deployments: two from the Pacific Fleet and two from the Atlantic Fleet. The Atlantic Fleet ships each provided 124 days of forward presence (with the balance of time spent in transit or in port calls outside their area of operations). The Pacific Fleet ships provided 90 days of presence each, reflecting the longer sailing times from the West Coast to the Indian Ocean. In all, that control group of four crews and four ships provided 428 days of presence over an 18-month period, or an average of 107 days per ship per crew. Over the same period, the *Gonzalez* provided more forward presence—453 days— using three crews (and, in effect, three ships), for an average of 151 days per ship per crew. That figure represents an improvement of 40 percent over the traditional single-crew method and 19 percent over the results of the Sea Swap test with Spruance class destroyers.

The increase in forward presence in the third Sea Swap experiment suggests that if the Navy normally needs 100 surface combatants to provide a given level of presence, the same capability could be provided with 72 surface combatants using this variant of rotational crewing. Thus, rather than needing a rotation ratio of 5 to 1 for single-crewed surface combatants, the Navy could reduce that ratio to about 3.5 to 1 with Sea Swap.[8]

The Navy's Conclusions About Sea Swap and Future Policy

The Navy reported that the results of the FFC Sea Swap experiment were positive, for the most part. Rotational crewing saved fuel costs by requiring fewer transits of the Pacific Ocean. The material condition of the *Gonzalez* at the end of its deployment was not substantially different from that of ships that deployed with single crews— although the Navy is awaiting a final evaluation of the ship's condition after its regular shipyard overhaul.[9] Crew morale and readiness were about the same among the rotating crews and those on single-crewed ships. Crew retention, however, was somewhat lower than on other ships. Overall, the Navy concluded that the Sea Swap concept works but that it requires increased oversight on the part of Navy staff to execute and increased effort and coordination on the part of crew members to ensure smooth transitions between crews.

According to the Navy's report, rotational crewing has several other advantages. From the combatant commander's perspective, the rotationally crewed ship in the FFC experiment remained in-theater for nearly the full 18 months, with none of the gaps in coverage that can occur if a relief ship arrives late. In addition, allied and friendly navies appreciated the familiarity of working with the same U.S. ship, even though the crew and command of the ship changed. From the Navy's perspective, rotational crewing generally eliminated the possibility that a ship's—and thus its crew's—deployment could be extended beyond the normal six months.[10] Because the ship remained in the theater of operations, crews could be swapped out every six months. But with a traditionally crewed ship, if its relief ship was not available and forward presence absolutely had to be maintained, the ship could have its tour of duty extended.

The Navy's report also identified several drawbacks of the third Sea Swap experiment. First, because rotational crewing was not "business as usual," it required some adjustment by the different crews, in that they would not be deploying with the ships on which they had trained. Some shore infrastructure and logistical coordination were required, particularly during crew exchanges, when ships being left in the United States needed personnel to support them. Thus, a large-scale use of Sea Swap could require an increase in shore-based infrastructure and personnel in order to provide enough sailors to take care of several ships whose crews had left for overseas exchanges at the same time. The Navy has not estimated how many additional personnel might be needed or at what cost.

The Navy concluded its interim report by stating, "No additional Sea Swap Initiatives are currently planned. However, the Sea Swap multi-crewing concept is executable and works extremely well for ships with high demand but low numbers and most especially in the case of 'sun-setting' a particular class of ships."[11] As noted above, when the Navy is planning to retire a ship class, it can avoid a substantial amount of maintenance to make old ships ready for their last deployments if it can simply rotate those ships' crews to a vessel that is already deployed overseas.

Ships with "high demand but low numbers"—such as coastal patrol ships or mine-countermeasures ships—are ones for which there are many more potential missions than vessels available to perform them. The Navy appears to have concluded from the Sea Swap experiments that it can get more use from high-demand ships by rotating crews to them instead of, for example, building more of those ships to meet the demand.

Logically, however, the effectiveness of multicrewing should depend on the characteristics of ships rather than on their numbers or the demand for them. The Navy's statement that multicrewing works well on ships with high demand and low numbers means, in effect, that crew rotation would work well on similar ships regardless of their numbers or demand. (Whether rotational crewing would be necessary on such ships is another matter.) In communications with CBO after releasing its interim report, the Navy recognized that there is no distinction in the viability of Sea Swap between ships that are in high demand but have low numbers and other ships that cannot be characterized that way. Thus, although the Navy currently has no plans to employ Sea Swap on large surface combatants, if it needs to provide more forward presence with those ships in the future than is feasible under traditional crewing procedures, and if it is unwilling or unable to expand its force of those ships, using Sea Swap could be a viable option to fill the gap.[12]

CBO's Analysis of the Potential Effects of Expanding Crew Rotation

In recent years, the Navy has begun issuing annual reports that detail its plans for ship construction over the next three decades. The defense authorization act for 2007 directed CBO to examine how much forward presence could be provided under the Navy's long-term shipbuilding plan with the widespread use of crew rotation. The remainder of this paper looks at the amount of presence that the Navy's surface combatant force might be able to provide in the future under various types of crew rotation and the potential costs of such a change.

Requirements for Forward Presence and Plans for Multiple Crewing under the Navy's Long-Term Shipbuilding Plan

The latest long-term shipbuilding report envisions expanding the Navy's battle-force fleet from its current size of about 280 ships to 313 ships by 2020.[13] The surface combatant force—which today comprises 74 cruisers and destroyers and 30 frigates—would consist of 94 cruisers and destroyers and 55 littoral combat ships by 2020 (see Figure 3). Under that plan, by 2040, the Navy will have finished purchasing seven DDG-1000 guided missile destroyers and 19 CG(X) guided missile cruisers and will be replacing the Arleigh Burke class destroyers with a new antiair guided missile destroyer, the DDG(X).

Based on its analysis of wartime needs—which stresses the importance of forward-deployed and early-arriving forces—the Navy has set its long-term requirement for large surface combatants at 88 cruisers and destroyers.[14] Of that number, 21 are supposed to be forward deployed at any given time (including ships on routine deployment from the United States and those based in Japan). Similarly, analysis of the need for littoral combat ships in future conflicts and for other missions that may occur at the same time—such as maritime interception or counterterrorism operations—suggests to the Navy that it must have an average of 23 LCSs overseas at any given time. The Navy believes it can achieve that level of presence with a fleet of 55 LCSs. From 2020 through the succeeding 20 years, the Navy's shipbuilding plan would acquire enough small and large surface combatants to meet both of those forward-presence requirements (see the top panel of Figure 4).

The expected rotation ratio for littoral combat ships is smaller than the ratio for large surface combatants because the Navy's plan anticipates using a rotational crewing concept for LCSs that is similar to the one now employed on Cyclone class coastal patrol boats. Specifically, the Navy envisions using four crews to operate three LCSs based in the continental United States, of which one ship would be forward deployed at any given time. That approach is often abbreviated as the 4/3/1 crewing concept. However, the first two LCSs (which are now under construction) will use a blue/gold dual-crew system—perhaps similar to that of mine-warfare ships— until enough LCSs have been commissioned into the fleet to allow for multiple crewing.

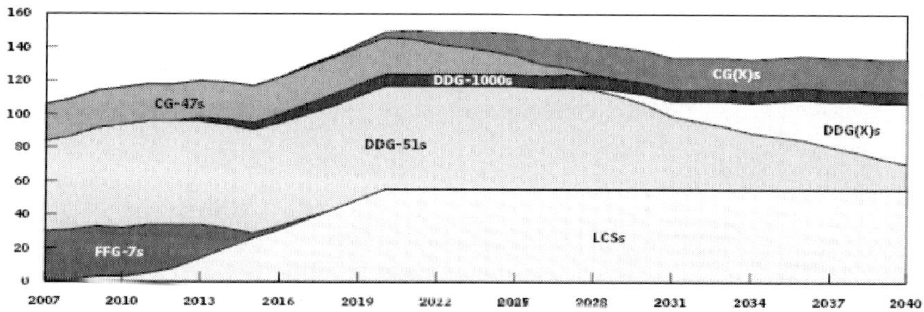

Source: Congressional Budget Office based on data from the Navy.

Notes: CG-47s = Ticonderoga class cruisers; CG(X)s = future guided missile cruisers; DDG-1000s = Zumwalt class guided missile destroyers; DDG-51s = Arleigh Burke class destroyers; DDG(X)s = future antiair guided missle destroyers; FFG-7s = Oliver Hazard Perry class guided missile frigates; LCSs = littoral combat ships.

CBO adjusted its assumptions about LCS purchases to reflect changes in that program since the publication of the Navy's 2008 shipbuilding plan. CBO assumed future purchases and retirements would occur at levels intended to keep the LCS force steady at 55 ships.

Figure 3. The Navy's Inventory of Surface Combatants Under Its Long-Term Shipbuilding Plan.

The assumption that the Navy will use 4/3/1 crewing for LCSs once they enter the fleet in large numbers may not hold true, however. When CBO asked how many LCSs would be needed to start implementing the 4/3/1 concept, the Navy stated that it "is reviewing future manning options, and the use of a 4:3 crewing concept is among the options being considered."[15] A decision not to employ that crewing concept could have implications for the amount of forward presence that LCSs could provide. For example, if the Navy determined that rotational crewing was not feasible for littoral combat ships and used a conventional single-crewing approach instead, the planned force of 55 LCSs would be able to keep only about 17 ships forward deployed at one time, rather than the stated requirement of 23 ships. To meet that forward-presence requirement with single-crewed LCSs, the Navy would have to build 85 ships instead of 55 (see Figure 5).

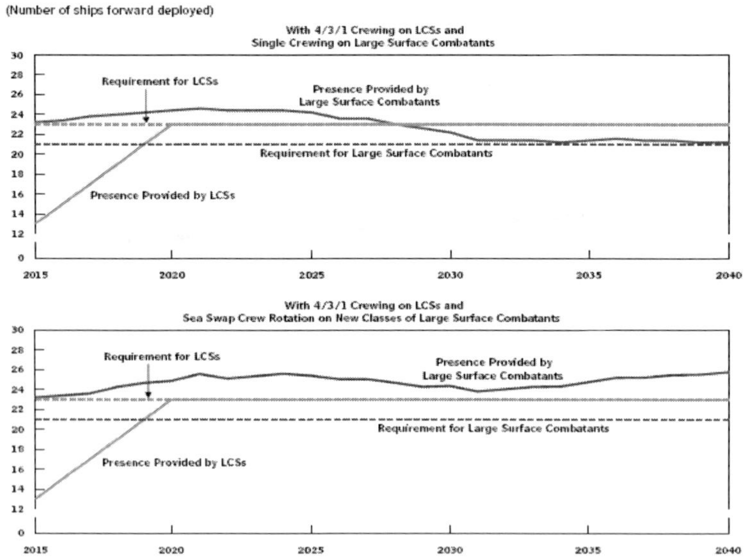

Source: Congressional Budget Office.

Notes: Under 4/3/1 crewing, four crews would operate three ships, one of which would be forward deployed at any given time.

CBO adjusted its assumptions about purchases of littoral combat ships (LCSs) to reflect changes in that program since the publication of the Navy's 2008 shipbuilding plan. CBO assumed that future purchases and retirements would occur at levels intended to keep the LCS force steady at 55 ships.

Figure 4. Forward Presence Provided by Surface Combatants Under the Navy's Long-Term Shipbuilding Plan.

Effects of Widespread Crew Rotation under the Navy's 313-Ship Plan

To analyze the possible impact of crew rotation on the fleet envisioned in the Navy's long-term shipbuilding plan, CBO had to make various assumptions.

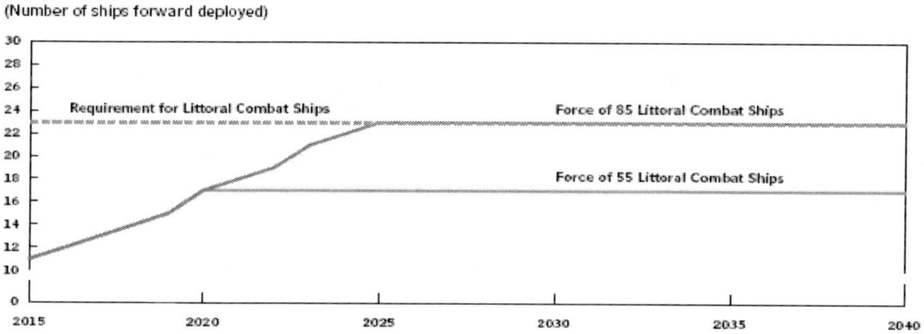

Source: Congressional Budget Office.

Figure 5. Forward Presence Provided by Single-Crewed Littoral Combat Ships.

For example, CBO defined the phrase "widespread use of crew rotation" from the 2007 defense authorization act to mean continuing crew rotation for ship classes that use it now, employing the 4/3/1 concept on littoral combat ships, and applying the Sea Swap rotation concept to all future classes of large surface combatants. (The Navy has not analyzed or conducted crew rotation experiments on other types of ships, such as amphibious ships or aircraft carriers.)[16] CBO chose to limit its analysis to future classes of large surface combatants because, in theory, introducing widespread crew rotation to new classes would allow the Navy to plan for and design the ships in ways to facilitate crew rotation.

Specifically, CBO assumed that the planned DDG-1000 guided missile destroyers, CG(X) future cruisers, and DDG(X) future guided missile destroyers (replacements for Arleigh Burke class destroyers) would employ the Sea Swap approach. Ships would be divided into groups of three, with one ship deploying for 18 months and the crews of the other two ships rotating to it every 6 months. At the end of 18 months, the deployed ship would return to its home port in the United States, and one of the other two ships in the group would deploy for an 18-month period, with the cycle of 6-month crew rotations continuing (see Figure 6).

In general, CBO assumed that crew rotation would not begin with a class of ships until at least a year after the third ship of the class had been commissioned. (Typically, a newly commissioned ship needs about a year to be made ready for regular, routine deployments.) Given that assumption and the shipbuilding schedules in the Navy's long-term plan, crew rotation on large surface combatants would not begin for about 10 years.

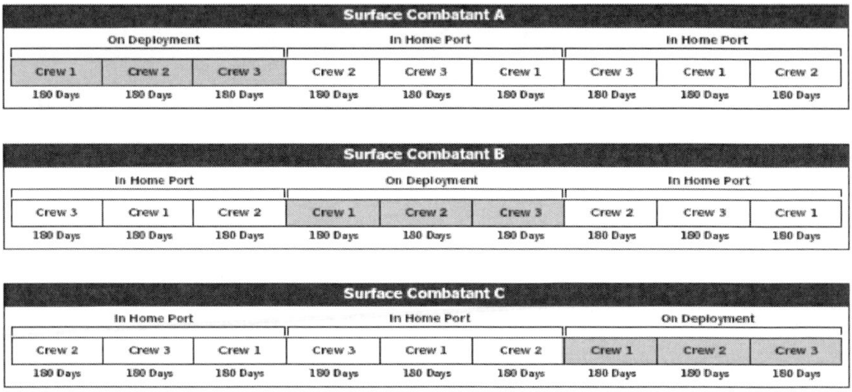

Source: Congressional Budget Office.

Figure 6. Notional Three-Ship Crew Rotation for Future Large Surface Combatants on 18-Month Deployments.

The Navy would employ Sea Swap on DDG-1000 class destroyers starting in 2018. (Because that class of ships is limited to seven, CBO assumed that crew rotation would begin once all of the ships had been commissioned.)[17] The first CG(X)s would employ crew rotation beginning in 2021, and the first DDG(X)s starting in 2030.

Overall, using the Sea Swap approach on those ships would enable the Navy to provide much more overseas presence with large surface combatants that its requirement calls for (see the bottom panel of Figure 4 on page 11). Today, the Navy maintains an average of about 23 large surface combatants overseas at any given time, and it says that it requires at least 21 over the long term. Under the widespread use of crew rotation, that number would rise to 25 ships by 2020 (when 6 destroyers would be using Sea Swap) and to 26 ships by 2040 (when 57 cruisers and destroyers would have rotating crews).

CBO did not attempt to estimate in detail the potential costs or savings to the Navy of using the Sea Swap concept on a widespread basis. Such estimates are uncertain and would be determined by, among other things, the cost of fuel 20 to 40 years in the future and the potential schedule of ship deployments. The Navy has told CBO that existing shore personnel can support at least one crew rotation at any given time and, therefore, that using Sea Swap does not entail any additional personnel costs.18 But if 57 ships were using crew rotation, then presumably 18 to 20 exchanges would be taking place every six months involving crews from San Diego or Norfolk (the main U.S. naval bases for the Pacific and Atlantic Fleets). Depending on ship schedules, two or three crew exchanges could occur in a given month, which would require as many as 42 additional personnel at each of those bases to serve as caretaker crews for the ships left vacant during the exchanges. However, the costs of those additional personnel would be offset by the savings on fuel from making fewer transoceanic trips.

Effects of Widespread Crew Rotation with a Smaller Fleet

In previous analyses, CBO concluded that implementing the Navy's current long-term shipbuilding plan would probably be more expensive than the Navy anticipates.[19] Building a fleet of 313 ships would cost an average of $17.3 billion per year (in 2008 dollars) between 2008 and 2037, the Navy estimates. CBO estimates that shipbuilding costs would average $22.7 billion a year over that period. Both figures are significantly higher than the annual average of $11.5 billion that the Navy has spent on ship programs since 2002.

Over the past 17 years, whenever budget constraints have forced the Navy to scale back its fleet, it has reduced the major components of the fleet (aircraft carriers, submarines, surface combatants, and amphibious ships) by roughly equal proportions. If funding constraints prevented the Navy from meeting its 313-ship goal and the service responded with across-the-board cuts, it could end up with a fleet of about 210 battle-force ships by 2040— including 54 large surface combatants and 40 LCSs (reductions of about 40 percent and 30 percent, respectively, from currently planned levels).[20] Such a fiscally constrained fleet would require annual spending for shipbuilding of $14.5 billion per year, CBO estimates—about the same as the amount the Navy has requested for 2008. The surface combatant force would consist of five DDG-1000 Zumwalt class destroyers rather than seven, 11 CG(X) cruisers instead of 19, and 38 antiair guided missile destroyers (intended primarily for fleet air defense) rather than 62 (see Figure 7).

Under the Navy's current plan to use single crews on large surface combatants and rotating crews on LCSs, that smaller surface combatant force would not meet the Navy's requirements for forward presence (see the top panel of Figure 8). By the late 2020s, Arleigh Burke class destroyers would be retiring in greater numbers than they were being replaced. With the fiscally constrained fleet described above, the Navy would be able to keep only 16 large surface combatants forward deployed in 2040, compared with the requirement of 21, and only 18 littoral combat ships, compared with the requirement of 23.

If such a scenario unfolded, the Navy could close the gaps in forward presence by using a blue/gold dual-crew rotation—similar to that planned for guided missile submarines—on some of its new large surface combatants and LCSs. With that crewing system (shown in Figure 1 on page 3), the Navy expects that its four SSGNs will be enough to keep two submarines forward deployed at all times and a third forward deployed almost five months of the year. That approach results in a rotation ratio of 1.67 to 1, compared with 5 to 1 for single-crewed surface combatants or 3 to 1 for LCSs under the 4/3/1 concept.

If nine of the Navy's CG(X)s and three of its DDG(X)s employed a blue/gold system and the rest used single crews, the 54 large surface combatants in the fiscally constrained fleet would be able to keep at least 21 forward deployed at any given time through 2040 (see the bottom panel of Figure 8). That result includes seven single-crewed cruisers and destroyers based in Japan, a number that CBO assumed would remain constant through 2040. In addition, if 23 of the 40 LCSs in the smaller fleet used a blue/gold crewing system, they would be able to maintain an overseas presence of 23 ships, including those based in Japan. That approach would have the advantage of meeting the Navy's presence requirement for LCSs in 2018, two years earlier than under the Navy's plan. It should be noted, however, that a fleet with fewer ships could be less flexible in responding to crises and less able to recover from losses suffered in combat.

With an SSGN-type blue/gold crewing scheme, there would be twice as many crews as ships, and nondeploying crews would conduct their training onshore rather than on ships. Whether such a concept would work with large surface combatants and LCSs is difficult to evaluate because it has not been tried. Other than the limited Sea Swap experiments, the Navy has no experience with rotational crewing on large surface combatants. Adapting the SSGN crewing concept to cruisers and destroyers would be a much more ambitious project that would require planning and experimentation as well as investment in training and maintenance facilities. (Issues related to the cost of such a change are addressed in the next section.)

Previous CBO analyses concluded that probably the most important factor in making a blue/gold crewing system work—especially one as ambitious as the SSGN model— is rigorous configuration control in the design and construction of the class of ships, including some redundancy in key systems.21 Neither the CG(X) future cruisers nor the DDG(X) future destroyers have been designed yet. The Navy is currently studying what capabilities the CG(X) should have; after that analysis is complete, the Navy will begin designing the ship, with the first one due to be authorized in 2011. The DDG(X) is even further off, with the first ship expected to be authorized in 2022. Thus, the Navy can still design its future large surface combatants to operate with dual crews, should that prove necessary in the 2020s. Other elements needed to support a blue/gold system, such as more-extensive training and maintenance infrastructure, could also be developed by the 2020s.

The Navy has not yet commissioned the first LCSs, so it has no practical experience of how a blue/gold or 4/3/1 crewing concept would work for that class. In addition, the Navy has officially told CBO that it does not yet know how many LCSs will be based in Japan and how many will be assigned to the Atlantic or Pacific Fleet. The final determination of those issues will affect what form of, and to what extent, alternative crewing methods would be used for the LCS if the Navy could not afford to buy all 55 planned ships of that class. The service's current experience with rotational crewing on small ships, such as coastal patrol ships and mine-countermeasures ships, suggests that it would be possible to adapt dual crewing to the LCSs.

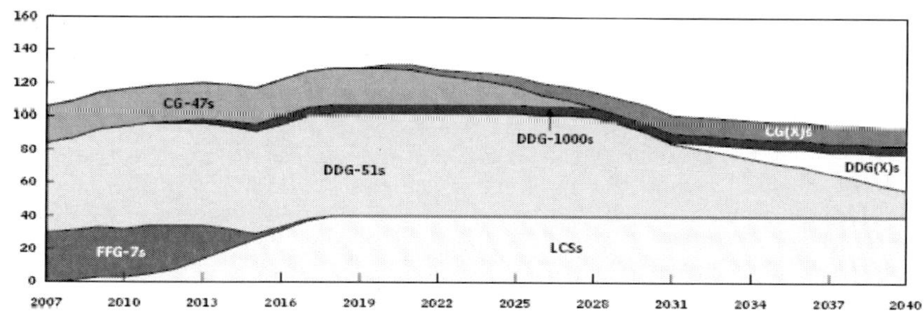

Source: Congressional Budget Office.

Note: CG-47s = Ticonderoga class cruisers; CG(X)s = future guided missile cruisers; DDG-1000s = Zumwalt class guided missile destroyers; DDG-51s = Arleigh Burke class destroyers; DDG(X)s = future antiair guided missle destroyers; FFG-7s = Oliver Hazard Perry class guided missile frigates; LCSs = littoral combat ships.

Figure 7. The Navy's Inventory of Surface Combatants Under a Fiscally Constrained Fleet.

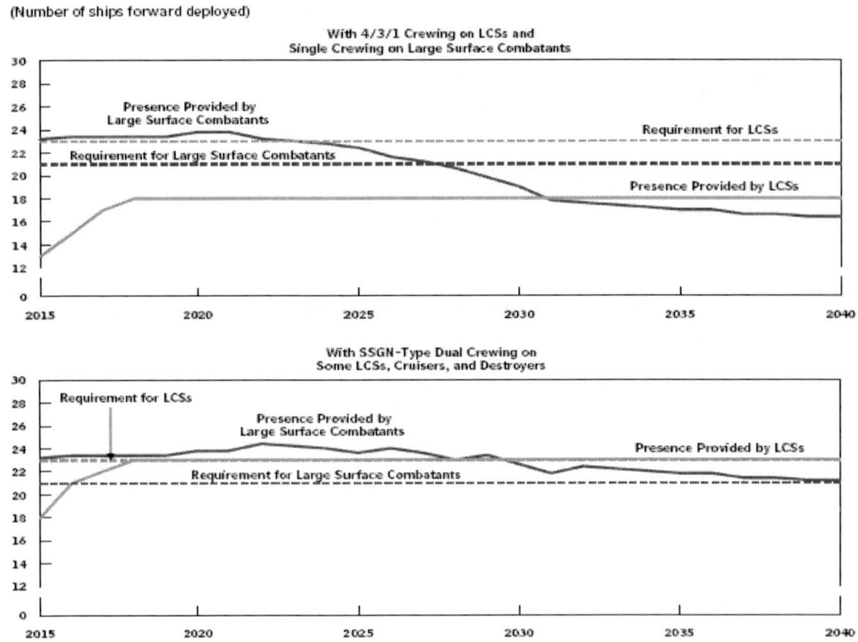

Source: Congressional Budget Office.

Notes: These scenarios assume that funding constraints cause the Navy to reduce its fleet to about 210 ships over the long term, rather than the 313 ships envisioned in its latest shipbuilding plan.

Under 4/3/1 crewing, four crews would operate three ships, one of which would be forward deployed at any given time.

LCSs = littoral combat ships; SSGN = guided missile submarine.

Figure 8. Forward Presence Provided by Surface Combatants Under a Fiscally Constrained Fleet.

Alternatively, the Navy could choose a more mixed solution to address shortfalls in forward presence with a fiscally constrained fleet. For example, if the Navy based 8 large surface combatants in Japan (up from 7 today) and used the Sea Swap three-crew version of crew rotation on all 46 remaining cruisers and destroyers, it could keep 21 large surface combatants forward deployed at a time. However, it is not clear that employing Sea Swap on 46 ships is a lesser challenge than adapting a blue/gold crewing system to 12 cruisers and destroyers. Similarly, if the Navy based 15 littoral combat ships overseas and used its 4/3/1 crewing concept on the other 25, it could maintain a forward presence of 23 ships. Finding countries in various regions willing to base 15 LCSs, however, would require negotiating with their governments, with no certainty about the outcome.

Cost Implications of Rotational Crewing

The costs or savings from rotational crewing—both onetime and recurring costs or savings—vary depending on the particular crewing concept. The type of rotational crewing with the highest relative costs (compared with those of the same or a similar ship operated by a single crew) is the blue/gold system for ballistic missile and guided missile submarines.

One-time costs for that form of dual crewing include designing and building the ships with rigorous configuration controls to facilitate the use of alternating crews and with more-redundant and more-rugged systems to withstand the longer times that dual-crewed ships spend at sea. Other one-time costs include more-extensive training and maintenance infrastructures. For example, the Navy keeps a larger supply of spare parts on hand (valued at more than $1 billion) for dual-crewed Trident submarines than for single-crewed attack submarines (whose inventory is valued at less than $200 million). The dedicated Trident training and maintenance facilities themselves would cost a total of about $1 billion to replace at both Trident submarine bases.

The Trident blue/gold model also incurs higher recurring costs for routine operations. A Trident submarine costs about one-third more to operate than a single-crewed attack submarine. That difference mainly occurs because of the higher personnel costs of having two crews per submarine, but part of the difference reflects higher maintenance costs for Trident submarines. (Excluding personnel costs, operating costs for a dual-crewed ballistic missile submarine are $46 million per year, compared with $32 million per year for a single-crewed attack submarine.) Some of the difference may also be attributable to the different sizes of the ships: SSBNs weigh more than 18,000 tons, whereas Los Angeles class attack submarines weigh about 7,000 tons.

The Sea Swap crew rotation experiments, by contrast, involved no one-time start-up costs and produced savings in operating costs, according to the Navy's report on the experiments. Having fewer transoceanic trips saved fuel costs, although those savings were partially offset by the costs of flying the crews overseas and putting them up in hotels during crew exchanges, among other expenses. Overall, the Navy's analysis concluded that the 18-month Sea Swap deployment of the *Gonzalez* cost about $10 million less than three 6-month deployments of single-crewed Arleigh Burke class destroyers. As noted above, using Sea Swap on all of the Navy's new surface combatants (a total of 57 ships by 2040) might require increasing the number of shore-based personnel in Norfolk and San Diego by 42 people each to facilitate crew exchanges. The costs of those additional personnel, however, would be more than offset by the savings generated from the widespread use of Sea Swap under the Navy's 313-ship plan.

Employing an SSGN-type blue/gold crewing system on large surface combatants and littoral combat ships under the fiscally constrained fleet could entail substantial startup costs as well as higher operating costs for those ships compared with single-crewed versions. The Trident experience suggests that the Navy would need to build dedicated training and maintenance facilities and keep a large supply of spare parts readily available. Designing the ships from the outset specifically to use a blue/gold system would also be necessary.

With respect to future large surface combatants, constructing a single class of 12 ships for a blue/gold system—rather than 9 ships of one class and 3 of another— would reduce the need to build separate training facilities and spare-parts pools.[22] Thus, in a fiscally constrained fleet, rather than purchase 11 CG(X)s, the Navy could buy 12 and not plan to base any of them in Japan. It could use dual crews on the entire class, which would eliminate the need for dual crews on DDG(X)s. The same concept would apply to the LCSs; at least 23 of those ships would need to be of the same design. (The Navy is currently building two versions of the LCS and is not expected to settle on a single design until 2010.)

With those changes, total operating costs for large surface combatants and littoral combat ships in the fiscally constrained fleet would still be less than under the Navy's plan. The 88 large surface combatants and 55 LCSs envisioned in the Navy's plan would require 88 and 73 crews, respectively. The 54 large surface combatants and 40 LCSs in the fiscally constrained fleet would require 66 and 63 crews, respectively. The dual-crewed ships would have higher maintenance costs than single-crewed versions. But whatever costs were associated with dual-crew systems would be exceeded by the savings from not buying 34 large surface combatants and 15 LCSs included in the Navy's plan.[23]

End Notes

[1] The Ethan Allen, Benjamin Franklin, James Madison, and Lafayette classes were also designed and constructed specifically as ballistic missile submarines. They, along with the George Washington class, composed the famous "41 for Freedom" ballistic missile submarine force delivered in the 1960s.

[2] Attack submarines and surface combatants are not considered on-station until they arrive in their areas of operations overseas.

[3] Similarly, the various Navy ships that have their home ports in Japan (which include an aircraft carrier, amphibious ships, surface combatants, and support ships) also count as being forward deployed all of the time, even during maintenance periods. However, the families of Japan-based crews generally live in Japan, whereas the families of Cyclone crews remain in Virginia.

[4] In a crisis, that time can be cut considerably by increasing the ship's transit speed and eliminating unnecessary stops along the way.

[5] See Secretary of the Navy Donald C. Winter, *Report on Navy Surface Ship Rotational Crew Programs in Compliance with Section 342 of Fiscal Year 2007 National Defense Authorization Act* (February 15, 2007), p. 15. That document is an interim report. The Navy's final report was expected in June 2007, although as of this writing, it had not yet been issued.

[6] Government Accountability Office, *Force Structure: Navy Needs to Fully Evaluate Options and Provide Standard Guidance for Implementing Surface Ship Rotational Crewing*, GAO-05-10 (November 2004).

[7] That criticism also applied to Pacific Command's experiment with Arleigh Burke class destroyers. The Navy did not compare the condition of the multicrewed ship in that experiment with the conditions of similar ships after their deployments.

[8] That 5-to-1 rotation ratio is CBO's estimate of a rough fleetwide average, based on the 6-to-1 ratio used by Central Command and the 4.5-to-1 ratio used by European and Pacific Commands.

[9] The Navy states in its interim report: "Using the Gonzalez post deployment Critical System Assessment ... in October 2006 as a reference point, the material condition of the Experiment and the Control Group ships were similar. However, the full assessment of Gonzalez material condition will include review and assessment of her post deployment maintenance availability scheduled to begin March 2007. These results will be included in the final report." See Winter, *Report on Navy Surface Ship Rotational Crew Programs*, p. 13. (The final report has not yet been released.)

[10] The last crew in the rotation could have its deployment extended, however, unless the Navy was prepared to conduct another crew exchange, which was not part of the Sea Swap experiment.

[11] Winter, *Report on Navy Surface Ship Rotational Crew Programs*, p. 15.

[12] However, section 342(b) of the John Warner National Defense Authorization Act for Fiscal Year 2007 (P.L. 109-364; 120 Stat. 2154) prohibits the Navy from implementing any new crew rotation experiment or program on surface ships until October 1, 2009.

[13] See Department of the Navy, *Report to Congress on Annual Long-Range Plan for Construction of Naval Vessels for FY2008* (February 2007).

[14] The 313 ships in the long-term plan (including the 88 cruisers and destroyers) are the requirement that the Navy has set for its fleet, which it says it needs to meet by 2020. Under

the current schedule for commissioning and decommissioning ships, however, the Navy would have more than 88 large surface combatants until 2028.

[15] Department of Defense information paper on LCS crewing furnished to the Congressional Budget Office on June 29, 2007.

[16] In 2003, the Navy considered experimenting with crew rotation on an amphibious ship. It abandoned that effort, however, when its preliminary analysis determined that crew rotation would be too complex and difficult to execute on such a ship, particularly in conjunction with the Marine Corps, whose units would be aboard the Navy ship and would need to rotate along with the ship's crew.

[17] CBO assumed that one of the seven planned DDG-1000s would be based in Japan with a single crew. The others would be divided into two groups of three and would use rotational crewing as outlined above.

[18] Department of Defense information paper furnished to the Congressional Budget Office on April 2, 2007.

[19] See the statement of J. Michael Gilmore, Assistant Director for National Security, and Eric J. Labs, Senior Analyst, Congressional Budget Office, *The Navy's 2008 Shipbuilding Plan and Key Ship Programs,* before the Subcommittee on Seapower and Expeditionary Forces of the House Armed Services Committee, July 24, 2007. That testimony updated the analysis in Congressional Budget Office, *Options for the Navy's Future Fleet* (May 2006).

[20] For a detailed discussion of alternatives for smaller fleets, see Congressional Budget Office, *Options for the Navy's Future Fleet,* Chapter 3. That analysis looked at five options for the Navy if total spending for ship and aircraft operations and procurement was constrained to $43 billion per year. (For example, money saved on aircraft procurement and operating costs could be applied to ship procurement.) The fiscally constrained fleet discussed here is the same as Alternative 1 in that report.

[21] See Congressional Budget Office, *Increasing the Mission Capability of the Attack Submarine Force* (March 2002), and *Transforming the Navy's Surface Combatant Force* (March 2003). During the decade or more that it can take to build a class of ships, electronics and other systems are frequently updated, which means that the last ships in a production run may have very different systems than their earlier counterparts. Configuration controls would be intended to ensure that the ships of a class were as similar to each other as possible so that they all resembled the onshore training systems used by nondeploying crews and so that individual crew members could fill in on a ship other than their own, if necessary, with minimal retraining.

[22] The Trident submarine fleet consists of 14 ships, so a class of 12 dual-crewed surface combatants would not be unprecedented in terms of the size of the force.

[23] For more details about the costs of specific ship classes, see Congressional Budget Office, *Options for the Navy's Future Fleet.*

INDEX

G

H

I

J

K

L

M

N

O

P

T

U

V

W